THE FATHERS
OF THE CHURCH

A NEW TRANSLATION

VOLUME 112

THE FATHERS
OF THE CHURCH

A NEW TRANSLATION

OECUMENIUS
COMMENTARY ON THE APOCALYPSE

Translated by

JOHN N. SUGGIT
Rhodes University
Grahamstown, South Africa

THE CATHOLIC UNIVERSITY OF AMERICA PRESS
Washington, D.C.

The paper used in this publication meets the minimum requirements of the
American National Standards for Information Science—Permanence
of Paper for Printed Library Materials, ANSI z39.48 – 1984.

LIBRARY OF CONGRESS CATALOGING-IN-PUBLICATION DATA
Oecumenius, Bishop of Tricca.
[Oecumenii commentarius in Apocalypsin. English]
Commentary on the Apocalypse / Oecumenius ; translated by John N. Suggit.
p. cm. — (The Fathers of the Church, a new translation v. 112)
Includes bibliographical references and index.
ISBN-13: 978-0-8132-0112-2 (cloth : alk. paper)
ISBN-10: 0-8132-0112-8 (cloth : alk. paper)   1. Bible. N.T. Revelation—
Commentaries—Early works to 1800.   I. Suggit, John.   II. Title.
III. Series: Fathers of the Church ; v. 112.
BS2825.53.O3513 2006
228'.077—dc22
2005024588

CONTENTS

ACKNOWLEDGMENTS

Some years ago the late Dr. Alastair Kirkland, who was engaged on writing a commentary on the book of Revelation, asked Mrs. Barbara Churms to produce an English translation of Oecumenius's commentary. After Alastair's tragic murder in 1997 Barbara asked me to look over and revise her translation, which followed the edition of Hoskier.

The present work, which represents a thorough revision of Barbara's version, has now become almost a new translation. While acknowledging my indebtedness to Barbara Churms, without whom I would never have learnt about Oecumenius, I must be held responsible for any errors or infelicities of expression. I am alone responsible for the Introduction and for the footnotes. We both hope that the version will be of interest to those concerned with the Revelation as well as to those who might care to see a good example of exegetical principles followed in the sixth century.

I am indebted to the editors of the Fathers of the Church series in the Catholic University of America, and especially to Joel Kalvesmaki and Carole Burnett for their help and encouragement. Marc de Groote's edition of the original Greek has been invaluable.

John Suggit
July 2005

ABBREVIATIONS

Byz neugr Jahrb	*Byzantinisch-neugriechische Jahrbücher.*
GCS	Die griechischen christlichen Schriftsteller der ersten drei Jahrhunderte.
GNB	Good News Bible.
JTS	*Journal of Theological Studies.*
LXX	Septuagint (ed. A. Rahlfs).
Oec	Marc de Groote, *Oecumenii commentarius in Apocalypsin* (Leuven: Peeters, 1999).
RSV	Revised Standard Version.
StudP	*Studia Patristica.*
VC	*Vigiliae Christianae.*

SELECT BIBLIOGRAPHY

Critical editions

de Groote, M. *Oecumenii commentarius in Apocalypsin*. Leuven: Peeters, 1999.
———. "The New Edition of Oecumenius' Commentary on the Apocalypse." *StudP* 34 (2001): 298–305.
Hoskier, H. C. *The Complete Commentary of Oecumenius on the Apocalypse*. Ann Arbor: University of Michigan, 1928.
Schmid, J. "Der Apokalypse-text des Oikumenios." *Biblica* 40 (1959): 935–42.

The Date, Provenance, and Person of Oecumenius

Durousseau, C. "The Commentary of Oecumenius on the Apocalypse of John: A Lost Chapter in the History of Interpretation." *Journal of the Chicago Society of Biblical Research* 29 (1984): 21–34.
Lamoreaux, J. C. "The Provenance of Ecumenius' Commentary on the Apocalypse." *VC* 52 (1998): 88–108.
Monaci Castagno, A. "Il problema della datazione dei commenti all' Apocalisses di Ecumenio e di Andre di Caesarea." *Atti della Accademia delle Scienze di Torino. Classe di Scienze morali, storiche e filologiche* 114 (1980): 223–46.
Schmid, J. "Okumenios der Apokalypsen-Ausleger und Okumenios der Bischof von Trikka." *Byz neugr Jahrb* 14 (1938): 322–30.

Background of Christological Controversies, Third to Sixth Centuries

Grillmeier, A. *Christ in Christian Tradition*, vol. 1: *From the Apostolic Age to Chalcedon (451)*, 2d ed. Atlanta: John Knox Press, 1975.
———. "Reception and Contradiction: The Development of the Discussion about Chalcedon to the Beginning of the Reign of Justinian." Part One in *Christ in Christian Tradition*, vol. 2: *From the Council of Chalcedon (451) to Gregory the Great (590–604)*, 2d ed. London: Mowbray, 1987.
Kelly, J. N. D. *Early Christian Doctrines*, 3d ed. London: Black, 1965.
Lampe, G. W. H. "Christian Theology in the Patristic Period." In *A History of Christian Doctrine*, ed. H. Cunliffe-Jones and B. Drewery, 121–48. Edinburgh: T & T Clark, 1978.
Prestige, G. L. *Fathers and Heretics: Six Studies in Dogmatic Faith with Pro-*

logue and Epilogue. The Bampton Lectures for 1940. London: SPCK, 1948. (See especially pages 94–178.)

Sellers, R. V. *Two Ancient Christologies.* London: SPCK, for CHS, 1965.

Oecumenius's Relationship to Origen and Origenists

Bethune-Baker, J. F. *An Introduction to the Early History of Christian Doctrine.* 6th ed. London: Methuen, 1938. (See especially pages 145–54.)

Crouzel, H. *Origen.* Trans. A. S. Worrall. Edinburgh: T & T Clark, 1989.

Diobouniotis, C., and von Harnack, A. "Der Scholien-Kommentar des Origenes zur Apokalypse Johannis." *Texte und Untersuchungen* 38.3. Leipzig: Hinrichs, 1911.

Kelly, J. N. D. *Early Christian Doctrines.* (Full reference above.)

Malaty, T. Y. *The School of Alexandria.* Book Two: *Origen.* Jersey City: St. Mark's Coptic Orthodox Church, 1995. (With many English texts of Origen.)

Prestige, G. L. *Fathers and Heretics: Six Studies in Dogmatic Faith with Prologue and Epilogue.* (See especially pages 43–93. Full reference above.)

Preuschen, E., ed. *Origenes Werke. 4te Band: Der Johanneskommentar.* GCS 10. Leipzig: Hinrichs, 1903.

Trigg, J. W. *Origen.* London: Routledge, 1998. (With selected English texts of Origen.)

Turner, C. H. "Origen Scholia in Apocalypsin." *JTS* (Oct. 1923): 1–16.

Miscellaneous

Jugie, M. "La mort et l'assomption de la Sainte Vierge: Étude historico-doctrinale." *Studi e testi* 114: 43–45. Vatican City: Vatican Library, 1944.

INTRODUCTION

INTRODUCTION

Although there is still considerable doubt about the identity and date of Oecumenius, it is certain that his commentary is the first Greek commentary on the book of Revelation, which was later used by Andreas in the beginning of the seventh century and by Arethas in the tenth century.[1] It is therefore of considerable interest and importance not only for helping to establish the text of Revelation, but more importantly as exemplifying methods of interpretation which may lead readers to appreciate Oecumenius's valiant attempt to make sense of the most difficult book of the New Testament. His efforts, and those of Andreas, may well have contributed to the eventual formal acceptance in the East of Revelation as part of the New Testament canon at the Third Council of Constantinople in A.D. 680.[2]

The introductory notes simply raise some of the problems without attempting to solve them. They also draw attention to several interesting remarks in Oecumenius's commentary, which is of particular importance because of what seems to be an ambivalent relationship between Oecumenius and Origen.

1. Who was Oecumenius?

The commentary was discovered by Franz Diekamp in 1901,[3] but it was not until H. C. Hoskier produced the first printed edi-

---

1. M. de Groote, *Oecumenii commentarius in Apocalypsin* (Leuven: Peeters, 1999), provides not only details of the use made by Andreas and Arethas of Oecumenius, but also a synoptic list of the parallel passages.

2. C. Durousseau, "The commentary of Oecumenius on the Apocalypse of John: A lost chapter in the history of interpretation," in *Journal of the Chicago Society of Biblical Research* 1:29 (1984): 23.

3. J. C. Lamoreaux, "The provenance of Ecumenius' commentary on the Apocalypse" in *VC* 52 (1998): 88–108; see especially p. 89.

tion of the text in 1928[4] that serious efforts were made to iden-
tify its author and date. Hoskier was specially concerned with
establishing what he called "the foundation text" of Revelation.
He felt confident that Oecumenius was the bishop of Tricca
who wrote his commentary "towards the beginning of the seventh century,"[5] instead of the earlier accepted date of the tenth
century. There are, however, problems with both the date and
the identity of Oecumenius. The evidence of the date is given by
Oecumenius himself in 1.3.6[6] when, commenting on Revelation
1.1 ("what must soon take place"), he says that "a very long time,
more than five hundred years, has elapsed since this was said."
Oecumenius elsewhere dates the Revelation to the end of the
reign of Domitian, when John was exiled to Patmos,[7] presumably
about A.D. 95 when Domitian had started persecution against
those who refused to accept him as Master and God,[8] a persecution which included philosophers, Jews, and others.[9]

If Revelation was written about A.D. 95, "more than five hundred years" later would give a date at the end of the sixth century. There is no doubt that Oecumenius's commentary was written
before that of Andreas, which can be dated to the early part of
the seventh century, so that the end of the sixth century gives the
terminus ante quem. The situation is, however, complicated by references to correspondence between Severus, bishop of Antioch,
who died in A.D. 538, and Oecumenius, who was described in
a monophysite catena as "a careful man, who is very orthodox
[i.e., monophysite], as the letters which Mar Severus sent to him
show, from the sixth discourse of those which he composed on
the revelation of the Evangelist John."[10] The evidence for recognizing Oecumenius as the correspondent of Severus and as the
commentator on Revelation would seem to be incontrovertible,
were it not for Oecumenius's own statement that more than five

---

4. *The Complete Commentary of Oecumenius on the Apocalypse*, edited with notes
by H. C. Hoskier (Ann Arbor: University of Michigan, 1928).
5. Hoskier, 4.
6. The references are to the sections given by de Groote in his edition, where
the sub-sections are given in brackets.
7. Rv 1.9; Oec 1.21; Eusebius of Caesarea, *Chronicon Paschale* 250c.
8. Suetonius, *Domitian* 13.2.   9. Dio Cassius, *Epitome* 67.14.
10. Lamoreaux, 92.

hundred years had elapsed since the Revelation was written. Oecumenius, however, does not seem to have been always exact in some of his statements, as is shown by inconsistencies in his interpretation of some passages in Revelation. Further, it looks as though the period of "more than five hundred years" may refer not strictly to the date of the writing of Revelation, but to the date of the crucifixion of Jesus and the delay in the occurrence of the parousia. Lamoreaux supports the view that Oecumenius was a contemporary of Severus, in spite of de Groote's opinion that Oecumenius was not Severus's correspondent.[11]

The letters of Severus show that Oecumenius was married. He is described as a count (κόμης), which was primarily a military title, implying an official position in the Emperor's household.[12] He seems to have been "a layman from aristocratic circles," living in Isauria, in Asia Minor, who was particularly interested in discussing the person of Christ.[13] He must therefore not be confused with the bishop of Tricca (in Thessaly) of the tenth century. Oecumenius is anxious to proclaim his orthodoxy, but his commentary does not display a detailed knowledge of the intricacies of Christological or Trinitarian doctrine. Severus of Antioch was himself described by G. W. H. Lampe as a moderate monophysite, being "a monophysite in phraseology rather than in substance," at a time when "'Chalcedonian' struggle was really only a sham fight as far as theology was concerned."[14]

A further point to be noted in connection with the date of Oecumenius is his approval of Evagrius as being "all-knowledgeable."[15] Evagrius, a loyal supporter of Origen, was formally condemned with Origen at the Second Council of Constantinople in A.D. 553. In view of Oecumenius's insistence on his own orthodoxy and his reluctance to mention Origen in his commen-

11. Lamoreaux, 101–8.
12. A. Souter, *A Glossary of Later Latin to 600 A.D.* (Oxford: Clarendon Press, 1996), s. v. *comes*, 60. Compare B. Daley, "Der Kommentar des Oecumenius zur Johannesapokalypse," in *Handbuch der Dogmengeschichte* IV / 7a (Freiburg: Herder, 1986), 223.
13. Lamoreaux, 100–101.
14. G. W. H. Lampe, *A History of Christian Doctrine*, ed. H. Cunliffe Jones and B. Drewery (Edinburgh: T & T Clark, 1978), 143.
15. Oec 6.3.12: ὁ τὰ γνωστικὰ μέγας.

tary, it is unlikely that he would have referred to Evagrius in such terms after 553.

2. Oecumenius's theology

There is no doubt that Oecumenius considered himself to be orthodox, not only in steering a middle course between Nestorius and Eutyches,[16] but in upholding the teaching of the Chalcedonian Definition. But he does this along the lines of Cyril of Alexandria, whose views he greatly appreciated, calling him "our blessed father Cyril."[17] Cyril's language can easily be regarded as monophysite. Part of the problem arose from confusion in the terminology employed, where οὐσία ("being"), φύσις ("nature"), and especially ὑπόστασις ("being," "subsistence," often regarded, together with πρόσωπον, as corresponding to the Latin *persona*), were not clearly and universally defined. In opposition to Nestorius, Cyril talked of "the one incarnate ὑπόστασις of the Λόγος," which drew attention to the one person of Christ, as opposed to the duality of persons, human and divine, which Nestorius considered were to be found in the incarnate Christ. Cyril's phrase was often quoted as "one incarnate nature (φύσις) of the Λόγος" and sometimes as "one nature of the incarnate Λόγος."[18] The kind of monophysitism which Oecumenius envisaged seems to have been in line with the Chalcedonian Definition of A.D. 451 as understood by Cyril.

This Christological perspective is expressed at the beginning of his commentary, with his assertion that the Word "has become for us and for our salvation a human being, not by divesting himself of his divinity, but by assuming human flesh, animated by a mind. In this way he who is Emmanuel is understood to have been made one from two natures, divinity and humanity, each being complete according to the indwelling Word and according to the different specific characteristic of each nature, without being confused or altered by their combination into a

16. Oec 1.2.3.
17. Oec 12.13.6.
18. Cyril of Alexandria, *Ep.* 17.8. See R. V. Sellers, *Two Ancient Christologies* (London: SPCK, 1940) especially 95–100 and 202–20.

unity, and without being kept separate after the inexpressible and authentic union."[19] By such words Oecumenius refutes the doctrines of Apollinarius as well as of Nestorius and Eutyches. A similar view is repeated in the final chapter of the commentary, with its allusion to the Chalcedonian Definition,[20] from which the monophysitism of Oecumenius is little different. It should, however, be noted that although Oecumenius uses the term ὁμοούσιος ("of one substance," "of one essence," or "of one being") in the full theological sense denoting the relation between the Son and the Father and the Spirit, he also uses it with a wider meaning, as when he says that Mary is "of the same substance as we are," and describes Christ as "incarnate and of the same essence as we are."[21]

Oecumenius's understanding of human free will at times seems to approximate to that of Pelagius. An interesting passage tells how after the Ascension "both the Devil himself will carry on his own customary activity, and human beings on earth in their usual way will follow their free will," thus enabling human beings to be trained like athletes to display their courage in the face of their sufferings, which is essentially the view of Origen.[22] Oecumenius shares with Origen his views on the need of discipline in the Christian life, and therefore of the exercise of free will, though always dependent on the grace of God.[23] In commenting on "freely" in Revelation 21.6 Oecumenius says that "no one can ever contribute anything worthy of future prosperity, even by completing innumerable tasks."[24] Similarly a favorite term of Revelation, παντοκράτωρ ("sovereign lord"), found elsewhere only in the Old Testament, makes it clear that God is all-powerful and does not need any help to effect his purposes: when God uses angels and human beings to carry out his work, he is showing them

19. Oec 1.3.3.
20. Oec 12.13.6.
21. Oec 6.19.2; 12.3.20.
22. Oec 11.3.16–20; Origen, *Homilies on Numbers* 14.2 and *De principiis*, Pref. 4; T. Y. Malaty, *The School of Alexandria*, Book Two: *Origen* (Jersey City: St. Mark's Coptic Orthodox Church, 1995), 69; J. W. Trigg, *Origen* (London: Routledge, 1998), 20.
23. Origen, *Homilies on Genesis* 10; Trigg, 95.
24. Oec 11.14.4.

a kindness, "for those who help another in need are not benefiting the recipient so much as themselves."[25] Both Origen and Oecumenius recognize the paradox that while God is always in control, the actions of human beings are carried out by the use of their own free will. This paradox of human life is, we might note, not confined to Christian authors, but is reflected both in the Old Testament and even in the works of Homer.

Oecumenius prefers to stress the mercy and kindness of God rather than his justice and threat of punishment. He therefore has difficulty in interpreting some of the texts of Revelation. "The precious blood of Christ has been shed on behalf of all people, but unprofitably on behalf of some," whose refusal to accept the gift offered was the act of their own free will.[26] The punishment of sinners is tempered by the merciful goodness of the Lord, and in a rather tortuous way he argues that the only real torment that sinners will undergo will be their exclusion from the bounty of God's goodness.[27] His views, however, of their final destiny are ambivalent, and he tries to combine the opinions of those fathers who accept the restoration of sinners with the view of Scripture that their punishment will be everlasting.[28]

Oecumenius has a high view of Mary ever-virgin, the God-bearer (Θεοτόκος), and sees her as the woman of Revelation 12. She is described "as equal to an angel, as a citizen of heaven," and "as one who has nothing in common with the world and the evils in it, but wholly sublime, wholly worthy of heaven, even though she sprang from our mortal nature and being. For the Virgin is of the same substance as we are." Oecumenius thinks that "it would have been more consistent to say that the woman was not clothed with the sun, but that the woman clothed the sun contained in her womb. But in order to show in the vision that even when the Lord was conceived, he was the protector of his own mother and of all creation, the vision said that he clothed the woman."[29] M. Jugie considers Oecumenius's in-

---

25. Oec 8.25.3–4.
26. Oec 8.7.6–7.
27. Oec 8.13.3–8. Compare 9.19.2–4.
28. Oec 5.19.1–4.
29. Oec 6.19.2–9.

terpretation of the woman of Revelation 12 to be more original and inspiring than that of the later Andreas.[30] Oecumenius's theological views will be considered further in the following section, which deals with the complex relationship between him and Origen. Enough has been said to show that Oecumenius attempts to be very orthodox, while being open to some original interpretations of Revelation. He is modest enough to claim that he is "as far away from the working of the Spirit" as he is "from the divine and highest wisdom," and he relies "on those who are judged to be fathers of the church,"[31] so that he believes that he writes with authority, in spite of his modest doubts.

3. Oecumenius and Origen[32]

Lamoreaux draws attention to Oecumenius's "commentary's place in the history of polemic against Origen," and believes that though the themes are subtle, they are so frequent that they may be seen as an orthodox attempt to replace the eschatological vision of Origen and his followers.[33] There is, however, little doubt that Oecumenius was much indebted to Origen (and to the school of Alexandria in general) for his methods of biblical interpretation. Oecumenius, like Origen, was more interested in the spiritual or intellectual meaning of the text than in its literal meaning. Both frequently use the Greek νοητός, often contrasted with words meaning "sensible, perceptible," or the like.[34] Both take the text of Scripture very seriously. Origen accepts the Scriptures as "the work of the world's Creator."[35] Both recognize the importance of the Psalms and frequently quote them. Some of Oecumenius's interpretations seem to be directly due to Ori-

---

30. M. Jugie, "La mort et l'assomption de la Sainte Vierge," *Studi e Testi* 114 (Vatican City: Vatican Library, 1944), 45.

31. Oec 1.1.3–4.

32. The references from Origen are culled from Trigg, Malaty, and E. Preuschen, ed., *Origenes werke: 4te Band: Der Johanneskommentar,* GCS 10 (Leipzig: Hinrichs, 1903).

33. Lamoreaux, 88.

34. See, e.g., Oec 1.17.2, and Origen, *Commentary on John* 1.8.44.

35. Origen, *Commentary on Psalms 1–25* 5; Trigg, 71.

gen, as in the mention of barley, which is described by Oecumenius as "the teaching according to the law of Moses, as being ripe fodder, more fitting than wheat, for nourishing the infant Israel," whereas wheat signifies "the proclamation of the gospel as being the proper food for mature people." Origen talks of barley as "the food especially of beasts or of peasants.... This word sows barley in the Law, but wheat in the Gospels."[36]

A further indication of Oecumenius's dependence on Origen is shown in 9.11.5, where in commenting on Philippians 1.1 he calls "the saints 'beings'[37] because they are in Christ and held in God's intimacy and memory." He here follows the argument of Origen, who omits the words "in Ephesus" in Ephesians 1.1 and regards "the saints who are" as referring to God's people sharing in the life of YHWH as "He who is" in Exodus 3.14.[38] Both Oecumenius and Origen are here indebted to Plato.

Oecumenius in his Commentary never mentions Origen, even though he could have used him as support for his belief that the author of Revelation was the fourth evangelist,[39] while he calls Methodius, a consistent opponent of Origen's teaching, "very wise."[40] Origen was an explorer, struggling to combine his deep appreciation of the Scriptures with a Platonist search for a coherent philosophy of God and human life. Several of his views were later found to be unwise and untenable, so that while some of his followers (like Gregory the Wonderworker) became devoted disciples, others shared completely opposite views: "some grovelled in his shadows, others gloried in his lights."[41]

It is therefore not surprising that Oecumenius does not expressly condemn Origen, but he is careful to emphasize his own orthodox views of the person of Christ, so making it clear that he does not subscribe to any subordinationist doctrine that was at times attached to Origen, who was frequently accused of being responsible for the teaching of Arius and Arianism. Epiphanius,

---

36. Oec 4.10.4; Origen, *Homilies on Genesis* 12.5; Malaty, 181–82.
37. Greek, ὄντες, "those who are."
38. J. A. Robinson, *St Paul's Epistle to the Ephesians*, 2d ed. (London: Macmillan, 1928), 292, quoting Cramer's *Catenae*, ad loc.
39. Origen, *Commentary on John* 1.1.1–6; Oec 1.1.4–6.
40. Oec 1.1.5.
41. G. L. Prestige, *Fathers and Heretics* (London: SPCK, 1948), 85.

for example, in the late fourth century, called Origen "the spiritual father of Arius, and the root and parent of all heresies."[42] It looks as though Oecumenius is attacking Origenist doctrines in arguing against any understanding of the Logos as a creature (κτίσμα).[43] There is no doubt that certain expressions used by Origen seemed to indicate a gradation within the persons of the Godhead, so that the Son is "second to the Father, and the Holy Spirit again is inferior."[44] These were the views that Oecumenius appears to be combating in his consistent defense of Cyrilline orthodoxy, as indicated above, and as reinforced by his remarks on the Son as coeternal and consubstantial with the Holy Spirit.[45] On the other hand, Origen was himself certainly responsible for his important contribution to Nicene orthodoxy in his teaching on the eternal generation of the Son,[46] to which Oecumenius appears not to refer. Many of the problems raised by Origen's successors were due to taking his statements in isolation from his teaching as a whole, as was particularly seen in the case of Arius and Arianism.

In spite of the importance of considering the Christology of Origen, there were two other areas in which his views were specially open to attack. The former of these arose from his belief, largely derived from Plato, of the immortality of the soul, so that the human soul of the pre-incarnate Jesus was alone of all human souls so closely linked to the Logos (God) that he was seen to be the unique Son of God, and was revealed as such by his incarnation. Such a view was implicitly and clearly denied by Oecumenius with his insistence that the incarnation involved an *assumption* (πρόσληψις) of "human flesh, animated by a mind."[47] The incarnation did not merely signal a changed mode of being of the Logos, effected by the perfect adherence of the human soul to God, as Origen seems to have held, but entailed the assumption by the Logos of human nature and a human soul. The

---

42. Epiphanius, *Adversus haereses* 64.4; Malaty, 214.
43. Oec 3.3.2–4.
44. Origen, *De principiis* 1.3.5. Compare *Contra Celsum* 5.39; 7.57.
45. Oec 11.3.8–9.
46. Origen, *Commentary on John* 1.29.204; Trigg, 136.
47. Oec 1.3.3.

difference between this and Origen's view is, however, not always easy to see.[48]

It is in the realm of eschatology that Origen was "without a doubt the most controversial figure in the development of early Christian eschatology."[49] Origen envisaged the restoration (ἀποκατάστασις) of all things to their beginning, so that "all rational beings will return to their original unity with God," including the possibility that the Devil will himself be saved.[50] This conflicted with the usual orthodoxy which condemns the wicked to eternal punishment. Oecumenius has a certain sympathy with Origen's view, in that he moderates the latter's understanding of the eternal punishment of the wicked, as mentioned above, but he never envisages the restoration of the Devil to share in unity with God.[51]

In a similar vein Origen expressed strong doubts about the bodily resurrection of the dead, holding that "the soul's attainment of likeness to God also entails incorporeality."[52] According to a letter of Justinian to the patriarch Menas, Origen affirmed that "in the resurrection the bodies of men rise spherical," to which Oecumenius perhaps alludes in 8.25.5 in his description of one of the primal elements as "circular." Origen's objections to a doctrine of bodily resurrection are vehemently denied by Oecumenius, who considers that God is capable of bringing together again after death the elements that constitute the body.[53] In the sixth century there was still much controversy about the beliefs of Origenists if not of Origen himself, which Oecumenius was at pains at least implicitly to deny.

In his commentary as a whole Oecumenius, while recognizing a certain dependence on Origen, is always ready to show originality in his scriptural interpretation. He is, for example, at pains to show that the 144,000 of Revelation 14 are not the same as

48. Origen, *Commentary on John* 1.28.195–197.
49. Trigg, 29, quoting Brian Daley.
50. Trigg, 31; Origen, *De principiis* 1.6.3; 1.7; Malaty, 887.
51. Oec 9.11.4–5; 10.15.5–7.
52. Trigg, 32; Origen, *De principiis* 3.6.2.
53. Oec 11.10.1–6. According to Justinian, Origen described the risen body as σφαιροειδής; see J. N. D. Kelly, *Early Christian Doctrines* (London: Black, 1965), 472. Oecumenius describes one of the primal elements of the body as κυκλοφορικός.

those of Revelation 7 and that the two groups must be distinguished, whereas Origen argues that the two groups refer to the same people.[54] Again in his remarks on Revelation 3.7 Oecumenius takes "opening" and "shutting" to refer to acquitting and condemning, while Origen understands them to indicate methods of interpreting Scripture.[55] All in all, therefore, it is not unlikely that Oecumenius is subtly challenging many of Origen's views.

4. Oecumenius's hermeneutical methods

Following the example of Origen, Oecumenius is particularly concerned to discover the spiritual meaning of the text. In this regard he is frequently moved as much by pastoral considerations as by his desire to discover the true meaning of Revelation, an aim that has often eluded modern commentators. Although he is never afraid to use his imagination, his allegorical methods always arise from his understanding of Scripture and the teaching of the church. So, for example, he takes the clouds of Revelation 1.7 to refer to the holy angels, as he does, too, in 14.14, where, however, he suggests that the cloud may here refer to the Θεοτόκος, Mary.[56] In Revelation 7.16 the sun is taken to refer to temptation, with a reference to Psalm 120.6—"The sun shall not burn you by day."[57] In Revelation 8.7 the burning of the trees and the hills must not be taken literally: fire means "the distress and deep pain of the sinners when they see the saints 'caught up in the clouds to meet the Lord,' while they themselves have stayed on earth, dishonored and considered of no account. When the text says *trees* and *grass* were burnt up, it refers allegorically to sinners because of their folly and the insensibility of their soul, their woodenness all ready for burning."[58]

His understanding of "the woman clothed with the sun" in Revelation 12.1 has already been mentioned.

Oecumenius is not sure how to understand Revelation 13.3, which he thinks would be known only to the inspired evangelist himself, but he is still ready to attempt an interpretation. "As

54. Oec 8.7.3; Origen, *Commentary on John* 1.1.2–7.
55. Oec 2.13.5; Origen, *Commentary on Psalms 1–25* 1–3; Trigg, 70–71.
56. Oec 1.15.2 and 8.17.1–2.　　　57. Oec 5.3.10.
58. Oec 5.9.3.

it appears to me, it indicates something of this sort: the mortal blow that the Devil received in one of his heads through the piety of Israel was healed again through the idolatry of the same people,"[59] thus allowing free range to the Devil.

At Revelation 19.1 Oecumenius links the great crowd of angels in heaven with the ninety-nine sheep of the parable. Following an unnamed Church Father, he takes the ninety-nine to refer to the holy angels, while the one who strayed was humanity as a whole.[60]

A remarkable interpretation attributes the binding of Satan for a thousand years to the time of the Lord's incarnate life. Oecumenius reaches this conclusion by referring to scriptural texts that say that a thousand years in God's sight are a day, and that Isaiah considers the day of salvation to refer to the whole period of the Lord's incarnation. During the incarnate life of Jesus Satan was prevented from exercising his power over the Lord, but after the resurrection Satan was again set free so that he could tempt disciples to refuse to respond to the Lord by the use of their free will, before he was finally destroyed.[61] Origen, too, denied any literal interpretation of millenarianism, though he did not anticipate Oecumenius's original contribution.[62]

In Revelation 13.18 Oecumenius recognizes the regular use of gematria to explain the number of the beast as 666, and gives various possibilities, but does not mention that the number probably refers to Nero.[63] Throughout his commentary Oecumenius notes the importance of numbers, and recognizes seven and ten as being specially noteworthy.

5. Oecumenius's text of Scripture

The manuscript tradition of the book of Revelation is rather different from that of the other books of the New Testament, presumably because its authenticity was doubted for so long before its acceptance into the canon. Hoskier in his edition of Oe-

---

59. Oec 7.11.11.
60. Oec 10.7.1.
61. Oec 10.17.1–11; 11.6.4.
62. Origen, *De principiis* 2.11.2–3; Malaty, 298.
63. Oec 8.5.6.

cumenius's text was particularly interested in attempts to discover the foundation text of Revelation. Some of the variants would seem to be due simply to scribal errors, as in Revelation 7.14, where ἐπλάτυναν was misread for ἔπλυναν, which was presumed in the later comment. The same is probably true of Revelation 3.8, where instead of "name" (ὄνομα) Oecumenius reads "law" (νόμον).

Oecumenius's text of Revelation 6.9 reads, "the souls of those who had been slain for the word of God, and for *the church* which they had," instead of *the witness*. He explains this by describing the people of the old covenant as the synagogue or church of those who believed in God.[64] His text of Revelation 15.6 includes an interesting variant, which reads (with some manuscripts of Revelation) λίθον ("stone") instead of λίνον ("linen"), no doubt referring to Ezekiel 28.13. More interestingly, however, he backs this up by referring not only to the regular texts, Isaiah 28.16 and Psalm 117.22, but also to Romans 13.14, where he apparently read, "Put on our stone Jesus Christ."[65] Interestingly Origen, too, addresses Christ as "stone," because "he is part of the building made out of living stones in the land of the living."[66]

Some manuscripts of Revelation 4.8 read "nine times" or "eight times" or "seven times" before the *trisagion*. Oecumenius apparently understood this as denoting "seven times," and he comments accordingly, though he does not mention "seven times" in his citation of the text.[67] This is an example of his occasional lack of care in ensuring that the text on which he comments is the same as that which he has previously cited. In commenting on Revelation 7.1–6 he accepts the genuineness of Luke 23.34 in spite of the doubts of Cyril of Alexandria.

6. The manuscripts of Oecumenius's commentary

The manuscript tradition is described in detail by de Groote.[68] The only complete manuscript is that of the first half of the

64. Oec 4.12.1 and 4.13.5.
65. Oec 8.22.2; 23.4.
66. Origen, *Commentary on John* 1.36.265.
67. Oec 3.9.5–6.
68. M. de Groote, *Oecumenii commentarius*, pp. 9–55.

twelfth century, designated by M (Messina), which is therefore accepted as normative. But since M and later manuscripts agree in recognizing uncertainties and errors in the text, the archetype remains problematic. De Groote provides the stemma showing the relationship between the MSS, and at times conjectures corrections that he has incorporated in his printed edition. It is that which has been followed in the translation. All significant changes to the text of Revelation (as in Nestle-Aland, 27th ed.) have been mentioned in the brief notes at the end of each chapter. The translation has always attempted to reproduce what Oecumenius wrote, even when the text in the commentary is different from the original citation.

7. *Some notes on the translation*

As far as reasonably possible, the translation has attempted to give a literal rendering of the text without being too ponderous. The Greek νοητός has regularly been rendered as "spiritual" rather than as "intellectual," and παντοκράτωρ as "sovereign Lord" or the like.

The references to the books of the Old Testament, including the numbering of the Psalms, are always to the Septuagint, or (in the case of Daniel) to Theodotion's version. Consequently at times the translation may seem strange to readers of the usually accepted text.

Oecumenius's commentary is full of quotations from, and allusions to, Scripture. These references have been reproduced almost entirely from the editions of Hoskier and especially de Groote, and are printed as footnotes on each page.

The references to patristic authors are reproduced from de Groote's edition, where further information is provided.

COMMENTARY ON THE APOCALYPSE

CHAPTER ONE

"ALL SCRIPTURE IS inspired by God and profitable," a sacred text said somewhere.[1] For it was by the Spirit that all those who proclaimed to us the saving gospel—prophets, apostles, and evangelists—were given wisdom. But blessed John was certainly holier than all other preachers and more spiritual than any other spiritual person. For he was "lying on the breast"[2] of the Lord, and evoking through his kisses more abundant grace of the Spirit. That is why he was also called "son of thunder."[3] For he boomed out under heaven with his divine teachings. (2) So his present treatise, insofar as it concerns both plain and polished mysteries, could be rightly considered the most mystical. For he does not only speak to us about present events, but also about those which have happened and those which are still to come. For this is the mark of consummate prophecy, to encompass the three periods. For even those who are not Christians introduce their own seers who knew "the events of the present, the future and the past,"[4] though they have, I think, been held in disdain by our prophets. For their diviners never had knowledge of everything, nor did even the demonic powers at work in them. (3) So it is necessary for those attempting to interpret spiritual things to be spiritual and wise regarding divine matters, since it is for "spiritual people to judge spiritual matters,"[5] according to the divine apostle. I, however, am as far away from the working of the Spirit as I am from the divine and highest wisdom; therefore it is with rashness rather than assurance that I have undertaken this essay, for

1. 2 Tm 3.16.
2. Jn 13.25.
3. Mk 3.17.
4. Homer, *Iliad* 1.70; cf. Hesiod, *Theogony* 38.
5. 1 Cor 2.13.

"wisdom will not make its way into a crafty soul, nor does it dwell in a body embroiled in sins,"[6] as Solomon and the truth testify.

(4) Therefore I have deliberately chosen the practice of refuting all ill-considered criticism of it, though it is not unknown that some have attempted to say that the present work is both spurious and inconsistent with the rest of the writings of John. I, however, testify to its genuineness because of the sayings which are spiritually profitable and which contain nothing which is not divine and worthy of the author. I have relied, too, on those who are judged to be fathers of the church who have both received and confirmed it: (5) the very great Athanasius in the *Exposition of the Canonical Books of Both the Old and the New Testaments*,[7] blessed Basil in his concise dissertation *Concerning the Son*,[8] Gregory the theologian in his book on *The Coming of the Bishops*,[9] very wise Methodius in his book *On the Resurrection*,[10] Cyril the great in work and word in the sixth book of *The Treatise in Spirit and Truth*;[11] in addition to these, blessed Hippolytus, too, in his *Interpretation of Daniel*.[12] (6) For it would not have found any mention in these such trustworthy fathers if there had been anything wholly spurious and worthless in it. It would have been possible to quote other holy fathers, too, in support of the book, if I did not know that moderation is valued by the wise. For if "the threefold cord will not quickly be broken," according to Ecclesiastes,[13] the sixfold cord could scarcely be broken. (7) What, therefore, does the holy disciple of Christ, glorying in the divine love, tell us by means of the Revelation? So we must now turn to the divine oracles themselves, to his intercessions calling for help.

2. *The Revelation of Jesus Christ, which God gave him to show his slaves what must soon take place, and which he made known by sending it through his angel to his slave John, (2) who bore witness to the word of*

---

6. Wis 1.4 (LXX): κατάχρεῳ ἁμαρτίας; Oec: κατάχρεῳς ἁμαρτίαις.
7. Athanasius, *Ep.* 39.
8. Basil, *Adversus Eunomium* 2.14.
9. Gregory of Nazianzus, *Orationes* 42.1.
10. Methodius, *De resurrectione* 2.28.5.
11. Cyril of Alexandria, *De adoratione et cultu in spiritu et veritate* 6.
12. Hippolytus, *Commentary on Daniel* 3.9.10.
13. Eccl 4.12.

God and to the testimony of Jesus Christ, to all that he saw (Rv 1.1–2).
3. In an introduction it is as well to indicate that in all his writings blessed John delighted in words appropriate to the divinity of our Savior, Jesus Christ. In the present work, however, he employs words appropriate to his humanity, lest he would seem to come to know him from his divine attributes, and not from his human attributes too. (2) For it is a sign of genuine theology to believe that God the Word has been begotten from God and the Father before all eternity and temporal interval, being coeternal and consubstantial with the Father and the Spirit, and joint-ruler of the ages and of all spiritual and perceptible creation, according to the saying of the most wise Paul in the epistle to the Colossians, that "in him all things were created, things in heaven and things on earth, things invisible and visible, whether thrones or dominions or principalities or authorities; all things have been created through him and for him, and he is the head of the body and of the church."[14] "He is the first-fruits, the first-born from the dead, that in everything he might be pre-eminent."[15]

(3) But it is also a sign of genuine theology to believe that in the last days he has become for us and for our salvation a human being, not by divesting himself of his divinity, but by assuming human flesh, animated by a mind. In this way he who is Emmanuel is understood to have been made one from two natures, divinity and humanity, each being complete according to the indwelling Word and according to the different specific characteristic of each nature, without being confused or altered by their combination into a unity, and without being kept separate after the inexpressible and authentic union. For Nestorius and Eutyches are both equally abominable, two diametrically opposed evils.

(4) Therefore, in order that John might present the doctrine of our Savior accurately and precisely, after dwelling on the divine aspects of the Lord, as I have said, in his other writings, he here made use of his human words and thoughts. Nevertheless, neither in the former did he present what is divine apart from what

14. Col 1.18. Oecumenius adds the word "and" (καὶ) to the usual New Testament text.
15. Col 1.16, 18.

is human, nor in the latter what is human apart from what is divine. He rather used a greater or lesser emphasis in his writings. (5) This is why he says, *The Revelation of Jesus Christ which God gave him,* as though he was saying, "Although the present revelation has been given by the Father to the Son, it has now been given by the Son to us," *his slaves.* By calling the saints *slaves* of Christ, he safeguarded his divine nature. For to whom would human beings belong, other than to the creator and maker of humankind? And who is the maker of humankind and of all creation? Nobody except the only Word and Son of God. For "all things were made by him," says the present writer in the gospel.[16]

(6) But what does he mean by adding *what must soon take place,* since those things which were going to happen have not yet been fulfilled, although a very long time, more than five hundred years, has elapsed since this was said? The reason is that all the ages are reckoned as nothing in the eyes of the infinite, eternal God. "For a thousand years," says the prophet, "in your sight, Lord, are as yesterday which is past, and a watch in the night."[17] On this account, therefore, he added *soon,* looking not to the actual time of the fulfillment of the future events, but to the power and eternity of God. For in fact, all temporal extension, even though it may be as long and protracted as possible, is short when compared to eternity. (7) He says, therefore, that Jesus Christ *made known* to me *what must take place,* not as appearing and speaking in person, but *through his angel* he initiated me into his mysteries. You see the truthfulness of this divine writer, in admitting that it was through an angel that the revelation came to him, and that he did not hear it from the mouth of the Lord. (8) The angel, says John, *bore witness to the word of God and to the testimony of Jesus Christ, to all that he saw:* he has used this method in the gospel, too, so preserving the trustworthiness of his teaching. He said there, "This is he who is bearing witness to these things, and who has written these things; and we know that his testimony is true,"[18] and now, he says, he is the witness of the

16. Jn 1.3.
17. Ps 89.4. Throughout this translation, the references to the Psalms are given in the Greek version (LXX).
18. Jn 21.24.

divine word which was seen by him, which refers to the present Revelation and the witness given by Christ, that is, "By means of the witness I am witness and author."

4. *Blessed is the one who reads and listens to the words of this prophecy, and those who keep what is written therein; for the time is near* (Rv 1.3).

5. He does not call blessed those who are only readers; in that case there would have been many so blessed (for there are very many readers), but he means those who both listen and so obey the exhortations in the prophecy, and those who faithfully keep and observe its precepts as divine laws. For, he says, *the time is near.* (2) For to everyone who keeps the commandments of God the time of blessedness is near at hand. He either means this, or that the time of the outcome of what is said is near. What is meant by *near* has been explained earlier.

6. He says, *John to the seven churches that are in Asia: Grace to you and peace from God, who is and who was and who is coming* (Rv 1.4).

7. This is the same as saying, "Grace to you from the God of us all." For the Father calls himself "being" when addressing the most wise Moses at the bush, saying, "I am who I am,"[19] (2) and the present blessed evangelist said "he was" about the Son, saying, "In the beginning was the Word, and the Word was with God, and the Word was God,"[20] and again in the first of the general epistles, "That which was from the beginning, which we have heard, which we have seen with our eyes, which we looked upon and which our hands touched, concerning the Word of life."[21] (3) And by *the one who is coming* he means the Holy Spirit. For not only was the Spirit present on the day of Pentecost, according to the narrative in Acts, but he is always present, too, to the souls worthy of receiving him.

8. *And from the seven spirits,* he says, *who are before his throne* (Rv 1.4).

19. Ex 3.14. 20. Jn 1.1.
21. 1 Jn 1.1.

9. The seven spirits are seven angels; but not as being equally honored or coeternal were they included with the Holy Trinity—far from it—but as genuine servants and faithful slaves. For the prophet says to God, "For all things are your slaves."[22] In *all things* the angels are also comprised. And again the same prophet says about them, "Bless the Lord, all his hosts, his ministers that do his will."[23] In this fashion, too, the apostle addressed Timothy when writing the first letter: "I charge you," he says, "before God and Jesus Christ and the elect angels."[24] (2) Further, by saying *who are before his throne* John gave added testimony to their rank as servants and ministers, and certainly not as having equal dignity.

10. *And from Jesus Christ,* he says, *the faithful witness, the first-born of the dead, and the ruler of the kings of the earth* (Rv 1.5).

11. Earlier he had written about the pre-incarnate Word of God, describing him as *he who was;* now he speaks about him as incarnate, saying, *and from Jesus Christ.* He does not separate him into two, but witnesses to both aspects of him at once, both that he is the Word of the Father and that he was made flesh. He is *the faithful witness;* (2) for according to the apostle "he bore witness before Pontius Pilate by a good confession."[25] But he says *he was* because he is God and Lord of all even though he is incarnate. Such witness is certainly the truth. For he calls the one who is *true* faithful and trustworthy. (3) *The first-born of the dead:* to this Paul, too, bears witness, saying, "He is the first-fruits, the first-born from the dead."[26] They call him *the first-born from the dead* as being the one who initiated the universal resurrection, and who "opened for us a new and living way," the resurrection from the dead, "through the veil, that is, his flesh" according to Scripture.[27] For all those who rose from the dead before the coming of the Lord were again delivered to death; for that was not the true resurrection, but a temporary remission of death. This is why none of those was called *the first-born from the dead.* But the Lord is called this, as he was both the origin and cause of the

22. Ps 118.91.   23. Ps 102.21.
24. 1 Tm 5.21.   25. 1 Tm 6.13.
26. Col 1.18.   27. Heb 10.20.

true resurrection. And just as he is a kind of first-fruits of the resurrection of human beings, so when he became a human being
he led the way, as it were from a porch, from death to life. For
concerning the Lord alone blessed Paul wrote in his epistle to
the Romans, saying, "We know that since Christ was raised from
the dead he no longer dies: death will no longer have any power
over him. For by his death he died to sin once for all, and by his
life he is alive to God."[28]

(4) He says, *the ruler of the kings of the earth:* Daniel also said
this to the king of Babylon, "until you know that the Most High
is lord over the kingdom of heaven, and he will give it to whom
he pleases."[29] So Christ is also the king of all those in heaven. But
now meanwhile he speaks about those on the earth. As he goes
on he shows him to be king of the holy legions in the heavens,
too.

12. *To him who loved us and washed us from our sins by his blood*
(2) *and appointed a kingdom for us,*[30] *priests to God and his prophets,
to him be glory and might for ever and ever, amen* (Rv 1.5–6).

13. The syntax of these words goes from the end to the beginning. He means that it was to him *who loved us* that *glory and might*
are due. For how did he not love who "gave himself as a ransom"
for the life of the world?[31] (2) *And to him who washed us from our
sins by his blood:* for he himself removed "the bond which stood
against us with its legal demands, and he nailed it to the" wood
of his "cross,"[32] paying for our sins by his own death, and with his
own blood setting us free from our transgressions. He did this by
"becoming subject unto death, even death on the cross,"[33] and
so healing our disobedience.

(3) *And appointed a kingdom for us:* and what is the advantage
of our becoming, as he says, *priests to God and his prophets*? That
human beings should have been considered worthy of these
both confirms for us the kingdom to come and promises inef-

28. Rom 6.9–10.
29. Dn 5.21.
30. Oecumenius here reads ἡμῖν ("for us"), with some manuscripts of
Revelation, instead of the usual ἡμᾶς ("us").
31. 1 Tm 2.6.   32. Col 2.14.
33. Phil 2.8.

fable glory in the present. For this is greater and more wonderful than washing away our sins in his own blood, and deserves to be called the gift of God, just as our appointment as priests and prophets of God without having made any kind of previous offering is the mark of such a gift.

14. *See, he is coming on the clouds of heaven, and every eye will see him, as well as those who pierced him; and all the tribes of the earth will mourn over him. Yea, Amen* (Rv 1.7).

15. Of his *coming on the clouds of heaven,* the Lord in fact spoke about himself, in the gospel according to Mark, saying: "And the powers in the heavens shall be shaken, and then they will see the Son of man coming in clouds with great power and glory."[34] For, I think, just as it is written in Acts that, when he was going up in the heavens on the day of his ascension, "a cloud took him from their sight," so he will again come with a cloud.[35] (2) I think that the Holy Scripture figuratively calls the holy angels *clouds* because of their lightness and being high above the world and walking on air, as though it was saying, "the Lord will come mounted on the angels of God as his bodyguard." For this is how the prophet also introduces him, saying, "And he mounted on cherubim and flew; he flew on the wings of the winds."[36]

(3) *And every eye,* he says, *will see him, as well as those who pierced him:* for his splendid second coming will not occur in a corner, nor secretly, as at first, when he visited the world in the flesh. The prophet clearly foreshadowed his first coming, saying, "And he will come down like rain on a fleece and like a shower falling in drops on the earth."[37] But his second coming will be open and clear so as to be seen by every eye, even by the very sinful and unholy, among whom must be classed those who drunkenly abused or pierced him.

(4) *And all the tribes of the earth,* he says, *will mourn over him*— that is to say, those who continued in unbelief and did not choose to bend their necks under his saving yoke. But the words *over him* you will understand to refer to his appearance and com-

34. Mk 13.25–26.
36. Ps 17.11.
35. Acts 1.9.
37. Ps 71.6.

ing. (5) Then to declare the certainty of that which is to happen he added, *Yea, amen,* all but saying precisely and unambiguously that these things will take place. For just as among Greeks *Yea* [ναὶ] expresses assent to what will happen, so also does *Amen* among the Hebrews.

16. *I am Alpha and Omega, says the Lord God, who is and who was and who is coming, the sovereign Lord, and Lord of creation* (Rv 1.8).
17. *Alpha* means the beginning, and *Omega* the end. Therefore he says, *I am the first and the last* (Rv 1.17), declaring by the first that God has no beginning, and by the last that he has no end. For since with human beings there is nothing that is without beginning and end, he used what is for us the beginning and the end, instead of saying, "without beginning and without end." This is also what God said through Isaiah: "I, God, am the first, and I shall be for the ages to come."[38] (2) He calls God *sovereign Lord, and Lord of creation,* of spiritual as well as of perceptible creation.

18. *I am John, your brother, and fellow-participant in your hardships and endurance in your kingdom* (Rv 1.9).[39]
19. He was writing to the faithful who had suffered much for the gospel and the preaching of Christ at the hands of those who persecuted the godly. He calls himself as being "in Jesus" as sharing both in their *hardships* and *endurance,* and in the kingdom of God, because of the way they deal with their hardships for the sake of the Word.

20. *I was on the island called Patmos on account of the word of God and the testimony of Jesus* (Rv 1.9).
21. He says "on account of Jesus"; for this is what being "in Jesus" means. And *on account of his word and testimony,* to which I testified when I proclaimed his gospel, *I was* (he says) banished

---

38. Is 41.4.
39. The manuscripts of Revelation have "in the kingdom and endurance in Jesus" (ἐν ... βασιλείᾳ καὶ ὑπομονῇ ἐν Ἰησοῦ), for which Oecumenius reads "endurance in (your) kingdom" (ἐν βασιλείᾳ ὑπομονή).

on Patmos. That he suffered this Eusebius narrates in his *Canonical Chronicle* in the time of the emperor Domitian.[40] (2) Then he goes on to say that, while he was living on the aforementioned island,

22. *I was in the Spirit on the Lord's day* (Rv 1.10). 23. The words *I was in the Spirit* indicate that he saw a vision which was not perceptible by the senses nor seen with physical ears or eyes, but with prophetic sense. Isaiah spoke about this spiritual hearing, when he went on to tell "me to understand early—early he went on to give me an ear to hear, and the discipline of the Lord opens my ears."[41]

24.(1–2) *And I heard a loud voice like a trumpet saying to me, "John, write what you see in a book and send it to the seven churches, to Ephesus, Smyrna, Pergamum, Thyatira, Sardis, Philadelphia, and Laodicea"* (Rv 1.10–11). 25. There are more cities in Asia than these, but he is ordered to write to those converted by him, and which had already received the faith of Christ. As for the unbelieving and those who turn away from the saving word, how could anyone even exhort them?

26. *And I turned to see the voice that was speaking to me, and on turning I saw seven golden lampstands, (2) and in the midst of the seven lampstands one like a son of man, clothed with a long robe stretching to his feet, and girt round his breast with a golden girdle. (3) His head and his hair were like white wool, just like snow, (4) and his eyes were like a flame of fire; and his feet were like burnished bronze refined in a furnace, and his voice was like the sound of many waters; (5) and he had in his right hand seven stars; and from his mouth was issuing a sharp two-edged sword; and his face was like the sun shining in full strength* (Rv 1.12–16). 27. The seven lampstands, as he himself goes on to explain, are the seven churches to which he had been commanded to

40. Eusebius of Caesarea, *Chronicon Paschale* 250c.
41. Is 50.4–5.

write. He called them *lampstands* as carrying in them the illumination of the glory of Christ. He did not call them lamps, but *lampstands*. The lampstand itself cannot illuminate; it carries in itself that which is able to illuminate. Christ illuminates his churches spiritually. (2) Just as the holy apostle exhorts those who have received the faith, "Be like stars in the world, holding fast the word of life,"[42]—and the star does not have light of its own but is capable of receiving light brought in from elsewhere—so also here the evangelist saw the churches as lampstands and not lamps. (3) For concerning Christ it is said, "You shine gloriously from the everlasting mountains"[43]—perhaps meaning angelic powers—and, again, addressing the Father, "Send out your light and your truth,"[44] and again, "the light of your face, Lord."[45] So those who share in the divine light are described in one place as stars and in another as lampstands. (4) He calls the lampstands *golden* on account of the honor and transcendence of those thought worthy of receiving the beam of divine light.

(5) *And in the midst of the seven lampstands,* he says, *one like a son of man:* for since the Lord himself promises to dwell in the souls of those who have received him and to walk in their midst, how could he not have been seen *in the midst of the lampstands?* (6) He calls Christ son of man as one who for us humbled himself as far as "taking the form of a slave,"[46] who became "the fruit of the womb," according to the divine hymn,[47] the womb of Mary, unwed and ever-virgin. Since Mary was a human being and our sister, naturally he who is born from her without seed as a human being is called God the Word and the son of man. He has carefully called him not a son of man, but *one like a son of man;* but he who is Emmanuel is also God and Lord of the universe. (7) The vision shows his varied appearance by his operations and powers, as it depicts his form. First he clothes him with a priestly dress, for the long robe and girdle are a priestly dress. He was addressed by God and the Father, "You are a priest for ever according to the order of Melchisedek,"[48] but the apostle, too, calls

42. Phil 2.15–16.
44. Ps 43.3.
46. Phil 2.7.
48. Heb 5.6; Ps 109.4.

43. Ps 75.3.
45. Ps 44.3.
47. Ps 126.3.

Christ "the high priest and apostle of our confession,"[49] as being
in the priestly service and leading us to make our confession of
faith in him and the Father and the Spirit. (8) He puts a golden
girdle around him, whereas the priests according to the [Mo-
saic] Law had a girdle of embroidered cloth. The difference between slaves and a master had to be pointed out, that is, the difference between the shadow of the law and the truth shown by
the new girdle.

(9) *His head,* he says, *and his hair were like white wool* and *like
snow:* for God's secret purpose in Christ is new in its appearance,
but it is before all ages in its intention. For the blessed apostle
has written about it as "the secret purpose which has been kept
hidden in all past ages and from generations, which has now
been revealed to those of his holy people whom he wished."[50]
Therefore, the age-old intention of the purpose revealed in
God's good pleasure is represented by the hoariness of the head
and its comparison with wool and snow.

(10) He says, *and his eyes were like a flame of fire:* this either
means that the flame of fire has the form of light—since Christ
both is light and calls himself light, saying "I am the light and
the truth"[51]—or it exposes the danger and the threat against the
seven churches to whom the facts of the Revelation are passed
on, in that they were not fully following his laws.

(11) *And his feet,* he says, *were like burnished bronze:* he refers
to the bronze mined on Mount Lebanon as being pure even
in itself and as rendered even purer when it has been refined
in a furnace and cleansed of its slight impurity. In this way the
steadfastness and constancy, as well as the brightness and glory,
of faith in Christ is signified when it has come to assurance. For
the apostle calls Christ "a rock,"[52] and Isaiah calls him "a precious
stone" in the foundations "of Sion."[53] (12) Else he means that
the burnished bronze is the copper-colored frankincense which
medical men are accustomed to call male.[54] This is fragrant when
burnt; for the fiery furnace represents the symbol of the burn-

49. Heb 3.1.
51. Jn 8.12; 14.6.
53. Is 28.16.
54. The Greek (ἄρρην) means "male" or "masculine."
50. Col 1.26–27.
52. 1 Cor 10.4.

ing of incense, which is the foundation of the preaching of the gospel—for the feet are the foundation of the rest of the body, which is Christ. For he is fragrant, and with spiritual fragrance he gives charm to the things in heaven and the things on earth. (13) Paul, too, calls Christ "a foundation" in writing the first epistle to the Corinthians, saying, "Like a wise master-builder I have laid a foundation, and another builds upon it. Let each one take care how he builds on it. For no one can lay any other foundation than that which is laid, which is Jesus Christ."[55] (14) That Christ is spiritually sweet-smelling, the bride in the Song of Songs who has experienced his sweet scent bears witness. In one place she says, "and the fragrance of your oils is above all spices," and in another, "your name is oil emptied out,"[56] and the Lord himself also describes himself as sweet-smelling in the words to the bride, saying, "I am a flower of the field, a lily of the valleys."[57] What then? Did not Paul, too, after becoming sweet-smelling from his communion with Christ, say, "for we are the fragrance of Christ";[58] and again, to us "he reveals the fragrance of the knowledge of him"?[59]

(15) *And his voice,* he says, *was like the sound of many waters,* and reasonably so; for how could his *voice* have come *to all the earth and* his gospel *to the ends of the world,* unless it had been clearly heard, not as a perceived loud sound, but by the power of the preaching?

(16) *And he had,* he says, *in his right hand seven stars:* he himself goes on to interpret these stars, saying they were the angels of the seven churches, about whom blessed Gregory spoke at the coming of the bishops: "with reference to the presiding angels, I believe that each is a guardian of each church, as John teaches in the Revelation."[60] I think that he calls the holy angels *stars* on account of the abundant light of Christ, which is in them. (17) They are in his right hand. They have been thought worthy of the most honorable position by God's side, and, as it were, they rest in the hand of God.

55. 1 Cor 3.10–11.
56. Song 1.3 (source of both quotations).
57. Song 2.1.   58. 2 Cor 2.15.
59. 2 Cor 2.14.
60. Gregory of Nazianzus, *Orationes* 42.9.

(18) *And from his mouth,* he says, *there was issuing a sharp two-edged sword:* blessed David says to the Lord, "Gird your sword upon your thigh, O mighty one."[61] For he had not then commanded us to keep the laws of the gospel, to transgress which was destruction. Therefore the actual position of the thigh indicated the postponement of punishment; for it was not the most suitable position for killing. (19) But now the sword issues from his mouth, the metaphor symbolizing that those who disobey the injunctions of the gospel will be in mortal danger of being cut in two by the sword. This is made clear by what the Lord says in the gospels. The apostle, too, said, "For the word of God is living and active and keener than a two-edged sword,"[62] that is to say, holding out a threat against the disobedient. So this is described by John as *sharp,* which is the same as what Paul calls "very keen."

(20) *His face,* he says, *was like the sun shining in full strength.* Deservedly *like the sun,* for *the Lord is the sun of righteousness* according to the prophet Malachi.[63] But lest you should think that the light of the countenance of Christ, which "gives light to everyone, coming into the world,"[64] was a manifest body giving perceptible light, he added *by his power,* just as if he were saying: "The light of Christ is to be spiritually perceived, 'operating in power,'[65] not a physical appearance, but giving light to the eyes of the soul."

28. *And when I saw him,* he says, *I fell at his feet as though dead. And he laid his right hand upon me, saying, "I am the first and the last, and the living one; (2) I was dead, and see, I am alive for ever and ever, and I have the keys of Death and of Hades. (3) So write what you have seen, both what is and what is going to take place after this"* (Rv 1.17–19).

29. It is the habit of the holy prophets when seeing a vision to be struck with amazement and to exhibit human weakness. Divine matters far exceed human affairs, and surpass them in ways past all comparison. We know that this is what Joshua the son of Nun felt when he saw the commander-in-chief of the battle-line of the Lord, as did Daniel, "the man of desires," in the visions

61. Ps 44.4.　　62. Heb 4.12.
63. Mal 4.2.　　64. Jn 1.9.
65. Col 1.29.

seen by him.[66] (2) Therefore *I fell at his feet as though dead,* says the evangelist, struck with amazement by the sight. But *he laid his right hand upon me, saying, Do not fear.* Saint John would not have been able to stay alive as a result of being struck by the vision, if the saving right hand of the Son of God had not touched him, which could effect so many marvels with a single touch.

(3) And he says to me, *I am the first and the last,* as if he said, "I am the one who came to be with you in the flesh for the salvation of all of you at the end of the age, though *I am the first* and 'the first-born of all creation.'[67] So how can you suffer any evil from my appearance? For if while living and being a fountain of life for you I died and again came to life after trampling on death, how can you who have life because of me and my vision, ever become dead? (4) And if *I also have the keys of Death and of Hades,* so that those whom I wish I may put to death or preserve alive, and if I could send them down to Hades and bring them up in accordance with what has been written about me, and mine are, as the prophet says, "the ways of escape from death,"[68] I would not dispatch my worshipers and disciples to an untimely death." (5) Since, therefore, he will not die, he says, *write what you have seen, both what is and what is going to take place.* In saying *what is,* he means both past and present events, and in saying, *what is going to take place,* he means future events. Of the things seen in the vision by the holy one, some had already taken place. Even if he had gone back as far as he could, these events would not have preceded the beginning. So he mentioned *what is;* but the argument will go on to show some events that were past and some which were still to take place.

30. He speaks of *the mystery of the seven stars which you saw in my right hand, and the seven golden lampstands. The seven stars are the angels of the churches, and the seven lampstands are the seven churches* (Rv 1.20).

31. Now since he has made clear to him what the stars and what the lampstands are, he goes on to speak of the evidence

66. Jos 1.9; Dn 10.11 and 8.17.
67. Col 1.15.
68. Ps 67.21.

against each of the churches. He explains to the blessed evangelist how he is to lay a charge against the church which strays far away from the divine purpose, and how he is to commend the carefulness of those who observe part of the evangelical law, while in other cases he is to set right those which are stumbling. Christ, "who wills all people to be saved"[69] and wishes them to become heirs and partners of his own bounty, has ordered his word and teaching as an appropriate remedy for each of the churches, and has enjoined the evangelist to spread abroad the gospel and his teaching. (2) To him be glory for ever and ever. Amen.

69. 1 Tm 2.4.

CHAPTER TWO

HE FIRST TASK of my argument and commentary is completed. My next aim must be to describe the exhortations addressed to the churches. The first enjoins him to write to the church in Ephesus as presiding over the rest of Asia, saying thus:

2. *To the angel of the church in Ephesus write: Thus says he who holds the seven stars in his right hand, who walks in the midst of the seven golden lampstands: (2) "I know your works, your toil, and your patient endurance, and that you cannot bear evil men but have tested those who call themselves apostles, but are not, and you found them to be liars; (3) and you have patience, and you bore up for my name's sake, and you did not give up. (4) But I have this against you, that you have abandoned the love you had at first. (5) Remember then from where you have fallen, and repent, and do what you did at first in righteousness. Otherwise, I shall come to you and remove your lampstand from its place, unless you repent. (6) But you have this good point,[1] that you hate the works of the Nicolaitans, which I also hate. (7) He who has an ear, let him listen to what the Spirit says to the churches. I shall grant those who listen to eat of the tree of life, which is in the paradise of my God"* (Rv 2.1–7).[2]

3. By *the angel of the church of Ephesus* he means metaphorically the church in Ephesus. For it is not his own angel presiding over the church who has committed any sin who needs to hear *Repent,* since he is the most holy one and is therefore also on the right hand of the Lord, displaying the proof of his natural purity and sparkling light. (2) What need could there be to say to the one giving God's message to the evangelist, *Write* to him? For the di-

---

1. Oecumenius has added the word "good" (ἀγαθόν) to the text of Revelation.

2. In v.7 Oecumenius has added "my" (μου), the significance of which he goes on to discuss.

vine angel was present and was listening to what was being said. The holy angel was on the right hand of the one who was speaking, and when the holy one himself finally interprets the vision seen by him, he says, *He who has an ear, let him listen to what the Spirit is saying to the churches:* he did not say "to the angels of the churches," but *to the churches.* So then in the same way you are to understand that, wherever you find *write* these things *to the angel* of this *church,* he is referring not to the angel but to the church.

(3) What does he command to be written to the church in Ephesus? He says, *He who holds the seven stars in his right hand, who walks in the midst of the seven golden lampstands, says this:* this is the same as saying, "These are the words of him who treats with care and holds fast and embraces both the holy angels in heaven"—for these are the seven stars—"and human beings on earth." For these are the seven lampstands, as was said earlier. He walks in the midst of those who worship him, and says through the prophet, "I shall dwell among them and I shall walk about among them."[3]

(4) He says, *I know your works, your toil, and your patient endurance,* and "nothing of the good things which you do has escaped me,"[4] "who alone formed" your "hearts, and who understand all" your "deeds,"[5] (5) and, he says, *you cannot bear evil men,* since you have acquired the habit of hating evil.

And you tested those who called themselves apostles, but are not, and you found them to be liars: the Ephesians were fulfilling the divine command: "Do not believe every spirit, but test the spirits, to see whether they are of God."[6] Therefore they used to test those among them who were proclaiming the gospel, and after testing them they found some false apostles who were imparting spurious beliefs. He is referring to the followers of Cerinthus, who were contemporaries of the evangelist and were preachers of profane doctrines.

(6) He says, *You have patience, and you bore up for my name's sake, and you did not give up,* and very fittingly; for it is said, "Bear one another's burdens and so fulfill the law of God."[7] (7) *But,* he

3. Lv 26.12.
5. Ps 32.15.
7. Gal 6.2.

4. Jb 34.21.
6. 1 Jn 4.1.

says, *I have this against you, that you have abandoned the love you had at first. Remember then from where you have fallen, and repent, and do what you did at first in righteousness:* just as he said, "Your good actions have not escaped me,"[8] so he says that you did not fail to show love to those in need. Return therefore to your former welldoing, now that I have taught you where you have fallen short.

(8) But if, he says, you will not return to where you came from, *I shall come to you and remove your lampstand from its place, unless you repent. I shall come to you* does not indicate a movement involving a change of place of God who fills all things, but a change of attitude such as from long-suffering to punishment. By the removal of the lampstand, that is, the church, he means his abandonment of it, as a result of which sinners become involved in every kind of disturbance and tumult, so that they say, "My eye was troubled in my soul, and my heart was troubled with-in me."[9]

(9) He says, *But you have this good point, that you hate the works of the Nicolaitans, which I also hate.* He has placed their sin between two achievements, so that by the praises at each end he may assuage the rebuke in the middle, lest anyone be consumed by excessive distress. This Nicolaus to whom he is now referring had been a blasphemous and disgusting heresiarch. So those who were being overcome by his evil errors were rescued by the Ephesians, who were thus commended by Christ. (10) Then after the divine admonition the evangelist adds his own words, saying, *He who has an ear,* that is, who is obedient and submissive to the divine laws, *let him listen to what the Spirit says to the churches.* He said *the Spirit* either because the events of the Revelation were being carried out in the Spirit, or he calls Christ *Spirit,* as in fact he is and is understood to be God, just as of course he is also called the son of man, as he is and is perceived as man. For the Godhead as a whole is called *Spirit,* as the Lord himself says to the Samaritan woman when talking with her, "God is Spirit, and those who worship him must worship him in Spirit and truth."[10] (11) So what does the Spirit say? To him who conquers *I shall grant to eat of the tree of life, which is in the paradise of my God:* the phrase is

8. Jb 34.21.
9. Ps 30.10; 54.4.
10. Jn 4.24.

figurative, for by *the tree of life* he means the blessed and eternal life, which the saints will enjoy in the kingdom of God, which he has now called *Paradise*. He says that those who have been victorious over the temptations of the enemy and who have exacted vengeance are worthy of this. (12) But no one should take offense at the Lord's saying *of my God,* for all the words denoting humility are rightly ascribed to the mystery of the incarnation. For he has also said in the gospel, "I am ascending to my Father and your Father, to my God and your God."[11] This is what he published in the church of Ephesus.

4. He says, *And to the angel of the church in Smyrna write: These are the words of the first and the last, who was dead and came to life: (2) I know your tribulation and your poverty, but you are rich, and I know the slander of those who say they are Jews and are not, but are a synagogue of Satan. (3) Have no fear because of what you are going to suffer. See, the Devil is going to throw some of you into prison, that you may be tested, and you will be tested for ten days. Be faithful to death, and I will give you the crown of life. He who has an ear, let him listen to what the Spirit says to the churches. (4) He who conquers shall not be harmed by the second death* (Rv 2.8–11).

5. The Lord calls himself *first* because of his Godhead, but he calls himself *last* because of his humanity and the mystery of his incarnation. (2) He says, *he who was dead and came to life:* he who went to the trial of death, he means, and by death put death to death. (3) *I know your tribulation and your poverty:* do not say, as the disbelieving Jews said, "Why did we fast and you did not know? Why did we humble our souls and you took no notice?"[12] (4) He says, *but you are rich,* since you have Christ as your rich protector, even though "he became poor" for our sake,[13] "taking the form of a servant,"[14] and incurring the blasphemy of the spurious Jews. (5) So Judas is interpreted as "confession," and Israel as "those who spiritually see God."[15] Therefore the true Jews and

11. Jn 20.17.
12. Is 58.3.
13. 2 Cor 8.9.
14. Phil 2.7.
15. With a reference to the popular (but mistaken) belief that Israel etymologically means "man seeing God," as in Philo, *On Abraham* 57–58, *On*

the spiritual Israel would be those who confess Christ. "For he is not a real Jew who is one outwardly, nor is the external circumcision in the flesh" acceptable to God, as Paul says, "but he is a Jew who is one inwardly, and circumcision is that of the heart,"[16] and not of the flesh. Those Jews therefore who have remained in unbelief are found to be a blasphemous synagogue under the command of Satan.

(6) He says, *Have no fear because of what you are going to suffer. See, the Devil is about to throw some of you into prison, that you may be tested, and you will suffer tribulation for ten days;* for by the action of the Devil people ill-treat the godly. And God consents, making them more acceptable by their temptations. "But," he says, "take courage; your tribulation will soon be over and is of a short duration."

(7) He says, *Be faithful to death, and I will give you the crown of life:* this is true, for it is also said, "He who endures to the end will be saved,"[17] assuredly not the one who throws away his shield and shows cowardice in battle.

(8) *He who has an ear, let him listen to what the Spirit says to the churches. He who conquers shall not be harmed by the second death.* What is said is exceedingly accurate; for to the first death, which is the separation of the soul from the body, all alike, both righteous and sinners, are subject, so that the divine pronouncement may achieve its end: "you are dust, and to dust you shall return."[18] But the second death, of sin, which the Lord mentions when he says, "Leave the dead to bury their own dead,"[19] would not injure those who conquer their temptations.

6. *And,* he says, *to the angel of the church in Pergamum write: These things says the one who has the sharp two-edged sword: (2) I know where you dwell, where Satan's throne is; you hold fast my name, and you did not deny my faith even in the days of Antipas my witness, my faithful one, who was killed among you, where Satan dwells. (3) But I have a few things against you: you have some there who hold the teaching of*

---

the *Embassy to Gaius* 4, and found elsewhere as in Basil, *Enarrationes in prophetam Isaiam* 9.23.

16. Rom 2.28.   17. Mt 10.22.
18. Gn 3.19.   19. Mt 8.22.

Balaam, who taught Balak to put a stumbling-block before the sons of Israel, to eat food sacrificed to idols and commit fornication. (4) In the same way you also have some who hold the teaching of the Nicolaitans. (5) Repent: otherwise I will come to you soon and make war against them with the sword of my mouth. (6) He who has an ear, let him listen to what the Spirit says to the churches. To him who conquers I shall give a white stone, and on the stone a new name, which no one knows except the one who receives it (Rv 2.12–17).

7. And, he says, "you shall write to the church in Pergamum: I say to you, I who carry in my mouth a sword to exact vengeance on those who transgress my commandments." The sword in his mouth symbolizes the danger of those who are not obedient to the divine commands. He says, "you dwell at the throne of Satan." (2) All of Asia is given to idolatry, but especially Pergamum. But he also says, "although you were living in such a place, you kept my faith unsullied: you did not turn aside to follow the determination of the majority to do evil, but you even spoke against them in the days and feasts of the idols, like *my faithful witness,* who," he says, "boldly spoke in my name. As far as the plotters are concerned, you kept close to me right up to death in guarding the truth. (3) But since blame attaches even to the most holy, and since 'we all often stumble,' as Scripture says,[20] to you in spite of your faithfulness," he says, "I still have a complaint to make." For *you have some there who hold the teaching of Balaam, who taught Balak to put a stumbling-block before the sons of Israel, to eat food sacrificed to idols and commit fornication. In the same way you also have some who hold the teaching of the Nicolaitans:* in the words *he taught Balak* he explains the sort of teacher he had. The story of Balaam and Balak is clearly written down in Numbers; Numbers is a book of the very wise Moses. Josephus[21] recounts that by the plotting of Balaam the Midianite women had been sent to Israel to lead them to fornication and to apostatize from God. [The angel] says, "you have those from Nicolaus who do such things, and you do not banish them from you." (4) Then he says, *Repent: otherwise I will come to you soon and make war against them with the sword of my mouth.* "O the depth of the riches

20. Jas 3.2.
21. Josephus, *De antiquitatibus Iudaeorum* 4.126–140.

and wisdom" and goodness "of God!"[22] For he did not say, *I shall come to you and make war* "against you," but *I shall make war against them*, that is, the Nicolaitans. For he spared those in Pergamum who were faithful and godly. (5) He says, *He who has an ear, let him listen to what the Spirit says to the churches. To him who conquers I shall give him some of the hidden manna* of the mystery:[23] in other words he said, "I shall grant them to be filled with the spiritual and future blessings." (6) *And I shall give him a white stone;* that is, one which has won the victory and is bright with glory; *and on the stone a new name, which no one knows except the one who receives it:* for it is said, "What eye has not seen, nor ear heard, nor what has entered the human heart—all that God has prepared for those who love him."[24]

8. *And to the angel of the church in Thyatira write: These things says the Son of God, with eyes like a flame of fire and feet like burnished bronze:* (2) *I know your works, your love and faith and service and patient endurance, and your works, and that your last works were more than the first.* (3) *But I have this against you, that you tolerate the woman Jezebel, who calls herself a prophetess and is teaching and misleading my servants to commit fornication and to eat food sacrificed to idols.* (4) *I gave her time to repent, but she does not wish to repent of her fornication.* (5) *See, I am throwing her into a bed and those who commit adultery with her into great tribulation,* (6) *unless they repent of her practices. And I will strike her children dead. And all the churches shall know that I am he who searches minds and hearts, and I will give to each of you according to your works.* (7) *But I say to the rest of you in Thyatira, all who do not hold this teaching, those who have not learned the deep things of Satan, as they say,* (8) *I am not laying upon you any other burden, only hold fast that which you have until I come.* (9) *He who conquers and keeps my works until the end, to him I will give authority over the nations,* (10) *and he shall be a shepherd to them with a rod of iron, as when clay pots are broken in pieces,* (11) *as I myself have received au-*

22. Rom 11.33.
23. The phrase τοῦ μυστηρίου does not occur in Rv 2.17, and the sentence "I shall give him some of the hidden manna" (δώσω αὐτῷ τοῦ μάννα τοῦ κεκρυμμένου) is omitted in Oecumenius's text as first given in the lemma upon which he is commenting.
24. 1 Cor 2.9.

thority from my Father; and I will give him the morning star. (12) *He who has an ear, let him listen to what the Spirit says to the churches* (Rv 2.18–29).

9. He who addresses the evangelist explains more clearly his own proper title. He says, *These things says the Son of God, with eyes like a flame of fire,* symbolizing his striking and threatening attitude against sinners. *And feet like burnished bronze,* indicating the constancy and stability of faith in him, or the spiritual fragrance of the evangelical teachings, as has been said above. (2) He says, *I know your works, your love and faith and service,* as if he were saying, "I praise all your devotion." For he has put *I know* instead of "I praise," just as "I know you to be above all people"[25] was said to Moses, and "the Lord knows the way of the righteous."[26] He calls *service* aid to those in need. (3) He says, *And the last are more than the first:* he declares that as they progressed they grew in stature in fulfilling the commandments.

(4) *But I have this against you,* to show that to be completely sinless belongs to God alone. What do *I have* against you? *That you tolerate the woman Jezebel* and you do not banish her, *who calls herself a prophetess:* he describes the wickedness of this church in terms relating to Jezebel, the consort of Ahab. *She,* he says, *who calls herself a prophetess is teaching and misleading* many to commit fornication and *eat food sacrificed to idols:* he means either actual fornication or apostasy from God, according to what is said, "and they committed fornication by their practices,"[27] and again, "they committed adultery with a tree."[28] (5) But the Lord, who does not wish the death of a sinner, but his conversion and life, says, "I have given her time for repentance. But if she does not wish to repent, I shall do the same to her as to those committing adultery with her, in order that all may know," he says, "that I am God, for it is God's business to search the minds and hearts. For Scripture says, 'God, who examines the hearts and minds.'[29] (6) But to those who have nothing in common with the adulterous woman, who are more simple and do not know the crafty ways of the evil one, say this: 'I shall not place any heavier burden upon

25. Ex 33.12.   26. Ps 1.6.
27. Ps 106.39.   28. Jer 3.9.
29. Ps 7.10.

you. Your simplicity is sufficient for you. Only keep the teaching given to you until my second coming.'"

(7) And to him who conquers the evil one, he says, *I will give him authority over the nations and he shall be a shepherd to them with a rod of iron, as when clay pots are broken in pieces, as I myself have received authority from my Father.* This is what is said in the Gospels to those who were good stewards of the pounds and talents entrusted to them: "Be in charge of ten cities"; and to another, "be in charge of five cities";[30] and in Daniel, "And the kingdom shall be given to the saints of God."[31] For he shows by this that some kind of rule and authority will be given to the saints over the more inferior and those in need of correction. So he says he will shepherd them with harsh authority, but the unbelieving he will crush like clay pots.

(8) *And I will give him,* he says, *the morning star.* The prophet says of the Assyrian, that is, Satan, "How did the morning star which rises early in the morning fall from heaven?"[32] So he now calls him the morning star: he says, "I will make Satan subject to my servants." This is similar to what was said by the apostle: "God will soon crush Satan under your feet,"[33] and "You will tread on the asp and the basilisk, and you will trample the lion and the serpent underfoot."[34]

10. *And to the angel of the church in Sardis write: These things says the one who has the seven spirits of God and the seven stars: I know your works, that you have the name of being alive, but you are dead.* (2) *Keep awake, and strengthen what remains and is on the point of death, for I have not found your works fully accomplished in the sight of my God.* (3) *Remember then how you have received and heard [the gospel]; keep it and repent. So if you will not awake, I will come like a thief, and you will not know at what hour I will come upon you.* (4) *Yet you have a few names in Sardis who have not soiled their garments, and who walk with me in white, for they are worthy.* (5) *He who conquers shall be clad in white garments, and I will not blot his name out of the book of life. I will confess his name before my Father and before his angels.* (6) *He who has*

30. Cf. Lk 19.17, 19.
32. Is 14.12.
34. Ps 90.13.

31. Dn 7.22, 27.
33. Rom 16.20.

an ear, let him listen to what the Spirit says to the churches (Rv 3.1–6).
11. Concerning the seven stars, which he now also calls *the spirits of God*, an explanation has been given in what has gone before. But now one must hear what he says about the people in Sardis. (2) He says, *I know your works*, that your name is like that of one who is living a godly, virtuous life, but *you are dead* because of sins. It is customary in Holy Scripture to call *dead* those who are involved in sins, as Paul in his great wisdom writes about those who have changed their course from unbelief to the faith of Christ: "And you who were dead in your transgressions he made alive together with Christ."[35] And the Shepherd says that some have gone down into the water of the font as dead, and have come up again living.[36] (3) But, he says, awake from the sleep of sin *and strengthen what remains, which is at the point of death:* you still have, he says, a few works and practices which are not entirely dead. Therefore, guard them while they are still alive, even though they are already veering towards death. For *strengthen* means "make strong and powerful what is feeble and ready to fall." "Not one of your endeavors," he says, "is full of zeal, but some are dead and others are on the point of death." (4) So he says, "*Remember then how you received* the faith *and heard* the word concerning it, and *keep* alive those of your works which are still living. But *repent* of those which are dead."

(5) *If therefore you will not awake*, he says, "and if you will not arise from your sluggishness as one from sleep, I will come to you," he says, "as a chastiser when you are not expecting it." The holy apostle also says about some others, "When they say, 'peace and safety,' then sudden destruction" will come upon them "as travail comes upon a woman with child."[37] (6) He says, *You have a few names in Sardis who have not soiled their garments, and who walk with me in white, for they are worthy*, for whose sake I am for the present deferring my displeasure and am showing patience towards you. By "unsoiled garments" he means the bodies of the saints, as the patriarch Jacob said, "He washes his garment in

35. Col 2.13.
36. *Shepherd* of Hermas, *Similitude* 9.16.4.
37. 1 Thes 5.3.

wine";[38] and Isaiah says the same thing: "Why are your garments red, like those of one who has come from the wine-press, fully trampled down?"[39] Therefore the white garment symbolizes the purity of the body. (7) He means that *he who conquers* his passions *will be clad* in white in the life to come. "For the righteous will shine like the sun and the moon,"[40] he has himself promised in the gospels. (8) He says that the pure will be written in the book of those who live out that blessed and eternal life. The Lord also mentioned this text in the gospels, saying to his disciples, "Do not rejoice that the demons are subject to you," but "that your names are written in heaven."[41]

(9) And he says, *I will confess their name before my Father and before his angels.* He will confess them as faithful attendants and as willing servants. For in the gospels, too, it is written, If anyone "confesses me before men, I also will confess him before my Father who is in heaven."[42] To speak about his Father and his [Father's] angels does not prevent the holy angels from being his also; at one time they are his Father's, at another time they are his. For he says, according to Matthew, Then "the Son" of man "will send out his angels with a loud trumpet call, and they will gather his elect from the four winds, from one end of heaven to the other."[43]

1 2. *And to the angel of the church in Philadelphia write: These things says the holy one, the true one, who has the key of David, who opens and no one shuts, who shuts and no one opens,* (2) *I know your works: see, I have set before you an open door—no one is able to shut it—I know that you have but little power, but you kept my word and did not deny my law.*[44] (3) *See, I am making those of the synagogue of Satan who say that they are Jews and are not, but they lie—see, I will make them come and worship at your feet, and learn that I have loved you.* (4) *Because you kept the gospel of my endurance, I, too, will keep you safe from the hour of trial which is about to come upon the whole world, to test the in-*

38. Gn 49.11.   39. Is 63.2–3.
40. Mt 13.43.   41. Lk 10.20.
42. Mt 10.32.   43. Mt 24.31.
    44. The text as printed reads νόμον (law), though many manuscripts read ὄνομα (name), which is used later in this section.

habitants of the earth. (5) I am coming soon; hold fast what you have,
so that no one may seize your crown. (6) He who conquers, I will make
him a pillar in the temple[45] *of my God, and he shall never depart from it.*
And I will write on him the name of my God, and the name of the city of
my God, the new Jerusalem, which is coming down from heaven from my
God, and the new name. (7) He who has an ear, let him listen to what
the Spirit is saying to the churches (Rv 3.7–13).

13. To those *in Philadelphia* he says: *Write: these things says the*
holy one, the true one. The holy one is the Son of God. So also he receives witness from the seraphim, who combine the three accla-
mations of "holy" in the one lordship, since the Word possesses
nothing earthly or prone to sin, even if he has become flesh. For
"he did not commit sin, neither was deceit found in his mouth,"
according to the word of Isaiah the prophet.[46] (2) Because he is
and is called *the true one,* he truly is and is so called. He is called
God, and the address is not false. For he is truly God, Emmanuel, even if the accursed Nestorius does not accept this. He has
become a human being, without discarding his divinity, and he
is truly a human being, even if Eutyches, the man hated by God,
chafes at this. What he is, he truly is. This has nothing to do with
analogy, as Nestorians say, nor with semblance or appearance,
as Eutychianists say and the accursed and disgusting tribe of the
Manichaeans.

(3) He says, *he who has the key of David:* he calls authority a
key. For he who has been entrusted with the key of the house
has been entrusted with the authority to open and shut. And he
more clearly states this in the gospels in the promises to Peter.
For when he said, "I will give you the keys of the kingdom of
heaven," he immediately adds, "and whatever you bind on earth
shall be bound in heaven, and whatever you loose on earth shall
be loosed in heaven."[47] (4) Since therefore the key symbolizes
authority, by saying *he who has the key of David* he intimates that
just as David was king of the perceptible Israel, so am I king over
the spiritual Israel as well as over the perceptible Israel, even if

45. Greek ναός strictly refers to the temple itself, but Oecumenius at times
uses it to refer to the whole temple precinct.
46. Is 53.9.
47. Mt 16.19.

the superiority of his authority differs by incomparable excess. For what kind of equal honor can a human being have in comparison with God? This was also the message that the divine angel Gabriel brought to the Virgin about the Lord, saying, "And the Lord God will give him the throne of his father David, and he will reign over the house of Jacob for ever, and of his kingdom there will be no end."[48] Since, therefore, Christ introduced an image of the kingdom of David, he rightly says, *he who has the key of David.* (5) Then continuing with the figure of the key, he adds, *who opens and no one shuts, who shuts and no one opens.* For "God is the one who acquits; who is the one who condemns?"[49] God is the one who condemns; who is the one who acquits? He means that opening and shutting is acquitting and condemning.

(6) He says, *I know your works,* that they are God-fearing, and *I have given you the open door* to well being. Earlier he had said, *he who opens and no one shuts.* Therefore neither will anyone shut *the door* which *I have caused to be opened.* (7) He says, *you have little power, but you kept my word and did not deny my name:* Philadelphia is a little city; consequently, her power is also little. But in guarding the faith of Christ beyond her own strength she arose as it were undaunted, standing fast against those who harried the faithful. (8) Then as a recompense for her loyalty to him, he promises that many of the Jewish persuasion will run up to her and receive the faith of Christ. For this is what worshiping her feet symbolizes, to be chosen in the last days to be brought into the church—simply to be part of the church. This is also what the prophet said in welcome, "I chose to be admitted[50] in the house of my God rather than dwell in the abodes of sinners."[51] (9) Since, therefore, *you kept* my faith in patient endurance, *I, too, will keep you safe in the hour of* evil *trial.* He means the persecution of Christians that took place in the time of the emperor Domi-

---

48. Lk 1.32–33.

49. Rom 8.33–34.

50. This is the literal meaning of the LXX, which Oecumenius reproduces (ἐξελεξάμην παραρρίπτεσθαι). The usual English rendering of the Hebrew text is "to be a doorkeeper" (RSV) or "stand at the gate" (GNB).

51. Ps 83.11. Oecumenius adds "my" after "God" (τοῦ θεοῦ μου).

tian, who was "the second persecutor after Nero," as Eusebius[52] narrates in the *Ecclesiastical History* and in the *Canonical Chronicle*. This, too, was when the blessed evangelist was condemned to live on Patmos, a small and desolate island. (10) *I am coming soon*, he says, to support you. *Hold fast what you have, so that no one may seize your crown*. What are you to *hold fast?* Clearly, true love for the Lord; if you strive in this until the end you will have the crown of life. For the prize of victory is for those who endure.

(11) He says, "I shall make him who conquers temptations to rejoice for ever in the vision of God." For this is to be a pillar of the divine temple. For surely the pillar would never move for any good purpose from the place where it had been secured. (12) *And I will write on him the name of my God, and the name of the city of my God*, of the heavenly *Jerusalem, and the new name*. He is describing their enjoyment of God for ever and their dwelling in good quarters and the bliss, which, he says, they will have in the age to come. *The new name*, he says, is that which until now has nowhere been heard, which the saints who reign together with Christ will receive, who are named friends, brothers, and servants. But the new name exceeds even these. For these have not only been mentioned in Holy Scripture but have also come into the hearing of men. But the new name is nowhere named. (13) His saying *of my God* does not imply that God disowns as unworthy the condition of self-emptying or the humility of the humanity. For if he disowned this, who was it who compelled him to be hypostatically united with flesh and thus to weave together our salvation? (14) To him be the glory for ever and ever. Amen.

---

52. Eusebius of Caesarea, *Ecclesiastical History* 3.17; *Chronicon Paschale* 250c.

CHAPTER THREE

 HAVE DESCRIBED in the second chapter all the prophecies that he has decreed to be sent round to the six cities, to the churches in Ephesus, Smyrna, Pergamum, Thyatira, Sardis, and Philadelphia. Now this is what must be written to Laodicea:

2. *And to the angel of the church in Laodicea write: These are the words of the Amen, the faithful and true witness, the beginning of God's creation: (2) I know your works, that you are neither cold nor hot. I wish you were either cold or hot, because you are lukewarm, and neither hot nor cold. (3) I am going to spew you out of my mouth. (4) For you say, I am rich, I have grown wealthy, and I need nothing, but you do not know that you are wretched, pitiable, blind, naked, and beggarly. (5) I counsel you to buy from me gold refined by fire, that you may be rich, and new white garments to clothe you, and that the shame of your nakedness may not be seen, and salve to anoint your eyes, that you may see. (6) Those whom I love, I reprove and chasten; so be zealous and repent. (7) See, I am standing at the door and am knocking. If anyone should listen to my voice and open the door, I will come to him and have supper with him, and he with me. (8) He who conquers, I will grant him to sit on my throne, as I myself conquered and took my seat with my Father on his throne. (9) He who has an ear, let him listen to what the Spirit says to the churches* (Rv 3.14–22).

3. He says, *These are the words of the Amen:* this is equivalent to *The true one says these things* (Rv 3.7), as has been explained earlier. For *Amen* is "Yea." For in him is "Yea," and not "No" at all, as is said about him.[1] And the *faithful witness* has been mentioned earlier. So it is unduly verbose to go through the same

---

1. 2 Cor 1.19.

things twice. (2) He says, *the beginning*[2] *of God's creation:* perhaps
the Arians' anti-Christ workshop would light upon this saying, as
though the Son were described by these words as a creature. But
let us not take notice of their unholy words. We must examine
whether any such description occurs in another text, so that one
might be able to form a judgment by comparing similar terms.
(3) The wise apostle, writing to the Colossians, talks of the Son
"who is the first-fruit" and "the first-born of all creation,"[3] certainly not "the first-created." And the prophet says, "From the
womb before the morning-star I begot you,"[4] certainly not "I created you." But also Solomon: "Before all the hills he begets me."[5]
For "the Lord created me as the beginning of his ways,"[6] referring to the Lord's body animated by his mind. Saint Gregory[7] accepted this sense in his work *On the Son.* "He begets" refers to his
divinity. (4) Therefore since all have decreed to use "begetting"
and not "creation" in the case of the only Word and Son, what
is the meaning of the present text, *the beginning of God's creation?*
Nothing other than the ruler of God's creation, and he who has
the rule[8] over all things. For since the Father has made all things
through the Son, it follows that as the maker and craftsman
of the universe, who brings the universe into being from non-
existence, he rules over what has been brought into being by
him.

(5) He says, *I know your works, that you are neither cold nor hot.*
The one who is aglow with the Spirit is *hot*—for says the divine
apostle, "those who are aglow with the Spirit"[9]—but the one
who is deprived of the activity and visitation of the Holy Spirit is *cold.* (6) *But you,* he says, *are lukewarm:* he calls lukewarm
those who received a share in the Holy Spirit through baptism,
but who quenched the gift through sloth and concern for temporal things. This, too, is the divine command: "Do not quench

2. The Greek (ἀρχή) means both "beginning" and "rule," and Oecumenius
explores this double meaning.
3. 1 Cor 15.23; Col 1.15.   4. Ps 109.3.
5. Prv 8.25.   6. Prv 8.22.
7. Cf. Gregory of Nazianzus, *Orationes* 30.2.
8. "Rule" renders Greek ἀρχή, which also means "beginning." "Ruler"
renders ἄρχων.
9. Rom 12.11.

the Spirit."[10] *I wish you were either cold or hot, because you are luke-warm.* (7) He means, "If only you were aglow, inflamed by the action of the Spirit, or totally *cold* and entirely lacking the grace of the Spirit, and unbaptized, instead of being *lukewarm.*" For those who have the mind of the Spirit spread fire among men, "having their senses trained for distinguishing between good and evil,"[11] and they are spiritual; but those who have not yet received the grace of the Spirit, but still hope one day to receive it, are not numbered among the rejected. The lukewarm, on the other hand, have not only been deprived of life but have also lost the chance of ever being baptized again and being aglow. (8) He says, *I am going to spew you out of my mouth:* he has properly used the metaphor of lukewarmness; for all that is lukewarm, as medical men say, causes nausea and leads those who partake of it to vomit. That, too, is why they give those who do not vomit easily some lukewarm water to swallow, in this way encouraging them to vomit. And he says, "I am going to reject you from my intimacy." (9) What is the cause of such a condition? He says, "You set your hope on the uncertainty of riches,[12] and as if among thorns[13] you choked the gift of grace." You were not listening to him when he said, "If riches increase, do not set your heart on them."[14] He says that riches are worldly and temporary.

(10) You do not know *that you are beggarly and naked,* since you do not know the gifts of the Spirit, which endure. *I counsel you,* therefore, *to buy gold refined by fire, that you may be rich.* What is meant by gold refined by the spiritual fire is taught by the prophet, saying, "The promises of the Lord are pure promises, silver refined and tested in the ground, purified seven times,"[15] referring in this way to the proclamation of the gospel. (11) This then requires *from me* the power to instruct you and to bring you near to God. For one who has acquired this ability both shines with virtue and will be cleansed in soul and body. This is the *new white garments.* (12) *And,* he says, *salve to anoint your eyes, that you may see:* to some of those who could see only dimly the spiritual light of the Lord, a reproachful saying of Jeremiah says, "See,

10. 1 Thes 5.19.
12. 1 Tm 6.17.
14. Ps 61.11.
11. Heb 5.14.
13. Mt 13.22.
15. Ps 11.7.

neither your heart nor your eyes are sound."[16] Therefore, he counsels them to embrace cleansing repentance to get rid of such impairment, just as the barren fig-tree with its rather worthless existence was addressed[17] with manure.[18] (13) He says, *Those whom I love, I reprove and chasten:* how surpassing is the extent of the love of Christ! For he promises to love them in spite of their being the sort of people the text describes; wherefore he both reproves and chastens them so that they may be zealous for better deeds and repent of their previous sins. (14) He says, *See, I am standing at the door and knocking. If anyone should listen to my voice and open the door, I will come to him and have supper with him, and he with me.* The Lord is showing his own meekness and peacefulness. For the Devil batters "with an axe and a chisel" the doors of those who do not receive him, according to the voice of the prophet.[19] But even now the Lord says to the bride in the Song of Songs, "Open to me, my sister, my bride."[20] And if anyone will open to him, he will enter. Otherwise, he will pass by. The supper with the Lord signifies participation in the holy mysteries. (15) He says, *To him who conquers* the enemy *I will grant to sit on my throne,* that is, to reign together with me. For it is said by the most wise Paul, "If we suffer with him, we shall also reign with him."[21] (16) He says, *As I, too, have conquered, and reign with my Father:* for the Lord also said in the gospels, "Be of good cheer; I have overcome the world."[22]

4. *And after that I looked, and see, in heaven an open door! And the first voice like that of a trumpet which I heard speaking to me said, Come up here, and I will show you what must take place after this.* (2) *At once I was in the Spirit, and see, there was a throne in heaven, and on the throne was seated one* (3) *looking like an emerald* (Rv 4.1–3).[23]

16. Jer 22.17.
17. The word rendered "addressed" (ἐξαγόρευσις) also means "confession of sins."
18. Lk 13.6–9.
19. Ps 73.6.
20. Song 5.2.
21. Rom 8.17; 1 Cor 4.8.
22. Jn 16.33.
23. The omission, by a scribal error, of some words in Rv 4.3, due to the repetition of ὅμοιος at the start of two phrases, has meant that the one sitting

5. It is not that there is in heaven a door that is being shut and opened from time to time, but this is how it was shown to the evangelist so that he might see the things above the heavens. For when any door is opened, the things inside are necessarily observed. (2) He says, *And I heard·a voice,* which sounded like a trumpet and said to me: *Come up here,* he says, so that you may see the things which are going to take place. (3) And I went up *in the Spirit*—for the way up was neither bodily nor perceptible—and, he says, I see a throne, and God and a Spirit on it *like jasper and carnelian.* God is certainly not like these, nor like any perceptible thing, or like a body at all; he is invisible, incorporeal, and without form, whose invisible nature the seraphim indicate as they cover their faces with their wings.[24] God, too, when he spoke to Moses said, Nobody shall see "my face and live."[25] But also the evangelist himself denies this possibility, saying, "no one has ever yet seen God."[26] Therefore, God was not seen to be like anything, but it was from the acts of God that the vision was depicted in the Revelation. (4) For jasper—which is a precious stone—looks like emerald and is green, resembling an asp's poison, from which it also derives its name.[27] Carnelian is another precious stone, fiery bright and blood-red. (5) Jasper signifies for us God's ability to give life and to provide for our needs, since every nourishment of human beings and four-footed animals and birds and reptiles has its source, and thus its cause, originating from green plants. For the prophet says, "He causes grass to grow for the cattle, and green plants for the service of men, so as to bring food from the earth. And wine cheers a man's heart, making glad his face with oil."[28] And again, in creating the world, God says, "Let the earth put forth vegetation, seed yielding seed according to its kind."[29] (6) So jasper connotes these things. But by carnelian

---

on the throne is "like an emerald." Not only is this corrected below in 3.5.9, but Oecumenius shows his awareness of the missing words by his comments in 3.5.3 on jasper and carnelian (ἰάσπιδι καὶ σαρδίῳ).

24. Is 6.2.
25. Ex 33.20.
26. Jn 1.18.
27. "An asp's poison": the Greek is ἰός ἀσπίδος.
28. Ps 103.14–15.
29. Gn 1.11–12.

he describes the awe of God. "For our God is a devouring fire," says the hierophant Moses.[30] And the prophet, too, says of God, "You are awesome, and who can stand before you?"[31] In agreement with this, the wise apostle writes, "It is a fearful thing to fall into the hands of the living God."[32] (7) For since the goodness of God is pure, and therefore at variance with those who love sin and despise him, it does not lead them to repentance but to fearlessness in committing sin.[33] So God is rightly depicted as awesome, as well as being good and beneficent. Wherefore Paul, knowing that the disposition of those under instruction needs goads, and not only gentleness, wrote to the Corinthians, saying, "What do you wish? Shall I come to you with a rod, or with love and in a spirit of gentleness?"[34] And one of the saints also exclaimed, "Gehenna does not terrify you. The kingdom of heaven does not persuade you; we are talking to a heart of stone."[35] In this way the awesomeness of God and his readiness to punish was found useful to those undergoing discipline. (8) But carnelian is not the first with God; jasper is the first. For his nature is goodness itself, kindness, and gentleness, and he wishes to be our father rather than our tyrant. But, if it is permissible to say so, it is we who compel him to be awesome and ready to punish, so that he often puts aside his natural gentleness, and is driven to unnatural severity.[36]

(9) He says, *And round his throne was a rainbow in appearance like an emerald:*[37] the visible rainbow, which the divine Scripture calls *a bow* of God, which is caused by the reflection of the sun's light when it is intercepted and impeded by a thick cloud, has a variegated color of all kinds. That spiritual rainbow, however, circling the divine throne, was of a single color, for it was like an emerald. (10) It indicates all the holy and ministering spirits around God, wherefore he has called it *a rainbow,* even though it has a single color, so that from the variegated colors of the rainbow we may obtain an idea of the numerous ranks and differences of the divine angels. Yet all things are aglow with one col-

30. Dt 4.24.
32. Heb 11.31.
34. 1 Cor 4.21.
36. Cf. Rom 11.22.

31. Ps 75.8.
33. Rom 2.4.
35. Cf. Basil, *Homilia in divitias* 6.
37. See n. 23 above.

or. For all are alike beneficial and bear an imitation of their own master, with the emerald color bearing witness to the [angels'] providential beneficence, just as the color of jasper bears witness to God's providence.

(11) Perhaps a reader may be troubled by something here: Why is it that while the holy ranks of the incorporeal beings around God are compared to the more precious stone of the emerald, God himself is compared to the less precious, jasper and carnelian? The reason is that the account is now concerned not with the value of the objects seen but with the meaning of the colors. If anyone should meanly look for value, there is not a single thing with which God may be compared. (12) Nor should anyone complain that the Lord is compared to a stone, for Isaiah says about the Lord, "See, I am laying in Zion a corner-stone."[38] And the prophet says about him, "The stone which the builders rejected."[39] The wicked ranks of demons are described allegorically as mountains: for David himself said that "mountains were being changed, in the heart of the sea, and mountains were stirred up by his mighty power."[40] They are of such a size that it is not even possible to discover their height.

6. He says, *Round the throne were twenty-four thrones, and seated on the twenty-four thrones were twenty-four elders, clad in white garments, with golden crowns upon their heads. (2) From the throne issue flashes of lightning, and voices and peals of thunder, and before the throne seven torches of fire were burning, which are the seven spirits of God, (3) and before the throne there is a sea of glass, like crystal* (Rv 4.4–6).

7. Only God, the one who knows the hidden things, and he to whom they are revealed, would know who were the twenty-four elders seated on the thrones. My guess is that they were Abel, Enoch, and Noah, Abraham, Isaac, and Jacob, Melchisedek and Job, Moses and Aaron, Joshua the son of Nun, and Samuel, David, Elijah, and Elisha, the twelve minor prophets combined together as one, Isaiah and Jeremiah, Ezekiel, Daniel, Zechariah, and John, James the son of Joseph, and Stephen, the martyrs

38. Is 28.16.
39. Ps 117.22.
40. Ps 45.3–4.

of the New Testament. (2) One could have spoken of Peter,
Paul, and James the brother of John, whom Herod "killed with
a sword,"[41] and the rest of the band of the holy apostles, if they
had not had the promise from the Lord that they would sit, not
now, but in the new age, on twelve thrones, which are clearly
different from those mentioned here. For this is what the Lord
said to them in the gospel according to Matthew: "Truly I say
to you, that you who have followed me, in the new age when
the Son of" God "shall sit on his glorious throne, you too will sit
on twelve thrones, judging the twelve tribes of Israel."[42] (3) The
white garments are a sign of their purity in their lifetime; the
crowns are the sign of their conquest of their passions and spiritual enemies; (4) the issuance of lightning and sounds of thunder from the throne symbolizes once again the awesomeness of
God. Delight in the divine beauty is found not in some enjoyment of merriment and pleasure, but in awe and wonder. Because he knew this the prophet said, "Serve the Lord with fear,
and rejoice in him with trembling."[43]

(5) He says, *Seven torches of fire, burning before the throne, which
are the seven spirits of God:* seven is the number of the archangels,
says Clement in the sixth book of his *Stromateis*,[44] perhaps under
the influence of this text. He says that these seven spirits are like
torches of fire. For it is said about angels somewhere, "He who
makes his angels spirits, and his ministers a flame of fire,"[45] the
divine Scriptures meaning these whom we are now discussing.

(6) He says, *And before the throne there is a sea of glass, like crystal:*
the vision of the sea is the multitude; and the glass and the crystal denote the purity and the freedom from every defilement of
the holy spirits around God, who are as the sea in number; "for
a thousand thousand stood before him," says Daniel,[46] "and ten
thousand times ten thousand waited upon him"; and although
there are so many, all of them are pure, resembling glass and
crystal.

41. Acts 12.2.
42. Mt 19.28.
43. Ps 2.11.
44. Cf. Clement of Alexandria, *Stromata* 6.16.143.1.
45. Ps 103.4.
46. Dn 7.10.

8. *And round the throne are four living creatures, full of eyes in front and behind.* (2) *The first living creature is like a lion, the second living creature like an ox, the third living creature has a face like a man, and the fourth living creature is like an eagle in flight.* (3) *And each of the four living creatures has six wings around it; and within they are full of eyes; and day and night they have no rest, saying, "Holy, holy, holy is the Lord God, the sovereign of all, who is and who was and is coming"* (Rv 4.6–8).

9. This is not to say that these are those holy living creatures whom Ezekiel the prophet was deemed worthy to see. Each of those had both four faces and eight wings, and they sidled along on wheels called Gelgel,[47] even if those were many-eyed just like these. Here, each had one face, even if it was different, and six wings. And those were the cherubim, so called by Ezekiel,[48] but these, as I surmise, are the seraphim, who were shown to the blessed Isaiah,[49] even though Isaiah did not mention that they had any faces, but only that they covered their faces with their wings, nor did he mention a multitude of eyes, but that they were six-winged. (2) It is important to explain the symbolism of the visions shown to the evangelist. There was an error among some of the Jews, who held that while God made provision for the holy orders in heaven and loved to dwell only among them, he stood aloof and was not concerned about those on the earth because of the transgression of Adam. That is why they said in Isaiah's words, "Why have we fasted and you did not see it? Why have we humbled ourselves, and you took no notice?"[50] Their error arose from a scriptural text which said, "Lord in heaven, your mercy and your truth reach up to the clouds,"[51] as though the divine providence deemed it unworthy to proceed downwards on account of the sins on earth. (3) So the vision shows the evangelist that the providence of God extends through all things, both providing for those in heaven and condescending to those on earth, and this is the symbolism of the four holy living creatures which are around the divine throne. For since every perceptible

47. Ezek 10.13. "Gelgel" represents the Hebrew *galgal*, which probably is to be rendered "whirling."
48. Ezek 10.20.
49. Is 6.2.
50. Is 58.3.
51. Ps 35.6.

and earthly body is composed of the four elements—fire, earth, air, and water—each of the living creatures represents one of these. The lion represents fire, on account of the heat and the passion of the animal; the ox represents the earth, because the ox's work is on the earth; the man represents the air, for man is a heavenly creature and high in the air on account of the subtlety of his mind; the eagle represents water, for birds have their origin in water. (4) They are seen around the throne of God, since those who are signified by the living creatures, that is, those on earth, are deemed worthy of his concern and providence. Their being many-eyed represents the all-surveying oversight of God over them.

(5) *And they have no rest by day or by night.* He says this not because they continually spend a painful and burdensome life, so that they are unable to have any respite from toil or from demanding obligation, but because they never desist from giving praises to God, and from reveling in their songs to him. (6) Their saying *holy* seven times signifies often and incessantly.[52] The number seven has been handed down many times in Holy Scripture, such as "she who was barren gave birth to seven, and she who had many children grew weak,"[53] and "the seven eyes of the Lord which watch over all the earth,"[54] and "the righteous man" set free "seven times from his distress."[55]

(7) He says, *who is and who was, and is coming:* the holy and august Trinity is indicated here, as was said earlier. But it does no harm to say it again now, for "to write the same things is not irksome to me, but it is safe for those who read,"[56] the divine apostle declared. *He who is* was the name given to the Father by Moses. For he says to him, "I am who I am."[57] *He who was* is said about the Son by the evangelist himself, saying, "In the beginning was the Word, and the Word was with God, and the Word was God."[58] By *he who is coming* he means the Holy Spirit, for he always visits the souls who are worthy to receive him.

---

52. In Oecumenius's version of the text of Rv 4.8 some manuscripts add "seven times" (*septies*). He here appears to consider the number significant.

53. 1 Sm 2.5. 54. Zec 4.10.
55. Prv 24.16. 56. Phil 3.1.
57. Ex 3.14. 58. Jn 1.1.

10. *And whenever the living creatures give glory and honor and thanks to him who is seated on the throne, who lives for ever and ever,* (2) *the twenty-four elders fall down before him who is seated on the throne and worship him who lives for ever and ever, and they cast their crowns before the throne, saying,* (3) *"You are worthy, O Lord our God, to receive glory and honor and power, for you created all things, and by your will they existed and were created"* (Rv 4.9–11).

11. Together with the holy living creatures, he says, the elders give glory to God. Their casting their crowns before God indicates this: the crown is a symbol of victory and kingship. So when they cast them before the throne of God, they ascribe to God, the ruler of all people, his real and true kingship and universal victory, saying, "To you, Lord, glory is due in the sight of all people, because you brought all things from non-being into being, and by your will you gave substance to things which had no previous existence."

12. *And I saw in the right hand of him who was seated on the throne a little scroll written on the inside and outside, sealed with seven seals; and I saw a strong angel proclaiming with a loud voice,* (2) *"Who is worthy to open the little scroll*[59] * * *[60] *nor to look into it.* (3–4) *And many wept that no one was found worthy to open the little scroll or to look into it.* (5) *Then one of the elders said to me, "Stop weeping; see, the Lion of the tribe of Judah, the root of David, has conquered, to open its seven seals."* (6) *And I saw, and there between the throne and the four living creatures and amid the elders there was a lamb standing as though it had been slain, with seven horns and seven eyes, which are the seven spirits of God sent out into all the earth;* (7) *and he went and took it from the right hand of him who was seated on the throne* (Rv 5.1–7).

13. Holy Scripture describes for us a certain scroll of God in which all human beings have been written down. Perhaps it calls the *scroll* figuratively God's record of us, except that the prophet

---

59. In this section the text usually refers to βιβλίον ("a little scroll"), but sometimes to βίβλος ("a scroll"). The translation attempts to preserve the original, in spite of some confusion in the argument.

60. There is a lacuna in the text here, which is, however, filled later with the words "and to break its seals" (καὶ λῦσαι τὰς σφραγῖδας αὐτοῦ); see de Groote edition, p. 112.

names it *a little scroll,* saying, "Your eyes saw my unformed substance, and in your little scroll all people will be written."[61] On the other hand, Moses the most wise, pleading for Israel, who had sinned, wept aloud to God and cried, "But now, if you will forgive their sin, forgive—and if not, blot me out of your scroll which you have written."[62] (2) This is the scroll which the divine evangelist sees *written on the inside and outside. Inside* would be those people of Israel written down as God-fearing by their keeping of the law. *On the back,* and in a worse fate, would be those of the gentiles who were idolatrous before believing in Christ.

(3) The little scroll was in the right hand of God; it refers, I imagine, to the ways of the saints who were triumphant in the old covenant. The little scroll had been shut and sealed *with seven seals.* The number seven, being a perfect number, indicates that the little scroll had been truly and very securely shut and sealed up. (4) What does it mean that the little scroll had been closed? That nobody was considered to be worthy of the vision of God, except a very few. For in view of the transgression of Adam, how could what had been closed ever be seen? More people through their sins had caused the little scroll to be closed— and their number was innumerable—than those very few who were well-pleasing to God for it to be opened, and so the general free access to God had to be barred against those who were written within it, since "all had turned aside and had become corrupt," according to the prophet.[63] For even if a very few in number had triumphed in the old covenant, since they were but human beings, they were not considered worthy to regain for everyone the freedom which had been lost by sin. (5) So since the prophet understood this, he addressed God, "In the morning you will hear the voice" of my supplication, "and in the morning I will stand beside you and you will behold me."[64] By the spiritual morning he means the appearance of Christ, "the sun of righteousness,"[65] which put an end to the gloom of ignorance, as though in this way, and not otherwise, humankind might acquire freedom, so that God could both listen to those praying,

61. Ps 138.16.
62. Ex 32.32.
63. Ps 13.3.
64. Ps 5.4.
65. Mal 4.2.

and find them worthy of his regard, once Christ had abolished the wall of sin which separated us from God.[66] Before his visitation to humankind, "every mouth" had been stopped, "and the whole world had been put under God's judgment,"[67] according to Scripture. So the fact that the scroll was closed and sealed indicates, as has been said, the lack of a free approach [to God] by those whose names were written in the scroll.

(6) He says, *I saw a strong angel proclaiming, "Who is worthy to open the little scroll and break its seals?"* "No one, most divine angel," one would say to him; only the incarnate God, who took away sin and who canceled "the bond which stood against us"[68] and with his own "obedience" healed our "disobedience."[69] (7) He says, *And no one in heaven or on earth or under the earth was able to open the little scroll.* For neither did an angel accomplish this for us, as Isaiah says, "Not an envoy, nor an angel, but he himself saved them because he loved them,"[70] neither a living man, nor even one of the dead. "A brother cannot ransom himself—a man cannot ransom himself," as it is written somewhere.[71] (8) And why does he say, "I tell you to open the little scroll," when no human being was strong enough to look into it? For how could anyone of those filled with the mist of sin look into it in the presence of the divine throne, on which the scroll was laid? "The unworthiness of all of them caused me to lament." But one of the elders encouraged me, pointing to the one who had opened it. For he says to me, *See, the lion of the tribe of Judah, the root of David, has conquered, so that he can open the little scroll and its seven seals.* He, he says, who has conquered our conqueror, the Devil, is he who opened the little scroll and its seals. (9) And who was *the lion of the tribe of Judah?* Certainly the Christ, about whom the patriarch Jacob said, "He stooped down, he couched as a lion and as a lion's cub. Who will raise him up?"[72] That the Lord according to his humanity arose from Judah, the divine apostle is wit-

66. Cf. Eph 2.14.
67. Rom 3.19.
68. Col 2.14.
69. Rom 5.19. Some manuscripts begin chapter 4 at this point.
70. Is 63.9.
71. Ps 48.8.
72. Gn 49.9.

ness when he said, "For it is evident that our Lord Jesus" Christ "has arisen from Judah."[73] (10) One might be surprised that he did not say of him, "A shoot from the root of Jesse," or "A flower sprung up from the root," as Isaiah said,[74] but he called him *a root of David*. He says this to show that according to his human nature he was a shoot sprung from the root of Jesse and David; but according to his divine nature, he himself is the root, not only of David but of all visible and invisible creation, since he is the cause of the universe, as was also said earlier.

(11) He says, *And I saw in the midst* of all those around the throne of God *a lamb standing, as though it had been slain, with seven horns and seven eyes, which are the seven spirits of God sent out into all the earth, and he came and took it*—that is, the little scroll—*from the right hand of him who sat on the throne*. He called the Lord *a lamb* on account of his guilelessness, and his ability to provide. For just as the lamb is the provider with its yearly production of wool, so also the Lord "opens his hand and fills every living thing with delight."[75] This at least is what prophecy calls him, saying through Isaiah, "like a lamb he was led to slaughter, and like a sheep before its shearer he was dumb,"[76] and through Jeremiah, "I did not know I was like a guileless lamb led to be slaughtered."[77] (12) But the lamb is described not as slaughtered, but *as though it had been slaughtered*. For Christ came to life again, trampling death underfoot, and despoiling Hades of the souls in its possession. For the death of Christ was not an absolute death, but as it were a death cut short by the resurrection. But since the Lord after his resurrection continued to bear the symbols of death, the print of the nails,[78] having his life-giving body stained red by his blood, as Isaiah said, speaking in the person of the holy angels, "Why are your garments red, and your clothes like one who comes from the full-trodden wine-press?"[79]—on account of this he was *as one who had been slaughtered* in the sight of the vision. (13) The seven horns bear witness to his great strength, as the number seven, being the perfect number, often

73. Heb 7.14.   74. Is 11.1.
75. Ps 144.16.   76. Is 53.7.
77. Jer 11.19.   78. Jn 20.25.
79. Is 63.2–3.

indicates, as has also been said earlier. The horns are the symbol of power, according to the prophet who said, "And all the horns of the wicked I will break off, but the horn of the righteous shall be exalted,"[80] and Habakkuk has, "there are horns in his hands."[81] (14) *The seven eyes which are the seven spirits of God sent out into all the earth,* Isaiah interprets for us, saying, "And there shall rest upon him a spirit of wisdom and understanding, a spirit of counsel and might, a spirit of knowledge and reverence; a spirit of the fear of God will fill him."[82] These spirits, that is, spiritual gifts of grace, have been sent to everyone from God, but no one ever received them in the same way as they rested upon Christ in their work among practically all people. And he grew stronger in word and understanding.[83] For the spirits which he himself as God sent from above, these he himself received below as a human being. For he was both a human being and God. (15) To him belongs the glory for ever and ever. Amen.

80. Ps 74.11.
82. Is 11.2–3.
81. Hab 3.4.
83. Lk 2.40.

CHAPTER FOUR

O THEN WHEN ALL of those in heaven and on earth and under the earth had been unable to find a way to open the scroll[1] or to look upon it, as the previous visions showed, only Christ, the Son of God, who on our account has been born like us while remaining what he was, took the scroll.

2. *And when he had taken the scroll, the four living creatures and the twenty-four elders fell down before the Lamb, each holding a harp and golden bowls full of incense, which are the prayers of the saints; and they sing a new song, saying,* (2) *"You are worthy to take the scroll and to open its seals, for you were slain and by your blood you ransomed us for God from every tribe and tongue and people and nation,* (3) *and you have made them kings and priests to our God, and they shall reign on earth."* (4) *Then I looked, and I heard around the throne and the living creatures and the elders the voice of many angels, and their number was ten thousand times ten thousand, saying with a loud voice,* (5) *"Worthy is the Lamb who has been slain, to receive power and wisdom and wealth and might and honor and glory and blessing"* (Rv 5.8–12).

3. All worshiped the Lord after he had taken the scroll, since they already knew the salvation which he was going to effect for human beings and the punishment he was going to bring on the polluted demons. (2) The elders' holding harps indicates the harmony and concord of their confession of God, according to Scripture, "Sing praises to our God, sing praises."[2] (3) The incense symbolizes the offering of all the nations, for Malachi, speaking in the person of God, says to disobedient Israel, "I will not accept an offering from your hand, for from the rising of the sun to its setting my name has been glorified among the nations,

---

1. In this chapter βιβλίον has been consistently rendered by "scroll."
2. Ps 46.7.

CHAPTER FOUR 65

and in every place incense is offered in my name, and a pure sacrifice,"[3] predicting by these [words] the faith of the nations and their bringing of gifts. (4) *And they sing a new song:* for the song sung to God incarnate is new, since it had never been invented before the incarnation. (5) What was the song? *You are worthy,* he says, to effect this salvation for human beings, you who were slain for us, and with *your blood* you took possession of many from among those under heaven. (6) Very correctly he said *from every tribe and tongue and people and nation:* for he did not acquire possession of everyone (for many died in unbelief), but only those who were worthy of salvation. The prophet also said something similar, "Arise, O God, judge the earth, because you" will place "your inheritance among all the nations,"[4] where he does not simply say "all the nations."

(7) And he *made them kings and priests to our God, and they shall reign on earth.* You can indeed understand this literally, for the kings and presidents of the churches are [God's] faithful people and servants of Christ. But you can also understand *kings* to be those who control their passions and are not controlled by them. And you can understand *priests* to be those who present their own persons "as a living sacrifice, holy and acceptable to God," as Scripture says.[5] (8) And he says not only the elders but also the incorporeal powers of the angels were singing a triumphant song to Christ. Daniel also predicted their number as now mentioned. The song of the angels attributes seven different honors to Christ, because by the number seven they indicate that it is fitting for Christ to be crowned with ten thousand praises.

4. *And every creature in heaven and on earth and in the sea are yours, and I heard all that was in them saying, "to him who sits on the throne and to the Lamb be blessing and honor and glory and might for ever and ever." (2) And the four living creatures said "Amen," and the elders fell down and worshiped* (Rv 5.13–14).

5. The present words show the concordant hymn of praise

3. Mal 1.10–11.
4. Ps 81.8.
5. Rom 12.1.

from all creation in heaven and on earth to God, both the Father and the Word incarnate in human form,[6] with the Holy Spirit, too, of course, sharing in their praise.

6. *And when*, he says, *I saw that the Lamb had opened one of the seven seals, and I heard what was like the sound of thunder from the four living creatures saying, "Come."* (2) *And I saw, and there was a white horse, and its rider had a bow, and a crown was given to him, and he went out conquering so that he should conquer.* (3) *And when he opened the second seal, I heard the second living creature say, "Come!"* (4) *And out came another horse, bright red; its rider's task was to take peace from the earth, so that men should slay one another, and he was given a great sword* (Rv 6.1–4).

7. That the scroll was shut and sealed indicates that the people who were written in it were unable to speak, and that their mouths were stopped from all pleading in their defense before God, according to what was said earlier. The successive removal of the seals, then, symbolizes the resumption little by little of the openness and intimacy towards God that the Only-begotten by his incarnation made possible for us, making amends for our faults by his own acts of reparation. We must understand that the undoing of each seal denotes one of the works of the Lord effected for our salvation, and of his acts against our spiritual enemies. For the Lord's providence for us entails the destruction of their sovereignty. (2) No one should be surprised that before the Only-begotten became incarnate—for his works and deeds before his visit to us are shown in the vision to the blessed evangelist—yet the lamb is seen in the Revelation as slain. For the visions of the prophets were regularly a prediction of what was to take place in future. Thus a man was wrestling with Jacob,[7] who was the type of Christ. Thus Isaiah saw the prophetess who conceived and bore a son, whose name, too, was called "plunder quickly, despoil sharply."[8] Thus Daniel saw as "a son of man" the

6. Literally, "the Word who became a human being and was incarnate" (τῷ ἐνανθρωπήσαντι καὶ σαρκωθέντι Λόγῳ).

7. Gn 32.24.

8. Is 8.3.

pre-incarnate God, the Word, coming to the "Ancient of days."[9]

(3) Therefore, the first benefit of our savior Christ to our race, which loosed the first seal of the scroll and has begun our restoration to the place from which we were banished as a result of Adam's transgression, and the recovery of the intimacy with God which we lost, and the change of our inability to speak into frank confidence, was established by the physical birth of the Lord. This hallowed our birth, so that we may no longer begin life in lawlessness and be conceived in sin by our mothers, but that we may have a hallowed birth, since Christ through his own birth has blessed our human birth. The divine apostle is a witness to this great honor shown to human beings when he writes, "Otherwise your children would be unclean, but now they are holy."[10] (4) So when the first seal had been opened, he says, I saw someone approaching on a white horse from those spiritual holy creatures, with a bow, *and a crown was given to him, and he went out conquering so that he should conquer.* The white horse is a symbol of the gospel, as the benefit due to be conferred on human beings. The crown symbolizes might and victory. And he came out carrying the crown for Christ,[11] as for one who had begun to conquer the Devil, who had enslaved our race. He says *he went out so that the conqueror might conquer:* Christ was the conqueror, so that he might make a complete conquest, and [the rider] carried the crown for him as a symbol of victory.

8. This, then, is the first benefit. The second benefit of Christ towards us, which opened the second seal of the scroll and went on both to expunge our disgrace and to restore to us the vision of God, was for the Lord to be tempted to conquer the tempter, so that he might know not only that he was himself the conqueror, but also that the wretch had been defeated; instead of "biting the horseman's heel" and "tripping us up on our steps" to God, he was "falling back"[12] and was being sent off like a slave. It was with a man that he wrestled, even though God was in him: he heard the words "Begone, Satan!"[13] and in disgrace he went

9. Dn 7.13.   10. 1 Cor 7.14.
11. Jn 19.5.
12. Cf. Gn 3.15; Ps 139.5; Gn 49.17.
13. Mt 4.10.

away and for the first time came to know his own weakness—he
who boasts of "putting his throne above the clouds," and who
imagines that he will be "like the Most High," as Isaiah portrayed
him.[14]
(2) After this *a bright red horse came out,* urged on by one of
the holy living creatures, and the rider of the horse, he says, *was
given* authority *to take peace from the earth, so that men should slay
one another; and he was given a great sword.* The red horse is the
symbol of blood; that is why a sword was given to its rider, so
that he might destroy and cut to pieces the propensity for evil
found among the inhabitants of the earth. They all planned to
turn to idolatry. And, he says, *so that men should slay one another,*
that is, that they might destroy each other's eagerness to commit evil. For the Lord "did not come to bring peace on earth,
but a sword, and to raise up a son against his father and a bride
against her mother-in-law,"[15] and their new and God-fearing behavior against that which is old and condemned.

9. *And when he opened the third seal,* he says, *I heard the third living creature say, "Come." And I saw, and there was a black horse, and its
rider had a balance in his hand; (2) and I heard a voice in the midst of
the four living creatures say, "A quart of wheat for a denarius, and three
quarts of barley for a denarius; but do not harm the oil and the wine."
(3) And when he opened the fourth seal, I heard the fourth living creature say, "Come." (4) And I saw and there was a greenish horse, and its
rider's name was Death, and Hades will follow him, and authority was
given to them over a fourth part of the earth, to kill with sword and with
famine and with death, and by wild beasts of the earth* (Rv 6.5–8).
10. The third mercy of Christ to us broke the third seal, and
brought us from condemnation back to God the Father. This
mercy is his saving teaching and the benefits effected through
his divine miracles. For these contributed to the destruction of
the Devil. For through them we came to know who was naturally and truly God, "so that we might not be children, tossed
to and fro by every wind of doctrine,"[16] and might not worship
what our hands had made, exchanging the destructive demons

14. Is 14.13–14.   15. Cf. Mt 10.34–35.
16. Eph 4.14.

for the glory of God. For the divine teaching of the Lord drew to itself, as leaven draws flour,[17] those who were being taught by the Lord's voice, and were receiving the benefit of his miracles, which healed their souls more than their bodies.

(2) After this, *a black horse* came out, *and its rider had a balance in his hand:* the black horse represents sorrow and grief, now that the destruction of the Devil had been achieved by the divine instructions. On this account the Devil was grieving for his release, which was being deferred for so many ages. The balance is the symbol of equity and righteousness. For "the judge of righteousness had taken his seat on the throne. He rebuked the tribes" of demons, and the impious one,[18] their leader, was destroyed. (3) The balance therefore is the symbol of the righteous judgment of the Lord on our behalf, so that we may also say boldly to him, "You effected judgment and justice for me,"[19] so that we gentiles may know that we are human beings, and that we may not be like beasts dragged along "with bit and bridle"[20] and led astray by the destructive tyrants.

(4) *And*, he says, *I heard a voice in the midst of the four living creatures saying, "A quart of wheat for a denarius, and three quarts of barley for a denarius, but do not harm the oil and the wine."* The gospel and the teaching is described allegorically by Holy Scripture as *seed,* for it is written in Matthew, "The sower went out to sow,"[21] and again the better-disposed of the slaves said to their lord, "Sir, did you not sow good seed in your field? How then does it have weeds?"[22] Some of the seed is wheat, signifying the proclamation of the gospel as being the proper food for mature people, who "have their senses trained to discriminate between good and evil."[23] What is the barley? It is the teaching according to the law of Moses, as being ripe fodder, more fitting than wheat, for nourishing the infant Israel. (5) Therefore, the speaker, God, *in the midst of the four living creatures says, "A quart of wheat for a denarius and three quarts of barley for a denarius."* These words symbolize that there was a famine and scarcity among people of that time

---

17. Cf. Mt 13.33.
19. Ps 9.5.
21. Mt 13.3.
23. Heb 5.14.

18. Ps 9.5–6.
20. Ps 31.9.
22. Mt 13.27.

of the teaching both of the gospel of the Lord and of the law, as Scripture says, "I will give them not a famine of bread, nor a thirst for water, but a famine of hearing the word of the Lord."[24] (6) Even if those who despise all teaching and attention had especially to suffer this and that, he says, "*do not harm the oil and the wine*, forgive them and do not bring any punishment on them; I shall still have mercy on them," says God, "since they have hope of being spiritually gladdened by the divine proclamations of my only Son." For these are "the wine that" spiritually "makes glad a man's heart."[25]

(7) So he who was going to set out against the former disobedience would harm the mercy which was to be shown to them by God and the spiritual gladness which would come with faith. And why do I say only "spiritual"? For the teachings of the Lord also afforded discernible grace. And the prophet is witness when he said to the Lord, "grace has been poured upon your lips."[26] Josephus the Jew also, constrained by the truth, wrote the following about him in his eighteenth book of *The Antiquities*:[27] (8) "There was about this time a wise man, Jesus, if indeed one ought to call him a man, for he was a doer of wonderful works, a teacher of people who gladly speak the truth. He won over many Jews and many of the Greeks. He was the Christ. When Pilate, on the indictment of men of the highest standing among us, had condemned him to be crucified, those who had first come to love him did not cease loving him. On the third day he appeared to them restored to life, for the holy prophets had prophesied these and countless other marvelous things about him. And the tribe of the Christians, so called after him, has still not now disappeared."

11. The breaking of the fourth seal and of the rest marks the beginning of release from sin resulting from Adam's transgression. For release from this clearly brings affinity with God. For if "our sins separate us from God," as Isaiah says,[28] their destruc-

---

24. Am 8.11.
25. Ps 103.15.
26. Ps 44.32.
27. Josephus, *De antiquitatibus Iudaeorum* 18.63–64.
28. Is 49.2.

tion clearly restores our intimacy with him. What effected this release? (2) "The blows"[29] struck on Christ, by which we have been set free. For since by the pleasure of tasting we were condemned, we were healed by the opposite. Blows are the opposite of pleasure, with the pain which is felt from them. Christ paid on our behalf everything on account of which we had been brought down to the corruption of death, and he made payment through opposites: by "obedience" he paid for our "disobedience,"[30] by painful submission he paid for the pleasure [of sin], by his hands stretched out boldly on the cross he paid for the hands which rashly grasped the forbidden tree.

(3) After this, he says, by the summons of the fourth of the holy living creatures there came *a greenish horse, and its rider's name was Death, and Hades follows him, and authority was given them over a fourth of the earth.* The greenish horse is the symbol of wrath, for bile, as doctors call it, is greenish. (4) Death and Hades were sent for the spiritual overthrow of the sinful demons and to exact retribution from them for the destruction of humankind. But since the saving passion of Christ, by which he paid for all our sins, had not yet been described in the vision, the complete destruction of the demons had not yet come about, but only the fourth part. (5) This destruction he calls metaphorically slaughter and *a famine* of those who were formerly worshiping them and *death,* so laying bare the end of their tyranny by death, and their destruction *by the wild beasts of the earth;* he calls the demons' passions of arrogance and vanity *wild beasts of the earth.* These passions consume and devour them as they are being ousted from their dominion over human beings. Even though they are naturally incorporeal, the demons are earthly in that they exult in their earthly wrigglings.

12. *When he opened the fifth seal, I saw under the altar the souls of those who had been slain for the word of God, and for the church*[31] *which they had.* (2) *They were crying out with a loud voice saying, "How long,*

---

29. Mk 14.65.
30. Rom 5.19.
31. All manuscripts of Revelation read μαρτυρίαν ("testimony") in Rv 6.9, but Oecumenius certainly reads ἐκκλησίαν ("church"), as is shown again later.

Master, holy and true, how long before you will judge and avenge our blood on those who dwell upon earth?" (3) *And a white robe was given to each, and they were told to rest a little longer until the number of their fellow servants and their brethren should be complete, who were to be killed as they themselves had been* (Rv 6.9–11).

13. So the fifth salvation of the Lord given to the human race, the one which broke the fifth seal of the Lord and effected the removal of our sins and the restoration of our intimacy with God, was found in the bonds and wounds with which the Lord was held when he was brought before Pilate, and which he suffered at the hands of Pilate himself who showed a half-hearted reverence. Isaiah[32] spoke about these wounds and said that when the Lord was asked by the divine messengers, "What are these wounds in the middle of your hands?" he said, "Those with which I was struck in the house by my beloved friend."[33] For these wounds healed our wounds, with which we were struck as we were going down from Jerusalem to Jericho when we fell among robbers, who stripped and wounded us, leaving us half-dead, according to Luke's parable.[34] (2) But he has also undone our bonds, the cords of sin with which we were fast bound. For the prophet says, "The cords of sinners have ensnared me."[35] The Devil, then, was not aware that his wicked action was directed against himself, and that in his drunken violence against the Lord he was thrusting the sword into himself, as he fell out of his evilly created domain.

(3) After this, God's people in the old covenant who had earlier on given their witness were as yet silent and recalled nothing as being of concern to them. All these things had not yet been done to Christ; for even though he had been spat upon and slapped and hit, these things were done in a corner in the illegitimate council of the high priests, where the only witnesses were the servants and those summoned to the council. But when they saw the Lord bound and publicly scourged by Pilate in the presence of all the people of the Jews, they rose up togeth-

---

32. All manuscripts read Isaiah in place of the correct reference, Zechariah.
33. Zec 13.6.
34. Lk 10.30.
35. Ps 118.61.

er and recalled the intolerable treatment of their master and of themselves. (4) For, he says, *I saw under the altar the souls of those who had been slain for the word of God, and for the church which they had.* He says, "I saw the souls of the martyrs in the highest place, for they were under the altar which is above the heavens." (5) Then he says who these martyrs are—those who had been slain, he says, on behalf of the godly word of the old covenant and of the church, or synagogue, *which they had.*[36] For martyrs do not die only for their own sakes, but they bring about a benefit for the whole community. For their courage becomes an encouragement for others, and the knowledge of God is built up by the blood of God's people.

(6) *And they were crying out,* he says, *with a loud voice saying, "How long, Master, holy and true, how long before you judge and avenge our blood on those who dwell upon earth?"* They made their prayer not against human beings, but against the demons who make their home with mortal beings. For it was not the loving purpose of God's people to rise up against their own kind, but against those who were urging human beings on to their destruction. (7) After saying this they first receive *white robes.* This was the symbol of their cleansing by their own blood, and the removal of all pollution. (8) Next they hear, *Rest a little longer until the number of their fellow servants and their brethren should be complete, who were to be killed as they themselves had been:* for it was not right that those who had shown the same courage as they had should be thwarted and lose their crowns of martyrdom by the premature destruction of the demons who were drilling them.

14. *And I saw when he opened the sixth seal, there was a great earthquake, and the sun became black as sackcloth, the full moon was turned into blood, and the stars of the sky fell to earth (2) like a fig tree shedding its fruit when shaken by a gale, (3) and the sky vanished like a rolled scroll, and every mountain and island was removed from its place. (4) Then the kings of the earth and the potentates and the generals and the rich and the strong, and every one, slave and free, hid themselves in the*

36. See n. 31. In the Greek Old Testament, ἐκκλησία referred to the congregation of Israel, often described (e.g., in Ex 17.1) as συναγωγή.

caves and among the rocks of the mountains. (5) *And they called to the mountains and the rocks, "Fall on us and hide us from the presence of him who is seated on the throne, and from the wrath of the Lamb,* (6) *because the great day of their wrath has come, and who can stand?"* (Rv 6.12–17)

15. The breaking of the sixth seal accomplished our complete salvation: it destroyed death: it restored life: it robbed the conqueror of human beings of his crown, openly triumphing over him, as Scripture says: the Only-begotten "ascended on high";[37] "he took captivity captive, and he gave gifts to men."[38] (2) What is the breaking of the sixth seal? The cross of the Lord and his death, which were followed by the resurrection and ascension in response to the prayers of all spiritual and sensible creation, "opening for us a new and living way," the return from death to life through "the veil of his flesh."[39] All these benefits he effected not only for the living, but also for those who had gone before. For the Lord also "went" and "preached to those in Hades who had been disobedient," according to the divine apostle Peter,[40] and there, too, he saved believers, as Cyril also thinks.[41]

(3) After this, he says, *there was a great earthquake; and the sun became black as sackcloth, the full moon was turned into blood, and the stars of the sky fell to earth like a fig tree shedding its fruit when shaken by a gale:* the vision clearly describes for us the miracles which took place at the cross—the earthquake and the turbulence of the earth,[42] the darkness of the sun, and the changing of the full moon into blood. (4) Quite accurately, he added the word *full* to the moon; for the moon was filled with light even though it was not quite a full moon on the day of crucifixion, and in its fullness it beheld the passion. This is what usually happens in the illuminated part during lunar eclipses. The prophet Joel, too, predicted that this would come about, saying, "The sun shall be turned to darkness, and the moon to blood, before the coming of the great and wonderful day of the Lord."[43]

37. Ps 67.19. 38. Eph 4.8.
39. Heb 10.20. 40. 1 Pt 3.19–20.
41. Cf. Cyril of Alexandria, *Frag in 1 Pet 3:19–20.*
42. Mt 27.51.
43. Jl 2.31.

(5) The falling of the stars perhaps actually took place, but if not, the account symbolically means that the heavenly light ceased, and that it became completely dark. (6) *The sky vanished like a rolled scroll.* By the sky he means the heavenly powers of the angels, who themselves, too, were shaken, since they were unable to bear the insult done to their master, in heaven as here on earth. They rushed around like a scroll rolled up and shaken.

(7) He says, *And every mountain and island was removed from its place:* he calls the regiments of the haughty demons *mountains and islands*, according to what Scripture says of them: "the mountains were being moved in the heart of the seas."[44] Again he says of the islands that they are lifted high and raised up[45] by the vain folly of their attitude in the unstable and bitter distractions of this life.

(8) *And the kings of the earth,* he says, *and the potentates and the generals and the rich and the strong, and everyone, slave and free, hid themselves in the caves and among the rocks of the mountains. And they called to the mountains and the rocks, "Fall on us and hide us from the presence of him who is seated on the throne, and from the wrath of the Lamb, because the great day of their wrath has come, and who can stand?"* Again he calls the guilty demons *kings* and *potentates* and *generals* and *the rich* and *the strong*, since they have ruled over those upon earth through deceit and guile. *The slaves and the free* refer to those of the demons who are in power and those who are subject. (9) That they hid themselves in the caves and among the rocks of the mountains and even cried, *Fall on us and hide us,* is figurative. It symbolizes their attempts to escape the punishment being brought upon them by Christ. For if some unseen punishment and retribution was not being brought against them, what is the meaning of the saying in the prophet Isaiah spoken in the person of Christ, "I have trodden the wine-press alone, and from the nations no man was with me; I trod them underfoot in my anger and crushed them in my wrath, and I brought down their blood on to the earth"?[46] And what is the meaning of the words of the abominable demons in Matthew, "What have you to do

44. Ps 45.3.
45. Cf. Is 23.2–6.
46. Is 63.2–3.

with us, Son of God? Have you come to torment us?"[47] (10) One could also suppose that these things recounted in the Revelation were the sufferings not only of demons but also of the lawless Jews who erected the cross for the Lord, when they were oppressed by the war against the Romans and became fugitives in the mountains and caves and holes of the earth, and on every side were afflicted by hardship and stress.

16. *After this,* he says, *I saw four angels standing at the four corners of the earth to see that no wind should blow on earth or sea or against any tree.* (2) *Then I saw another angel ascend from the rising of the sun, with a seal of the living God, and he called with a loud voice to the four angels who had been charged to harm the earth and the sea and the trees, saying,* [*"Do not harm the earth]*[48] (3) *or the sea or the trees, until we have sealed the servants of our God upon their foreheads."* (4) *And I heard the number of the sealed, a hundred and forty-four thousand, out of every tribe of the sons of Israel*—(5) and he goes on to list groups of *twelve thousand* who were sealed from each tribe (Rv 7.1–6).

17. Here all that happened to the Jews in the war against the Romans is clearly shown to the evangelist. These things happened to them because of the cross and their madness against the Lord. (2) The four angels controlling *the four corners* of the land of the Jews were on guard lest any of the Jews deserving of death should escape, perhaps by making them too afraid to run away or by putting some difficulties in their way or causing an excessive longing for their country or their wives and those dearest to them. These are indicated figuratively by their control of the four corners of Judaea. (3) The control of the four winds, that they should not blow *on earth or sea or against any tree,* indicates that the Jews found no relief in the war, nor any consolation for their disasters, whether they were fighting on foot on land, or fighting on ships at sea—for they fought many naval battles according to Josephus[49]—or indeed whether they were busy with farming and the care of crops. Utter calamity overtook them all: their cities were being destroyed by fire, their land was being rav-

47. Mt 8.29.
48. A lacuna occurs in the text here, as apparently later on.
49. Cf. Josephus, *Bellum Iudaicum.*

aged, and their crops were being cut down. All this Josephus related accurately in his account of the destruction of Jerusalem. (4) *And I saw an angel ascend from the rising of the sun, with a seal of the living God, and he called with a loud voice to the four angels who had been charged to harm the earth and the sea, saying, "Do no harm until* the servants of our God have been sealed." The coming of the divine angel *from the rising of the sun,* and not from the sunset and the evening, symbolizes the gospel and the promise of good things. The present seal was foreseen by the prophet, too, in the Spirit when he said, "The light of your face, Lord, has been marked upon us."[50] (5) He correctly commands that for the time being nobody should be harmed, until those of the Jews worthy of being saved had been sealed, lest the righteous suffer unintentionally with the sinners.[51] (6) He says that they sealed a hundred and forty-four thousand. The number of Jews who believed in Christ were many more than this, who thereby benefited by their deliverance from the general universal destruction. So those who spoke to Paul when he was in Jerusalem attested, "You see, brother, how many myriads there are of believing Jews."[52] (7) It was reasonable that not only the believers should escape, but also those who ignorantly and through deception cooperated in crucifying the Lord, of whom he said, "Father, forgive them, for they know not what they do."[53] Even though Cyril[54] in the thirteenth book *Against Julian* says that this prayer of the Lord is not found in the gospels, at any rate we use it. It was not only these [who should escape], but also those who were not present at that time, or who were not living in Jerusalem, and therefore had no part in the unholy council of the accursed high priests concerned with the crucifixion, or though they were actually present had certainly not acquired any taint of guilt. Even though [the Lord] himself blessed the whole earth under heaven, it turned out contrary to the wishes of those who hated God and of the council of the criminals. It is likely that all these Jews [who escaped] were later sealed in the faith of Christ. For the angel would not otherwise have called them *the servants*

50. Ps 4.7.   51. Gn 18.23.
52. Acts 21.20.   53. Lk 23.34.
54. Cf. Cyril of Alexandria, *Contra Julianum* 13.

of God. (8) But though these were saved, the rest were in their wickedness utterly destroyed by flight and desertion to the Romans. "They became a spectacle to the world, to angels, and to men,"[55] though in a different sense from that which Paul said about the blessed apostles. Josephus again records that he reckons tens of thousands died by famine.[56] (9) The equal number of those from each tribe who were sealed and became believers symbolizes the equally valid zeal and the same understanding of the faith [among them all], even if in fact more from one tribe and fewer from another were saved and believed in Christ, who was dishonored by the Jews, (10) but is worshiped both by us and by all supernatural creation now and always, for ever and ever. Amen.

55. 1 Cor 4.9.
56. Cf. Josephus, *Bellum Iudaicum* 5.567–69.

CHAPTER FIVE

HE EVENTS WHICH the account described were shown to the blessed evangelist concerning those of the blood of Israel who had been sealed and were therefore saved, and who later also became believers. But in order that there should not be anything deficient in the Revelation, the divine oracle also shows him the countless myriads of the nations who later hastened to join the faith. These are they who are around the Lord and stand by the divine throne. (2) For since the Lord has not yet been described in the introduction to the Revelation as being present at his second coming, when God's people "are carried off to meet" the Savior "in the clouds," according to the divine apostle,[1] the vision shows them as already having been carried off and as having achieved the blessedness laid up for them. For what is more blessed than to be counted worthy to be with Christ and to behold the divine throne? See what he says:

2. *After this I saw, and see, a great multitude whom no one could number, from every nation, from all tribes and peoples and tongues, standing before the throne and before the Lamb, clothed in white robes, with palm branches in their hands. (2) And they cry out with a loud voice, saying, (3) "Salvation belongs to our God, who sits on the throne!" And the holy ones of the elders[2] stood around the throne and around the elders and the four living creatures, and they fell on their faces before the throne and (4) worshiped our God for ever and ever. Amen. (5) Then one of the elders addressed me, saying, "Who are these, clothed in white robes, and from where have they come?" I said to him, "Sir, you know."*

1. 1 Thes 4.17.
2. Not surprisingly, some manuscripts (PB) of Oecumenius read "all the holy angels" (πάντες οἱ ἅγιοι ἄγγελοι) instead of "the holy ones of the elders" (τῶν πρεσβυτέρων οἱ ἅγιοι) at Rv 7.11. The NT text reads "all the angels" (πάντες οἱ ἄγγελοι).

(6) *And he said to me, "These are they who are coming out of the great tribulation; they have broadened³ their robes and made them white in the blood of the Lamb.* (7) *This is why they are before the throne of God and serve him day and night within his temple, and he who sits on the throne will dwell among them.* (8) *They shall hunger no more, neither thirst any more; the sun shall not strike them, nor any scorching heat.* (9) *For the Lamb in the midst of the throne will be their shepherd, and he will guide them to springs of living water, and God will wipe away every tear from their eyes"* (Rv 7.9–17).

3. The innumerable myriads of the nations who received the faith of Christ and who had gained their share in blessedness were allotted the honored place of standing before the Lord and his Father's throne, as was said earlier. (2) Being *clothed in white robes* is a description of their purity during their life. The palm branches, which are a symbol of victory, indicate that they are promised the victory of Christ over their spiritual and earthly enemies. (3) *And they cry out, "Salvation belongs to our God and to the Lamb!"* confessing that salvation is with them, because they had preserved the servants of God who had been sealed from the total destruction of the world. (4) At the end of this act of thanksgiving, the ranks of worshipers in heaven, together with the elders, answered *Amen,* giving their approval to what was said. (5) Then the divine angels, too, offer their own praise to God, honoring him seven times with their worship, which, as has been mentioned earlier, symbolizes the ceaseless nature of the adoration of the angels; for seven is a perfect number.

(6) When one of the elders asked the evangelist who these were from the nations who were clothed in white robes, he did not ask out of ignorance but as a challenge to find out about them. So he goes on to say, *These are they who are coming out of the great tribulation.* For it was not a slight contest but a truly great one which the righteous had in overcoming the Antichrist.

(7) He says, *And they have washed their robes and made them white in the blood of the Lamb.* Yet it should follow that robes dipped in blood would turn out to be scarlet rather than white. So how did

---

3. De Groote's text reads ἐπλάτυναν ("they broadened") instead of ἔπλυναν ("they washed"), which is presumed in the later comment.

they become white? Because baptism enacted into the death of the Lord, as Paul in his great wisdom said,[4] purges all filth resulting from sin and renders those who are baptized in it white and pure. But participation in the life-giving blood of Christ also bestows this favor. For the Lord says concerning his own blood that it is being poured out "for many" and "on behalf of many, for the forgiveness of sins."[5] (8) Thus these *serve* God for ever, and God dwells among them. Indeed, the dwelling-place of God, said one of God's saints,[6] is where the souls of his saints continually remember him; therefore God naturally dwells with *those who serve him day and night.*

(9) *They shall hunger no more, neither thirst any more:* formerly those from the nations went through every trial; but now they will be sated with innumerable good things. (10) He says, *Nor shall the sun strike them:* in some places of the divine Scripture the sun metaphorically stands for temptation, as when the prophet says, "The sun shall not burn you by day, neither the moon by night,"[7] or as when the evangelist writes that the sun shone and scorched the seeds which had sprung up on stony ground,[8] interpreting the sun as temptation. Therefore he now says that temptation would in future never harm them, for they had been found worthy to be shepherded by Christ and nourished at the waters of life. (11) *And God,* he says, *will wipe away every tear from their eyes.* So those who have lived and struggled with unprofitable cares have no need of a *tear,* nor of "weeping and gnashing of teeth,"[9] but deserve everything good and wonderful.

4. *And when he opened the seventh seal, there was silence in heaven for half an hour.* (2) *And I saw the seven angels who stood before God, and seven trumpets were given them* (Rv 8.1–2).

5. Perhaps someone who has been exceedingly attentive would consider what has been said and would say to me as follows: "You there, what are you doing? Have you forgotten what was said in the introduction to the present Revelation? For it was there said, *And the first voice which I had heard was like a trumpet speaking to me,*

4. Rom 6.3.
6. Cf. Ps 14.1?
8. Mt 13.5.

5. Mt 26.28.
7. Ps 120.6.
9. Mt 13.42, 50; 24.51.

saying, Come up hither, and I will show you what must take place after this.[10] But you have been explaining to us not future events but things which have already taken place, in your account of the Lord's birth, his temptation, his teachings, his miracles, his beatings and bonds and the blows he suffered before Pilate, his cross and death, and his resurrection and ascension or return to heaven." (2) To such a one I would reply: "You have certainly heard, my friend, some of the future events, too, when we were describing the righteous from among the nations who were with Israel around the divine throne, and present with the Lord. But now you will hear more at the breaking of the seventh seal. For when the divine oracle said to the evangelist, *Come up hither, and I will show you what must take place after this,* this did not invalidate his vision of past events, but with them he indicated future events, too."

(3) Therefore, listen. The breaking of the seventh seal accomplished for us the final glory; for no longer as before was it the forgiveness of sins and our turning to God and God's turning to us, but the inexpressible benefits—being called sons of God, "heirs of God and fellow heirs of Christ,"[11] brothers and friends and children of Christ, reigning with him[12] and being glorified together with him,[13] and benefits "which no eye has seen, nor ear heard, nor the heart of man conceived."[14] (4) What is the breaking of the seventh seal? The second coming of the Lord and the consequent gift of his benefits. For even if some of those who have sinned are handed over for punishment, the aim of Christ and the plan of the incarnation is that all should become heirs of his kingdom. (5) So when the seventh seal was broken, he says, *there was silence for about half an hour,* in anticipation of the coming of the king of creation, when every angelic and supermundane power had been filled with the exceeding glory of his presence; this is why they fell silent.

(6) Then he says, *seven trumpets were given* to the seven angels so that they might sound their trumpets as at the institution of a king. By the same trumpets they were going to wake the dead

---

10. Rv 4.1.   11. Rom 8.17.
12. 2 Tm 2.12.   13. Rom 8.17.
14. 1 Cor 2.9.

from sleep. For the wise apostle, too, writing to the Thessalonians about God's works, says in his first epistle, that "the Lord himself will come down, with a shout of command, an archangel's voice, and a trumpet of God,"[15] and again, "For the trumpet will sound, and the dead will be raised imperishable."[16]

6. He says, *And an angel came and stood at the altar with a golden censer; and he was given much incense to be used for the prayers of all the saints upon the golden altar before the throne;* (2) *and the smoke of the incense rose with the prayers of the saints from the hand of the angel before God.* (3) *Then the angel took the censer and filled it with fire from the altar and threw it on the earth; and there were loud noises, peals of thunder, flashes of lightning, and an earthquake.* (4) *And the seven angels who had the seven trumpets made ready to blow them* (Rv 8.3–6).

7. He calls the altar a *censer* as being receptive of incense.[17] When Christ appears, the prayers of the saints, like some first-fruit and honored primal offering, are brought to him by our guardian angels, prayers which are naturally sweet-smelling, but which become sweeter-smelling with the cooperation of the holy angels. That is why it is said, *He was given much incense.* It was clearly God's gift to the angels to protect human beings and to make their prayers acceptable. Those who received the incense give the sweet odor for *the prayers of the saints.*

(2) He says, *And the smoke of the incense rose with the prayers of the saints from the hand of the angel.* You see that it is by the angel that the prayers of the saints became sweeter-smelling and worthy to be carried up *before God.* (3) Then he says that the divine *angel took the censer and filled* it with divine *fire and threw it on the earth; and there were loud noises, peals of thunder, flashes of lightning, and an earthquake.* Perhaps one of the angels threw some of this divine fire onto Mount Sinai, "and there were thunders and loud noises and trumpets and lightnings, and the mountain was wrapped in smoke" when God visited it.[18] Just as the thunders and the

15. 1 Thes 4.16.
16. 1 Cor 15.52.
17. The word (λιβανωτός) means both "censer" and "incense." Oecumenius appears to confuse the two meanings. In Rv 8.3 the word for incense is (θυμιάματα), but in his comment Oecumenius uses (λίβανος).
18. Ex 19.16–19.

terrors went forth then, so now these things preceded the glorious coming of the Lord. (4) Then the angels, too, blew their trumpets, signifying the coming of God. For at that time, too, the trumpets sounded loudly.

8. *The first angel blew his trumpet, and there followed hail and fire, mixed with blood, and it was cast upon the earth, and a third of the earth was burnt up* (Rv 8.7).

9. The righteous had been considered worthy of their share in blessedness, as I said at the end of the breaking of the sixth seal, being caught up before the coming of the Lord "in the clouds into the air," so that they might meet the Lord as he came,[19] according to the testimony of the apostle which was there presented to me. The vision then goes on to indicate the end of the rest of humankind, and the punishment of sinners. (2) When utter destruction is about to take place, it follows that there will also be different kinds of death and of requital of the impious. Most of them will be conducted through fire, "for that day will be revealed in fire," said the divine apostle writing his first letter to the Corinthians.[20] For if there are "many resting places," as the Lord says,[21] there are also different places of punishment. The same trumpets which bring about death for those on earth will also raise the dead after this. (3) Why, therefore, does he say that when the first angel blew his trumpet, *hail and fire* burned up *a third of those on the earth*? If one takes this quite literally, he will not find the true meaning of the saying. But if he reckons it as said metaphorically, he will have said nothing strange, the word *fire* meaning the distress and deep pain of the sinners when they see the saints "caught up in the clouds to meet the Lord,"[22] while they themselves have stayed on earth, dishonored and considered of no account. (4) When the text says *trees* and *grass* were burnt up, it refers allegorically to sinners because of their folly and the insensibility of their soul, their woodenness all ready for burning.

19. 1 Thes 4.17.   20. 1 Cor 3.13.
21. Jn 14.2.   22. 1 Thes 4.17.

10. He says, *The second angel blew his trumpet, and something like a great mountain, burning with fire, was thrown into the sea, and a third of the sea became blood, (2) a third of the living creatures in the sea died, and a third of the ships were destroyed* (Rv 8.8–9).

11. The divine apostle, writing to the Romans, says, "the creation was subjected to futility, not of its own will but by the will of him who subjected it in hope that the creation itself will be set free from its bondage to decay and obtain the glorious liberty of the children of God."[23] When will it "be set free"? When there will be "new heavens and a new earth according to his promises," as Peter preaches to us in his second epistle?[24] (2) When the earth is changed so that it might be freed from destruction and become new, it follows that the sea, too, should also change, for the sea is on the earth. But how could it itself be cleansed, except by means of cleansing fire? Therefore, fire falling on it changed it into blood, and it killed a third of the [creatures] in it. (3) This is taking a literal, physical view, but you could also understand *the sea* allegorically and according to the rules of metaphor as referring to the present life because of its turbulence and constant motion; fish and *ships* are then human beings wriggling in their salty and bitter sins, who will melt away in their grief because of their fruitless concerns in their lifetime.

12. *The third angel blew his trumpet, and a great star fell from heaven, blazing like a torch, and it fell on a third of the rivers and on the fountains of water. (2) The name of the star is Wormwood. A third of the waters became wormwood, and many people died as a result of the waters, because they had become bitter* (Rv 8.10–11).

13. Naomi long ago was given the name "bitter" because of her great distress over her children and other calamities. Bitterness then is a sign of extraordinary plagues. We sinners may some time suffer such bitterness, if we become embittered at the glory of the saints, seeing that when such good things had been prepared for human beings, we ourselves exchanged the pleasures of the present for those in the future. I think this is what the falling of the star means—a display of God's wrath which made the waters bitter. (2) Figuratively he calls human beings

23. Rom 8.20–21.   24. 2 Pt 3.13.

waters, according to the prophet's saying, "from the sounds of many waters, amazing are the surgings of the sea,"[25] and again, "The rivers have lifted up, Lord, the rivers have lifted up their voices, the rivers will lift up what has been worn away."[26] (3) These, then, are figurative expressions. But we must not reject the possibility that these and other such things were actually taking place then.

14. *The fourth angel blew his trumpet, and a third of the sun was struck, and a third of the moon, and a third of the stars, so that a third of the stars were darkened, and a third of the day did not shine, and likewise the night.* (2) *And I looked and I heard an eagle crying with a loud voice, as it flew in midheaven, "Woe, woe, woe, to the inhabitants of the earth, at the blasts of the remaining trumpets which the three other angels are about to blow"* (Rv 8.12–13).

15. We have been taught by Joel the prophet that "the sun" shall be turned "to darkness, and the moon to blood, before the great and terrible day of the Lord comes,"[27] meaning that on that day all these things will take place. Peter, too, said in his second epistle, "The day of the Lord will come as a thief, in which the heavens will pass away with a loud noise, and the elements will be dissolved with fire."[28] The Lord himself, too, in the hundred-and-ninth section of Matthew says, "Immediately after the tribulation of those days the sun will be darkened, and the moon will not give its light, and the stars will fall from heaven."[29]

We are now being taught through the Revelation that these things will come about at the consummation of the present age. (2) What is the meaning that not everything on the earth, in the sea, and in the rivers, as well as also the elements in the heavens, will experience the afore-mentioned sufferings, but only a third of them? This is also a sure proof of God's love of humankind. He was calling to repentance those of an earlier time by means of a partial and not a total onslaught against the elements. Those who do not turn to him he leads to total destruction in the future. (3) The prophet also says something similar: "He made a

25. Ps 92.4.   26. Ps 92.3.
27. Jl 2.31.   28. 2 Pt 3.10.
29. Mt 24.29.

path for his anger; he did not spare their souls from death."[30] For to go partly forward as on a road and to send forth part of God's wrath is the mark of one who opens a door to repentance by calling human beings to a change of purpose through fear of what is taking place [around them]. But if those among them do not go forward and make progress, "he did not spare their souls from death." (4) The eagle in midheaven, looking sadly at the misfortunes of those on earth, you will understand is a kind of divine angel sympathizing with the plight of human beings.

16. *And the fifth angel blew his trumpet, and I saw a star fallen from heaven to earth, and the key of the shaft of the bottomless pit was given to him, (2) and from the shaft came up smoke like the smoke of a great burning furnace, and the sun and the air were darkened with the smoke. (3) Locusts came out on the earth, and they were given power like the power which scorpions have on earth. (4) They were told not to harm the grass of the earth or any green growth or any tree, but only those who were without the seal of God upon their foreheads* (Rv 9.1–4).

17. Up to now the vision was describing for us the way and the kind of plagues with which the [elements] of earth and heaven, and with them human beings, were being consummated or changed. But now as though the consummation has already come about and the resurrection has been effected, he describes the punishments accorded to sinners. (2) He says, *I saw a star fallen from heaven to earth,* meaning that the star is a messenger of God because of its brilliance, which had come down on the earth, where the judgment of sinners will occur, at a certain place which one of the holy prophets named "the valley of Jehoshaphat."[31]

(3) He says, *The key of the shaft of the bottomless pit was given to him.* He calls Gehenna *a shaft of a bottomless pit.* That is why *there also came up from the shaft smoke* as of abundant fire, which was clearly lurking in the shaft. But the smoke symbolizes not only fire, but also darkness; for the word of the prophet, "The voice of the Lord cutting through a flame of fire,"[32] is interpreted by the saints as though it will cut through the illumination of the

30. Ps 77.50. 31. Jl 3.2.
32. Ps 28.7.

fire of Gehenna so that only scorching heat and darkness remain in it.

(4) He says, *The sun and the air were darkened with the smoke* of the shaft, not because these elements were darkened, but because those who had been thrown into the shaft were filled with darkness because of their punishment, and so were blind to the air and the sun. For this is what one of the holy prophets also said: "The sun" will be darkened "at noon,"[33] describing the disasters of the Jews, not that the sun was darkened, but that they suffered this in their affliction and could not see the sun; for the extent of their disasters was like being overcome with dizziness.

(5) He says, And from the smoke *locusts came out on the earth.* I think that he calls the worms *locusts,* about which Isaiah says, "Their worm shall not die, and their fire shall not be quenched,"[34] perhaps calling the biting sting of the soul and its persistent and creeping pain a worm. (6) He says, *And they were given power like the power which scorpions have on earth. They were told not to harm the grass of the earth or any green growth or any tree, but only those human beings who do not have the seal of God upon their foreheads* once the earth had been changed and renewed. For it is said somewhere about it, "You will send forth your spirit and they will be created, and you will renew the face of the earth."[35] (7) It was no longer a good thing for any adornment of the earth to be struck, neither a tree nor anything growing, except only human beings, and of these only those *who do not have the seal of God on their foreheads.* For those human beings who are completely holy and pure have received the place mentioned earlier on, being constantly with Christ and in sight of the divine throne. But those who are less holy but nevertheless who have been baptized, and who bear the sign of Christ *on their foreheads* and who have not been completely rejected, and have not gravely defiled themselves and their baptism by their unnatural deeds, but as it were are midway between good and evil, remain upon earth but escape punishment. (8) For if this were not so, why would the Lord have said to those who had made good use of the pounds entrusted to them, "Have authority over ten cities," and to another, "over five cities,"[36] as

33. Am 8.9.   34. Is 66.24.
35. Ps 103.30.

if they were going to rule over the inferior, while their subjects went altogether unpunished? For who would choose to rule those who were being punished and constantly gnashing their teeth, and bewailing their unspeakable sufferings? I am not of course referring to the saints, nor to people like them, but simply to people deserving our sympathy. Who would choose to rule over them, unless he himself, too, were going to suffer something similar to the incurable condition of those who were being punished? (9) The third part of human beings is handed over to punishment, since they are sinners and impious and have not received the faith of Christ. That is why it is said that those were struck who had not been sealed with the seal of God.

18. He says, *They were allowed not to kill them, but to torture them for five months, and their torture was like the torture of scorpions, when they sting someone.* (2) *And in those days people will seek death and not find it; they will long to die, and death flies from them* (Rv 9.5–6).

19. Is this why some of the fathers accepted the restoration of sinners, saying that they were to be chastised so far, but no further, as they had been cleansed by their punishment? But what is to be done, when most of the fathers say this, while the accepted Scriptures say that the punishment of those who were then being chastised is everlasting? What, therefore, should one say, or how should one reconcile these views? One must combine the opinions of both. (2) I say this as a suggestion and not as an affirmation; for I associate myself with the teaching of the church in meaning that the future punishments will be everlasting, since this is also what the Lord said in the gospel according to Matthew, "And these will go away into everlasting punishment,"[37] and Isaiah, "Their worm shall not die, and their fire shall not be quenched."[38] (3) So this is to be taken as a suggestion, taking a middle path between each view, because up to a certain time, which the present Revelation said is *five months*, using the number in a kind of mystical way, sinners will be most severely punished as if stung by a scorpion; but after this we shall be punished more gently, though we shall certainly not be entirely un-

36. Lk 19.17, 19.　　　　37. Mt 25.46.
38. Is 66.24.

punished, to such an extent that we may seek death and not find
it. For why would those who were not being punished at all need
to seek death? (4) He says, *Death flies from them,* for they pass all
their life in punishment.

20. *And the appearance of the locusts was like horses arrayed for war;
on their heads were what looked like crowns of gold; their faces were like
human faces, (2) their hair like women's hair, and their teeth like lions'
teeth; (3) their breasts were like iron breastplates, and the noise of their
wings was like the noise of many chariots with horses rushing to war. (4)
They have tails like scorpions, and stings, and in their tails is their power of hurting people for five months. (5) They have as their king the angel of the bottomless pit; his name in Hebrew is Abaddon, and in Greek
he has the name Apolluon. (6) The first woe has passed; two woes are
still to come* (Rv 9.7–12).

21. After this the blessed evangelist depicts for us the nature
of the worms in a way which is both subtle and fearful. In each of
the statements about them, one might wonder at the accuracy
of the account; for he did not say that they had lions' teeth and
scorpions' tails and human faces, but that there was in each a
sort of image disclosing a figurative picture, not the truth. (2) By
such means, therefore, either their fearsomeness and amazing
power is indicated, or he has truly sketched their shape.

(3) He says, *They have as their king the angel of the bottomless pit;
his name in Hebrew is Abaddon, and in Greek Apolluon.* The name
has either been invented to correspond with the aforementioned
events of the vision, or perhaps not only are there "ministering
spirits, sent to serve those who are to inherit salvation," according to the divine apostle,[39] but also spirits sent to punish those
who deserve to be punished, rather like the angel who in a single
night struck the hundred and eighty-five thousand of the Assyrians;[40] and those who destroyed by fire the five cities of Sodom.[41]

(4) He says, *The first woe has passed; two woes are still to come. Woe* is
the jargon denoting great distress and indicates present and future afflictions. So he says the one punishment has already been
mentioned; two will be mentioned later.

39. Heb 1.14.   40. 2 Kgs 19.35; Is 37.36.
41. Gn 19.2.

22. *Then the sixth angel blew his trumpet, and I heard a loud voice from the horns of the golden altar before God, (2) saying to the sixth angel with the trumpet, "Release the four angels who are bound at the great river Euphrates." (3) So the four angels were released, who had been held ready for the hour, the day, the month, and the year, to kill a third of human beings. (4) The number of the troops of cavalry was ten thousand times ten thousand; I heard their number. (5) And this was how I saw the horses in my vision and their riders with their breastplates of flame color, hyacinth-blue, and sulfur-yellow; and the heads of the horses were like lions' heads, and fire and smoke and sulfur issued from their mouths. (6) By these three plagues, a third of humankind was killed, by the fire and the smoke and the sulfur issuing from their mouths. (7) For the power of the horses is in their mouths and in their tails; they are like serpents with heads, and by means of them they wound* (Rv 9.13–19).

23. He says that when the angel sounded the trumpet, *I heard a voice from the horns of the altar.* By *the horns of the altar* he means those among the angels who are superior and distinguished above the others. He says the altar was *golden,* because he depicts the altar as wonderful since it was valuable and divine, made out of material which we consider precious. Just as we understood *the horns of the altar* to be rulers of the angels, so it is natural to understand *the altar* itself to be all "the ministering spirits,"[42] because they offer to God "a spiritual sacrifice."[43]

(2) What is the voice that was heard from the horns of the altar? *Release,* it says, *the four angels who are bound at the great river Euphrates.* (3) Holy Scripture told us about the rebel angel—I mean Satan and those who rebelled with him—how on the one hand we were told that they were "kept in eternal chains in the nether gloom,"[44] and on the other hand how they were condemned to the depth of the sea. (4) For it says in the second epistle of Peter, "For if God did not spare the angels when they sinned, but cast them into hell and committed them to pits of nether gloom to be kept until the judgment,"[45] and in the epistle of Jude it says, "The angels that did not keep their own position but left

42. Heb 1.14.
43. Rom 12.1, rendering the Greek λογικός, which is so rich in meaning.
44. Jude 6.
45. 2 Pt 2.4.

their proper dwelling he has kept in eternal chains in the nether
gloom until the judgment of the great day."[46] (5) The book of
Job says that the rebel has been thrown into the sea, expound-
ing allegorically in various ways his shape and size and the bitterness of his condition; he says, "He is mocked by the angels of
God."[47] And Isaiah cried out about him that "The sword of God
will be brought against the serpent, the fleeing snake, against
the serpent, the crooked snake, and he will destroy the serpent
in the sea on that day."[48] (6) And the prophet, too, after detail-
ing all created things, goes on to add this about those in the sea:
"This serpent, which you formed to sport in it."[49] In accordance
with these words the blessed prophet Ezekiel, too, when speaking about Egypt, says, "You were like a lion of the nations, and as
a serpent in the sea, and you were thrusting with your horns in
your rivers."[50]

(7) Yet no one ever told us that they had been bound in the
river Euphrates, or that they would ever be released, nor even
that human beings were to be punished by them. For Jude, in
saying that they had been bound "with eternal chains," denied
that they would ever be released. And when Isaiah said that the
serpent in the sea will be destroyed on the day of judgment, he
did not say that he would destroy others, but only the serpent.
So, too, the Lord in the gospels, when sending the sinners "to
the fire prepared for the Devil and his angels,"[51] denied that he
would use them as avengers and tormentors, but rather that they
were going to undergo punishment. (8) So how could anyone
understand the present saying to mean, on the one hand, that
they had been bound *in the river Euphrates* and that they will be
released and, on the other, that they themselves will punish the
sinners?

I suspect that the words are figurative, in line with the manner of the whole vision. I think he means by the angels those
who had been spiritually bound to the joyful contemplation of
God. For *the river* is used allegorically by Isaiah to refer to the divine: "See, I am turning to them as a river of peace, and as a tor-

46. Jude 6.
48. Is 27.1.
50. Ezek 32.2.

47. Jb 41.25.
49. Ps 103.26.
51. Mt 25.41.

rent enveloping the glory of the nations."[52] And the prophet says, "The waves of the river make glad the city of God."[53] And the Lord himself, in John, in the twenty-second section, said about the Spirit, "He who believes in me, as Scripture says, 'From out of his belly shall flow rivers of living water.'"[54] (9) He says, "Release them from the contemplation of God and send them to punish the impious." He means that these are those who have been appointed for the day of his presence. But who does he say the four angels are? Perhaps they are those designated in the Scripture: Michael, Gabriel, Uriel, and Raphael.

(10) After this they went out with an ineffably large army of cavalry. By this he means the invincible force of the holy angels, comparing it with a huge force of cavalry. (11) He says, *I saw their riders with their breastplates of flame color, hyacinth-blue, and sulfur-yellow:* fire is a symbol of wrath and punishment; blue indicates that those who were sent were heavenly, for heaven is blue like a hyacinth; being sulfur-yellow makes them pleasing to God, in that they are singing[55] to God, for it is pleasing to sing. Who rather than the holy angels would be pleasing to God? (12) Then the vision changes course and ceases to refer to the power of the holy angels, and now provides an image of lions and fire, of smoke and sulfur and snakes, all of which clearly indicate their fearfulness and irresistibility.

24. *The rest of humankind, who were not killed by these plagues, did not even repent of the works of their hands so as to stop worshiping demons and idols of gold and silver and bronze and stone and wood, which can neither see nor hear nor walk; (2) nor did they repent of their murders or their sorceries or their thefts* (Rv 9.20–21).

25. The prophet, plucking his spiritual lyre, told us of those who were being punished in Hades, saying with reference to God that "in death there is no one who remembers you; in Hades who will give you praise?"[56] so depriving them both of joy

with God and of repentance. For by not remembering God they were deprived of spiritual joy, as the same prophet writes elsewhere, "I remembered God and I rejoiced,"[57] and through not making confession they were deprived of repentance. For confession is the declaration of offenses resulting from a change of heart and conversion due to the pricking of conscience in one's soul. (2) For in fact, God has given us two kinds of life, the present and the future. In the present we have been permitted to conduct our life according to our opinion and ability, but in the future life we receive the consequent rewards or punishments for the actions of our lives. The present life is not one of judgment, unless someone perhaps may be profitably reminded to turn to repentance, nor is the future life one of behaving in such a way that we may be changed from a debased life to one better. (3) This being so, what is the meaning of the present saying about those who are being punished there—*And the rest of humankind, who were not killed by these plagues, and did not repent of the works of their hands?* He means by this not those who did not repent in their life there, but those who are still living and who did not repent of their various unlawful deeds after hearing and seeing what the future holds. By this aforesaid plague, perhaps they will not die the spiritual death—calling punishment death—while they eternally live out their life with the wicked, unless, of course, they will be punished by something worse, which he has prudently passed over in silence in his attempted explanation. (4) May all of us be free of these, by the grace and lovingkindness of our Lord Jesus Christ, to whom with the Father and the Holy Spirit be glory for ever and ever. Amen.

57. Ps 76.4.

CHAPTER SIX

N THE PRESENT chapter blessed John continues to explain to us the events after the sixth angel had blown his trumpet, all of which I have not discussed fully in a single chapter, as I saw the fifth chapter being lengthily prolonged. What other event does he write about?

2. *And I saw a mighty angel coming down from heaven, wrapped in a cloud, with a rainbow over his head, and his face was like the sun, and his feet like pillars of fire.* (2) *He had in his hand a miniature open scroll. And he set his right foot on the sea, and his left foot on the land,* (3) *and called out with a loud voice, like a lion roaring. When he called out, the seven thunders made their own voices heard.* (4) *And when the seven thunders had spoken, I was about to write, but I heard a voice from heaven saying, "Seal up what the seven thunders have said, and do not write it down"* (Rv 10.1–4).

3. So, therefore, all those who are still living and who have heard or even beheld the punishments of sinners, and have not repented but remained in their wickedness, as was said earlier, he says against these, *I saw an angel who had come down*[1] *from heaven,* bearing different forms of punishments. (2) He says that the look of him and his appearance was like this: He was *wrapped in a cloud.* The cloud symbolizes the incorporeality and invisibility of the holy angels, for the cloud is a type of what cannot be seen. For the prophet, indicating clearly the invisibility of God, says, "Clouds and darkness are round about him."[2] (3) And there is *a rainbow over his head,* just as if he were saying that the sum and excellence of the angels' good qualities is their brilliance. For

1. The comment here uses the aorist participle (καταβάντα), whereas the text cited for v. 1 has the present participle (καταβαίνοντα), as in the manuscripts of Revelation.
2. Ps 96.2.

they are angels of light.[3] (4) He says, *And his face was like the sun.*
And this is the proof of their original pure brilliance. But the
rainbow has a created brilliance, indicating the brilliance that
comes from the angelic virtues. So the brilliance of the rainbow
is not of a single form, but is variegated, indicating all the virtues
of angels. The sun symbolizes their sparkling nature. Wherefore
he was wrapped in the rainbow, for their virtues are wrapped
around us. But his face was like the sun, for among us the sun is
a wholly natural boon.

(5) *And his feet were like pillars of fire.* The fire indicates the retribution which he came to bring upon the impious. (6) He says,
He had in his hand a miniature[4] open scroll. Daniel mentioned such
little scrolls, saying, "The court sat in judgment before him, and
the scrolls were opened."[5] It was the miniature scroll in which
were written both the names and the iniquities of the exceedingly impious who were to be punished. Wherefore he spoke
of *the miniature scroll,* using a diminutive, since a scroll, or little
scroll—for both descriptions occur in Holy Scripture—is that
in which the names of all human beings have been written, as I
have already said—but *the miniature scroll* is that in which are the
names of the exceedingly impious. For those who worshiped images and were guilty of murder and witchcraft and were sick with
the other evils that he recounted are unlikely to be numerous
enough to fill a whole little scroll.

(7) He says, *And he set his right foot on the sea, and his left foot on
the land:* this indicates the huge size of the holy ones; but it also
shows that he was bringing retribution both to those who had
sinned on land and to those on the sea, such as pirates or those
who had harmed others at sea. (8) *And he called out with a loud
voice, like a lion roaring:* that the holy angel should roar like lions
is a symbol of his wrath against the impious. (9) He says, *And
when he called out, the seven thunders made their own voices heard.* By
the seven thunders he means the seven ministering spirits, which

3. 2 Cor 11.14.
4. In the text three different words are used for "scroll": βίβλος (scroll),
the diminutive βιβλίον (little scroll), and the further diminutive βιβλιδάριον
(miniature scroll).
5. Dn 7.10.

have been mentioned earlier. That is why the definite article is used. He means that *the seven thunders* are analogous to those seven spirits. (10) What does the cry of the seven spirits mean? It means that they give their entire support to the punishment of the sinners, offering a thanksgiving hymn to God, because he has done everything justly. At the same time also as they cried out, they disclosed the different forms of punishment.

(11) He says, *I was about to write* what was said by the seven spirits. *But I heard a voice from heaven saying, Seal up what the seven thunders have said, and do not write it down.* For *seal* means, "Have the recollection engraved in your mind," but being prevented from committing it to writing implies a purpose the reason for which is known to God. Perhaps the punishments were lighter than those normally considered appropriate and reflect the goodness of the one inflicting the penalty, and so tended to make them contemptible for people. (12) What do blessed Gregory and all-knowledgeable Evagrius say about these things? The former says, "The retribution" for Adam and his kind "is compassion for humankind; for this is how I believe God punishes." And in another place he says, "Neither is mercy without judgment, nor is judgment without mercy."[6] Evagrius says, "The deeper account of judgment may well escape the notice of the youth and the worldly; for they do not know" distress, "since their rational soul has been condemned to ignorance."[7]

4. *And the angel whom I saw standing on the sea and on the land lifted up his right hand to heaven, (2) and swore by him who lives for ever and ever, who created heaven and what is in it, the earth and what is in it, and the sea and what is in it, that there should be no more time, (3) but in the days of the seventh angel when he is about to sound his trumpet* (Rv 10.5–7).

5. This is said in the form of an ellipse; for he means that when the seventh angel *is about to sound his trumpet,* all the different and varied punishments of the wicked will be completed. But he says that this will not take place now when the trumpet

6. Cf. Gregory of Nazianzus, *Orationes* 38.12 and 45.8.
7. Evagrius Ponticus, *Gnostica* 36.

sounds in the vision, since the other events had not yet then occurred, (2) but only when the trumpet is sounded at the appropriate time. After this, he says, *the secret purpose of God will be fulfilled, as he announced to his servants the prophets* (Rv 10.7). For up
to the time of the judgment and the rewarding and punishment
of the good and the bad, the prophets prophesied, but after this
they said no more. Therefore, when in that age the seventh angel sounds his trumpet, all God's secret purpose will be fulfilled,
together with every prophetic prediction.

6. *And I heard a voice from heaven again speaking to me and saying, "Go, take the little scroll which is open in the hand of the angel who
is standing on the sea and on the land." (2) And I went to the angel
and said to him, "Give me the little scroll." And he said to me, "Take it
and eat; it will be bitter to your stomach, but in your mouth it will be as
sweet as honey." (3) And I took the miniature scroll from the hand of the
angel and ate it; it was as sweet as honey in my mouth, but when I had
eaten it, my stomach was made bitter. (4) And he said to me, "You must
again prophesy over many peoples and nations and tongues and kings"*
(Rv 10.8–11).

7. And the voice that *I heard from heaven,* I heard it *again,* he
says, *speaking to me.* What was it saying? "Take the little scroll
from the angel." (2) *I took* it, he says, *and ate it, and it was sweet
in my mouth,* but after eating it was bitter in my stomach. Since
the blessed evangelist both saw and heard the punishments imposed on the wicked, in order that it might be instilled by deed
and not only by report that the sins of humankind were hated by
God, being bitter and abominable, the teaching of the vision is
this—for as he was a holy and chaste man he did not know this
from experience—that in this way he might know that the wrath
of God against the wicked was just. For the little scroll contained
both the names and the transgressions of those who had sinned
very grievously, as was said earlier. (3) Therefore, he was commanded to eat it, that as though by tasting and a kind of spiritual
experience he might share through the vision in the bitterness
of sins. And when he ate it he found that they were sweet in his
mouth, but bitter in his stomach after eating; for that is just like
every sin. It is sweet while it is being performed, but bitter when

accomplished. It thus provides grounds for punishment, and even in repentance it makes bitter those who have performed it. This was also just like the tree forbidden by God in paradise which all expound allegorically as sin, since it introduced the knowledge of good and evil, of good in the taste, but of evil after the experience.

(4) He says, *And he said to me, "You must again prophesy over many peoples and nations and kings,"* just as if he were saying, "Since in a vision you have seen the consummation of the present age and God's wrath against the wicked, do not now think that the day of consummation is actually present; there is a long time meanwhile for you to prophesy to many nations and kings." So up till now blessed John has been prophesying by means of his gospel, his general epistles, and the present Revelation. For all that he has said and prophesied has been in the Spirit.

8. *And I was given a measuring rod like a staff, with the words "Rise and measure the temple of God and the altar, and those who worship there, (2) but leave out the court outside the temple, and do not measure it, for it has been given over to the nations, and they will trample over the holy city for forty-two months"* (Rv 11.1–2).

9. In what went before, the vision showed blessed John the multitude of the saints who were with Christ and who were looking upon the divine throne. Among them those from the nations were many times more numerous than those from Israel. But now he shows him something else—the number of those who had been honored in the time of the old covenant, and those in the time of the new covenant. And see how cleverly this is depicted for him. (2) A measuring rod is given him to measure *the temple of God and the altar* in the temple, obviously the one in Jerusalem, *and those who worship in it.* And he measured it; those who had pleased God in the times of the old covenant could be measured because of their scarcity. (3) *But,* he says, *leave out the court outside the temple and do not measure it, for it has been given over to the nations.* When he measured the temple and the altar and those sacrificing in it, he heard that he must leave out the court outside and widen it, definitely not measure it, since it was too large to be measured. He says the court has been given *to the na-*

tions; it is attached to the temple and also outside it, (4) just as
the new covenant is attached to the old. For [the writings of]
the new covenant spiritually and truly fulfill the shadows [of the
old], and yet they are different from it, as Jeremiah says, "Behold, the days are coming, says the Lord, when I will make a new
covenant with the house of Israel and the house of Judah, not
like the covenant which I made with their fathers when I took
them by the hand to bring them out of the land of Egypt."[8] (5)
He means that the *court of the temple* is the new covenant. Then
the vision speaks with mystical signs, saying that the Lord was
in the old covenant, too, who in the new covenant was called
"Christ" and "Beginning."[9] This is why Paul thinks it right to say
about Israel, "For they drank from the spiritual rock which followed them, and the rock was Christ."[10] He called *the court* of the
old covenant the new covenant, for the court is the entrance[11]
and the way into God, and is certainly not the temple. Therefore
he did not measure the court, which symbolizes both the court
and those within it; for both the new [covenant] and those who
have been set right in it exceed all comprehension, the people
because of their untold multitude and the covenant through the
subtlety and loftiness of its teachings.

(6) In saying, *because it has been given over to the nations,* he
means that the good things in the new covenant were given also
to Israel, but since those of the nations in it are more numerous than those honored from Israel, he has indicated the whole
by the majority, by saying that the court has been given to *the
nations.* (7) He says, *and they will trample over the holy city for forty-
two months—the city,* not the temple—calling the church *the city,*
about which it is said, "Glorious things have been spoken about
you, the city of God,"[12] "the heavenly Jerusalem,"[13] "the mother"[14] "of the first-born, those inscribed in heaven."[15]

(8) What does the period of forty-two months mean? It intimates that the time of the new dispensation on earth will be
short, and then will come the end. For the number forty consists

8. Jer 38.31–32 LXX = 31.31–32 RSV.   9. Jn 1.1.
10. 1 Cor 10.4.   11. Greek ἀρχή, "beginning."
12. Ps 86.3.   13. Heb 12.22.
14. Ps 86.5.   15. Heb 12.23.

of four tens and therefore is not a perfect number, and likewise the number two. In this way the argument shows that the establishment of the new covenant will not be of long duration in the present life. That is why Scripture calls the time of the new covenant, when the only Son became incarnate, "the last" hour and also "the eleventh" hour.[16] But in the future age it will be eternal. (9) By saying that those of the nations will trample on *the holy city,* that is, the church, he indicates that they will dwell in it.

10. *And I will give my two witnesses [authority] to prophesy for two thousand two hundred and sixty days, clothed in sackcloth. (2) These are the two lampstands*[17] *which stand before the God*[18] *of the earth. (3) And if any one would harm them, fire pours from their mouth and consumes their foes; if any one would harm them, this is how he must be killed. (4) They have the authority to close the sky, so that no rain should fall during the days of their prophesying, and they have authority over the waters to turn them into blood, and to smite the earth with every plague, as often as they please* (Rv 11.3–6).
11. Everything in the vision was shaped by the evangelist in connection with the design of the Lord in his incarnation—his birth, his temptation, his teachings, the insults to him, and indeed the cross and the resurrection, and the second coming, and in addition to these the rewards and punishments of the saints and the sinners. But nothing had been said about the accounts of the heralds of his second coming, so, as though by a turnabout, these matters are now explained. (2) It is clear to everyone that the divine Scripture predicted that Elijah the Tishbite would come, because Malachi says, "See, I will send you Elijah the Tishbite before the great and glorious day of the Lord comes, who will turn the heart of the father to his son, and the heart of a man to his neighbor, lest I come and smite the land with might."[19] And in Matthew's gospel the Lord says of the Bap-

16. Mt 20.6, 9.
17. Oecumenius omits "the two olive trees and" (αἱ δύο ἐλαῖαι καὶ), found in most manuscripts of Revelation, but includes it below.
18. Most manuscripts of Revelation read κυρίου (Lord); Oecumenius reads θεοῦ (God) here, but "Lord" below.
19. Mal 4.4–5.

tist, "and if you are willing to accept it, he is Elijah who is to come."[20] (3) We have not heard anything at all clear about any other herald, except that Genesis said about Enoch, "because he was well-pleasing to God he was taken up,"[21] and the wise apostle said about him, "By faith Enoch was taken up so that he should not see death; and he was not found, because God had taken him."[22] (4) An old tradition holds sway in the church: with Elijah the Tishbite, Enoch will also come as the precursor of the second coming of Christ, as he prepares to take his stand against the Antichrist; for they say that they came first and testified that the signs which the Antichrist would perform were deception and that one should not believe the wretch. (5) It is about these that the vision now says that *they will prophesy* for so many *days,* meaning either some mystical number or one which will actually be the truth. (6) They will do this, he says, *clothed in sackcloth.* For they will mourn over the disobedience of humankind at that time.

(7) He says, *These are the two olive trees and the two lampstands which stand before the Lord on the earth.* The blessed prophet Zechariah[23] saw a lampstand supporting seven lamps, and two olive branches, but the branches were set in two pipes of the lamps, as he said, "What are these two olive branches, which are in the two golden pipes?" And he heard the angel responding, "They are the anointed ones,[24] who stand by the Lord of all the earth." (8) Surely he is not speaking about them now? For it is with the definite article that he says, *these are the two olive trees and the two lampstands,* explaining this by reference to an accepted symbolism, except that he here called the two pipes *two lampstands.* That the two olive branches were interpreted as referring to the two peoples, those of the Jews and those from the nations, was not unknown to the saints. Nevertheless, he can also mean the two prophets who are now under discussion. (9) He says that if anyone would harm them, fire pours from their mouths and protects them, *and they have the authority to close the sky, so that no rain*

20. Mt 11.14.   21. Gn 5.22.
22. Heb 11.5.   23. Zec 4.11–14.
24. Literally, "the sons of fatness" (τοὺς υἱοὺς . . . τῆς πιότητος); i.e., those anointed with olive oil.

should fall during the days of their prophesying. This is very plausible, for if one of them, Elijah the Tishbite, had such authority even before the ministry of Christ, why should it be incredible that he should be seen as heralding Christ?

(10) He says, *And they have authority over the waters to turn them into blood and to smite the earth with every plague, as often as they wish.* For since "the coming" of the Antichrist will take place "by the activity of Satan with all power and false signs and wonders,"[25] as Paul says in writing the second epistle to the Thessalonians, the signs are [Satan's] instrument to draw [people] to agree and believe [in them]. That is why the two prophets who say that the Antichrist is a deceiver and a cheat will use all sorts of signs to draw their hearers to faith.

12. *And when they have finished their testimony, the beast that ascends from the bottomless pit will make war upon them and conquer them and kill them, (2) and he will put their dead bodies in the street of the great city which is allegorically called Sodom and Egypt, and where their Lord was crucified. (3) Those from the peoples and tongues and tribes and nations will gaze at their dead bodies and they will not allow them to be placed in a tomb, (4) and those who dwell on the earth will rejoice over them and make merry and give presents to one another, because these two prophets had tortured the inhabitants of the earth* (Rv 11.7–10).

13. He says, *And when they have finished their testimony:* for they will testify that this present one is not the Christ but is some deceiver and cheat and vandal, in so far as the Son of God will not come yet, but is he who must be believed as Savior and God, who long ago came for the benefit of humankind and is now at hand.

(2) He says, *the beast that ascends from the bottomless pit:* he calls the Antichrist a *beast* because he is cruel, inhuman, and greedy for blood. He calls the life of human beings a bottomless pit, bitter with its sins, distasteful, and never at rest with the proliferation of wicked spirits. For the wretch will not arise from any other source than our own human nature. For he will be a man "whose coming is due to the activity of Satan,"[26] as has just been

25. 2 Thes 2.9.
26. 2 Thes 2.9.

said. (3) Therefore he says *the beast will kill* the two witnesses, and he will cast their bodies unburied into the streets of Jerusalem. For he will reign there as king of the Jews, whom he will keep deceived as they comply with him and obey him in every way, as the Lord says according to John, "I have come in my Father's name, and you do not receive me; if another comes in his own name, him you will receive."[27] (4) He calls Jerusalem *Sodom allegorically*, not factually, because of its impiety and infamy at that time, and *Egypt*, as enslaving and oppressing the slaves of Christ, just as Egypt did to Israel. It was there, too, he says, that *their Lord*—that is, of the two witnesses—*was crucified.* (5) When those from every tribe who have been deceived by the Antichrist see the destruction of the witnesses, *they will rejoice over them* as though their own king was the victor. (6) Also the giving of presents to one another is an example of joy and delight. (7) He says, *because the two prophets had tortured the inhabitants of the earth*—not a physical torture, but by jeering at their sins and by refuting them and doing away with their deception they will torture them spiritually.

14. *But after the three-and-a-half days a breath of life from God entered them, and they stood up on their feet, and great fear fell on those who saw them.* (2) *Then they heard a loud voice from heaven saying to them, "Come up here!" And they went up to heaven in the cloud, and their enemies saw them.* (3) *And at that hour there was a great earthquake, and a tenth of the city fell down; seven thousand people were killed in the earthquake, and the rest were terrified and gave glory to the God of heaven.* (4) *The second woe has passed; behold, the third woe is soon to come* (Rv 11.11–14).

15. Since all these things were clearly taking place, and were going to occur in actual fact at that time, it is futile to spend time on what has already been established.

16. *Then the seventh angel blew his trumpet, and there were loud voices in heaven, saying, "The kingdom of the world has become the kingdom of our Lord and of his Christ, and he shall reign for ever and ever."* (2) *And the twenty-four elders who sat on their thrones before God fell*

27. Jn 5.43.

on their faces and worshiped God, saying, (3) *"We give thanks to you, Lord God, sovereign of all, who are and who were, because you have taken your great power and have entered on your reign.* (4) *The nations raged, but your wrath has come, and the time for the nations to be judged, and to reward your servants, the prophets and the saints, and those who fear your name, both small and great, and to destroy the destroyers of the earth."* (5) *Then God's temple in heaven was opened, and the ark of his covenant was seen within his temple; and there were flashes of lightning, noises, peals of thunder, an earthquake, and heavy hail* (Rv 11.15–19).

17. After the vision had set out as in an aside the account of the two witnesses, or prophets, and had gone through everything concerning them, it now comes to the matter in hand just from where it had started. It had started by describing the future reward of the saints, and by saying that there were more from the nations than from Israel, and that those in the new covenant who pleased God were more numerous than those in the old. (2) And he says that when the seventh angel sounded the trumpet, *there were voices in heaven saying that the kingdom of the world* now belongs to *God and his Christ.*[28] God is always reigning; he neither began, nor will he ever cease, to reign over heaven and earth and all things visible and spiritual in them; he is without beginning and also without end, being master and lord of all. But since human beings speak on earth of kings, and God in a way included those who were reigning with him, when the earthly kingdom of human beings is done away at the end of the present age, God alone will reign as king. That is why it is said that *the kingdom of the world* now belongs to *God and his Christ,* since the human kings on earth and the demonic tyrants had been destroyed and made an end of. (3) When the voice had sounded, he says, *the elders worshiped God,* and they themselves rendered their own thanksgiving, saying, *"We give thanks to you, Lord God, sovereign of all, who are and who were."* And he takes *You who are* to refer to the Holy Trinity, as well as *You who were,* even though *You who are* is especially said about the Father, and *You who were* about

28. Note that here, and a few sentences later, the author changes the construction used in the citation.

the Son; for being (*You who are*) refers to the Father, the Son, and the Holy Spirit. And we rightly say "You who were" of the Father, Son, and Holy Spirit. So the thanksgiving of the elders is offered up to the Holy Trinity.

(4) He says, *because you have taken your great power* from those on earth, and your kingly power which you had given them, and now you alone are king. (5) When the earthly kingdom was being destroyed, naturally *the nations raged*, as their domination was demolished—meaning by *nations* the ranks of the demons and the unbelievers.

(6) He says, *and your wrath came forth, and the lot*[29] *for the nations to be judged, and for rewarding your servants, the prophets and the saints.* He means that in the past you were very long-suffering with them, but since they did not benefit from your kindness, you now, that is, at the day of judgment, displayed your wrath against them, and all that was allotted and due to the nations came about and is present now. What then was [due to them]? Their judgment, and the reward given to the saints who had been ill-treated by them, and the destruction by retributory punishment of those who had ruined the earth, and, as it were, had defiled it by their own sins.

(7) He says, *Then God's temple in heaven was opened, and the ark of his covenant was seen within his temple.* After saying all this he now goes on to say that the hidden good things, and in addition some new mysteries, were revealed to the saints. For this is the meaning of the opening of the ark of the covenant. For that there are good things in the coming age which are hidden from human beings in this age is made clear by the saying, "what eye has not seen, nor ear heard, nor the heart of man conceived, what God has prepared for those who love him."[30] And again, that there are some mysteries and other knowledge at present unknown, the Lord makes clear when he said, "I shall not drink again of the fruit of" this "vine until that day when I shall drink it new with you in my Father's kingdom."[31] (8) The saints were

---

29. The text here reads κλῆρος ("lot"), whereas the citation from Revelation (Rv 11.18) rightly reads καιρός ("time").

30. 1 Cor 2.9.

31. Mt 26.29; Mk 14.25; Lk 22.18.

made worthy of this, but for the sinners *there were flashes of light-ning, noises, peals of thunder, earthquakes, and heavy hail,* which are the third woe. By using things well known to us he symbolizes the punishments coming upon the impious, and the terrors of God.

18. *And a great portent appeared in heaven, a woman clothed with the sun, and the moon was under her feet, and on her head a crown of twelve stars;* (2) *she was with child, and she cried out in her birth-pangs, in anguish for delivery* (Rv 12.1–2).

19. The vision wishes to give us a fuller description of the things concerning the Antichrist, of whom it has made a brief mention in what has gone before. The incarnation of the Lord, by which the world was subjected and made his own, became the occasion for the raising [of the Antichrist] and the endeavors of Satan. For this is why the Antichrist will be raised up: so that he may again cause the world to revolt against Christ, and persuade it to turn around and desert to Satan. Since again the Lord's physical conception and birth marked the beginning of his incarnation, the vision has brought into some order and sequence the events which it is going to explain, by starting its explanation from the physical conception of Christ, and by depicting for us the Mother of God. (2) For why does he say, *And a portent appeared in heaven, a woman clothed with the sun, and the moon under her feet?* He is speaking of the mother of our Savior, as I have said. Naturally the vision describes her as being in heaven and not on the earth, as pure in soul and body, as equal to an angel, as a citizen of heaven, as one who came to effect the incarnation of God who dwells in heaven ("for," he says, "heaven is my throne"),[32] and as one who has nothing in common with the world and the evils in it, but wholly sublime, wholly worthy of heaven, even though she sprang from our mortal nature and being. For the Virgin is of the same substance[33] as we are. The unholy doctrine of Eutyches, that the Virgin is of a miraculously different sub-

32. Is 66.1.
33. Greek, ὁμοούσιος, the term used to describe the unity between God the Father and God the Word.

stance from us, together with his other docetic doctrines, must
be banished from the divine courts.

(3) What is the meaning of saying that *she is clothed with the
sun, and has the moon under her feet?* The divine prophet Habakkuk says in prophesying about the Lord, "The sun was lifted up
and the moon stood still in its position for light."[34] He calls our
Savior Christ, or perhaps the preaching of the gospel, "the sun of
righteousness."[35] When this was exalted and increased, he says,
the moon, that is, the law of Moses, *stood still,* and no longer grew
in size. For after the appearance of Christ it no longer received
proselytes from the nations as before, but experienced annul-
ment and diminution. (4) Perhaps you could imagine that here
the holy Virgin is being protected by the spiritual sun. For this
is how the prophet, too, speaks of the Lord when he says about
Israel, "Fire fell upon them, and they did not see the sun."[36] And
the moon, that is, their worship according to the law and their
way of life according to the law, inasmuch as it has been brought
down and much reduced, is under her feet, overcome by the
evangelical splendor. He well named the requirements of the
law *the moon,* since they were brought to the light by the sun,
that is, Christ, just as the actual moon is given light by the actual
sun. (5) In line with this explanation, it would have been more
consistent to say that the woman was not clothed with the sun,
but that the woman clothed the sun contained in her womb. But
in'order to show in the vision that even when the Lord was conceived, he was the protector of his own mother and of all creation, the vision said that he clothed the woman. In the same
way the divine angel said to the holy Virgin, "The Spirit of the
Lord will come upon you and the power of the Most High will
overshadow you."[37] Overshadowing, protecting, and clothing all
have the same meaning.

(6) He says, *And on her head, a crown of twelve stars.* For the Virgin is crowned with the twelve apostles who proclaim the Christ
while she is proclaimed together with him. (7) He says, *She was*

34. Hab 3.10–11.
35. Mal 4.2. Oecumenius appears to confuse Habbakuk with Malachi.
36. Ps 57.9.
37. Lk 1.35.

with child, and she cried out in her birth-pangs, in anguish for deliv-ery. Yet Isaiah says about her, "before the woman in labor gives birth, and before the toil of labor begins, she fled and brought forth a male child."[38] Gregory, also, in the thirteenth chapter of his *Interpretation of the Song of Songs* talks of the Lord "whose con-ception is without intercourse, and whose birth is undefiled."[39] So the birth was free from pain. Therefore, if, according to such a great prophet and the teacher of the church, the Virgin has escaped the pain of childbirth, how does she here *cry out in her birth-pangs, in anguish for delivery?* (8) Does not this contradict what was said? Certainly not. For nothing could be contradictory in the mouth of the one and the same Spirit, who spoke through both. But in the present passage you should understand *the cry-ing out and being in anguish* in this way: until the divine angel told Joseph about her, that the conception was from the Holy Spir-it, the Virgin was naturally despondent, blushing before her be-trothed, and thinking that he might somehow suspect that she was in labor from a furtive marriage. Her despondency and grief he called, according to the principles of metaphor, crying and anguish; and this is not surprising. For even when blessed Moses spiritually met God and was losing heart—for he saw Israel in the desert being encircled by the sea and by enemies—God said to him, "Why do you cry to me?"[40] So also now the vision calls the sorrowful disposition of the Virgin's mind and heart "crying out." (9) But you, who took away the despondency of the unde-filed handmaid and your human mother, my lady mistress, the holy Mother of God, by your ineffable birth, do away with my sins, too, for to you is due glory for ever. Amen.

38. Is 66.7.
39. Gregory of Nyssa, *Homilia in Canticum Canticorum* 13.
40. Ex 14.15.

CHAPTER SEVEN

FTER PARTLY completing the vision of our universal lady, the holy ever-virgin Mary, Mother of God, he proceeds to give us another vision, saying,

2. *And another portent appeared in heaven; see, a great red serpent, with seven heads and ten horns, and seven diadems upon his heads.* (2) *His tail swept away a third of the stars of heaven, and threw them down to the earth. And the serpent stood in front of the woman who was about to bear a child, that he might devour her child when she brought it forth;* (3) *she brought forth a male child, one who is to rule all the nations with a rod of iron, but her child was caught up to God and to his throne,* (4) *and the woman fled into the desert, where she has a place prepared by God, so that she might find shelter there for one thousand two hundred and sixty days* (Rv 12.3–6).

3. At the start of the explanation of the vision it was said that the vision, in its wish to set out in greater detail the facts about the Antichrist, begins with the conception and birth of the Lord, which was why that vandal had been chosen by the universal foe and enemy of all to enslave again those who had been gathered together by the Lord. So it must now be said that the vision, in its wish to explain in detail all that concerns the Antichrist, reverts to the original event preceding the beginning already mentioned—I mean the birth of the Lord. This concerns Satan, and the way he was thrown down from heaven, even though he says this more clearly in the following vision, when he adds that he had also plotted against the Lord. In this way he laid some kind of prior foundation on which to build the future explanations of the Antichrist's affairs and his deeds.

(2) After this preface, we must move on to consider the text. He says, *And another portent appeared in heaven:* in this way the account is hitting at Satan, the prince of evil, because, although he

was a heavenly being, on account of his rebellion he has become an earthbound crawler. He depicts him in heaven so that the apostate might know from what state he has fallen and where he now is. (3) He says, *And see, a great red serpent:* he calls Satan *a serpent* because he is crooked. For that is what Isaiah, too, calls him, saying, "against the serpent, the crooked snake."[1] He is *red* because he is blood-sucking and irascible. (4) *With seven heads and ten horns, and seven diadems upon his heads:* the prophet knew well enough that he is many-headed. So he says of God, "You crushed the heads of the serpent; you gave him as food for the peoples of Ethiopia."[2] They say that he is many-headed since seven indicates many (as has been said more than once) as one who makes many crafty starts and designs against humankind by which he enslaves them; for the diadem is the symbol of tyranny. (5) The ten horns symbolize his immense power. For ten is a perfect number, and the horn is a sign of power. For [Scripture] says, "My horn shall be lifted up as the horn of a unicorn."[3] And anyone who reads the book of Job can discover that he is powerful.[4]

(6) He says, *And with his tail*[5] *he swept away a third of the stars of heaven, and threw them down to the earth.* For he cast down with himself a very great number of the angels, persuading them to rebel with him against God, and so he has made the heavenly beings earthy, and those who were bright as stars he has turned into darkness. *With his tail* means that he has done this by means of his uttermost and hindmost trespasses; for when he first considered his mad rebellion, and then went on consciously to nurture it in the arrogance of his purpose, he thus came to destroy the rest too.

(7) He says, *And the serpent stood in front of the woman who was about to bear a child, that he might devour her child when she brought it forth.* These are some of the events concerning the Lord: when he was to be born, the one who was planning to bring his power to an end carefully watched his opportunity so that when the Virgin gave birth he might destroy the child. So he did not miss his opportunity but stirred up Herod to destroy the manly male

1. Is 27.1.   2. Ps 73.13–14.
3. Ps 91.11.   4. Jb 1.12.
5. Note the slight difference from the original quotation.

child, who had nothing weak or womanish about him. For "before the child knows how to call 'father' or 'mother,'" Isaiah proclaims to us, "he will take the wealth of Damascus and the spoil of Samaria in the face of the king of Assyria."[6] (8) And who this one is who was born, this male child, reveal to us, John, more clearly. He who is, he says, *to rule all the nations with a rod of iron.* You have plainly told us, divine seer, that he is our savior and Lord, Jesus the Messiah. For he had been promised by his own Father, "Ask of me, and I will give you the nations for your inheritance, and the ends of the earth for your possession; you will rule them with a rod of iron, you will dash them in pieces like a potter's vessel."[7]

(9) *And,* he says, *her child was caught up to God and to his throne.* But the poisonous serpent was lying in wait and provoked Herod to destroy the children in Bethlehem, because [he thought] he would at all events find the Lord among them. But the child, by the forethought of his Father, escaped the plot. For Joseph heeded a divine warning to take the child along with his mother and escape to Egypt as Herod was about to seek the child's life. (10) *And the woman fled into the desert, where she has a place prepared by God, so that she might find shelter there for one thousand two hundred and sixty days.* So while the child was rescued from the serpent's plot, was the woman given over to destruction? No, but she, too, was rescued by the flight into Egypt, which was desert and exempt from Herod's plot. And there she lived, he says, and was sustained *for one thousand two hundred and sixty days,* which comprise almost three and a half years. The Mother of God spent all that time in Egypt until the death of Herod, after which an angel's divine message brought them back to Judaea.

4. *And war arose in heaven; Michael and his angels fought against the serpent. And the serpent and his angels fought;* (2) *but they did not prevail,* (3) *and there was no longer any place found for him in heaven. And the great serpent was thrown down, that old snake, who is called the Devil and Satan, the deceiver of the whole world; he was thrown down to the earth, and his angels were thrown down with him* (Rv 12.7–9).

6. Is 8.4.
7. Ps 2.8–9.

5. As though in a continual return to the starting-point, as already described, the vision now plans to describe an earlier beginning which had indeed been partly mentioned previously, as it prepares to tell us about the Antichrist; for the first beginning of the acts of the Antichrist was Satan's fall from heaven. The Lord, too, says of this, "I saw Satan fall like lightning from heaven."[8] (2) What, therefore, does it mean, *And war arose in heaven?* The divine Scripture says that Satan raised up his neck against God,[9] that is, stretched up an arrogant and stubborn neck against him and planned to revolt. But God, inasmuch as he is naturally good and long-suffering, was forbearing towards him. The divine angels, on the other hand, did not put up with the arrogance of their master, and drove him out of their company. He now says that Michael, one of the great rulers among the angels, made war against Satan and those under him. (3) And Satan *did not prevail* in the war against him, *nor was there any place* of refuge found for him, or any dwelling *in heaven, and he was thrown down to the earth.* He either actually suffered this, or because he had been stripped of angelic and heavenly rank, he was brought down to an earthly frame of mind. (4) Then, as though taking vengeance on God because of his fall, as he could not injure God, he injures God's servants, human beings, and leads them astray and tries to get them to revolt from God, thinking that in this way he would injure the master himself.

6. *And I heard a loud voice in heaven, saying, "Now has come salvation and power and the kingdom of our God and the authority of his Christ, for the accuser of our brethren has been thrown down, who accuses them day and night before our God. (2) And they have conquered him by the blood of the Lamb and by the word of their testimony, and they did not love their lives even unto death. (3) Rejoice then, O heaven and you that dwell therein! But woe to the earth and the sea, for the Devil has come down to you in great wrath, because he knows that his time is short"* (Rv 12.10–12).

7. Therefore, the holy angels, intimating their own joy which they had at the destruction of Satan, sing a song of victory to

8. Lk 10.18.
9. Cf. Jb 15.25.

God. They said, he says, *Now have come salvation and the kingdom, and the power of God* has shone out, *and the authority of his Christ,* showing that it is all-powerful. For by its cooperation, he says, we have conquered the enemy, *and the accuser of our brethren, who accuses them day and night before our God,* has departed from us. (2) What modesty of the holy angels! How they imitate their own master! They call human beings their *brothers.* And why is this amazing, when our common master did not refuse to call them this when he said, "I will tell of your name to my brothers; in the midst of the congregation I will praise you"?[10] (3) But why do they say of Satan, "He went away"? He was deprived of his dignity. There was no longer any room for him to stand before God, and to accuse human beings. (4) And he says, they themselves took vengeance on him in equal measure, and they conquered him who seemed to be invincible in venturing even against God. And they conquered by using as support and help the precious blood of Christ and the word of those who bore testimony to him, which they chose before their own lives. (5) After this, he says, *Rejoice,* all you angels of God, now that you have been delivered from the bitter sphere of Satan.

(6) He says, *Woe to the earth and the sea, for the Devil has come down to you in great wrath, because he knows that his time is short.* And "if he was going to harm the earth and the sea by the descent of Satan," someone might ask, "Why did he come down?" The answer is that for those who are self-controlled and have their hope in God, not only has it not been for their harm, but in fact for their benefit. He is exercising them like a gymnastic trainer, making them more acceptable by temptations and hardening them like iron. But he does harm the sluggish and fainthearted, who perhaps, even when the tempter was not around, were bad in themselves because they had turned their passions into their nature. (7) When they say, *Woe to the earth and the sea,* they do not mean, "woe to most of those who dwell on the earth and on the sea," but those who are *earth* and "ashes,"[11] according to Scripture, those who are earthbound in their mind,[12] as well as the capricious and perplexed and mentally unstable. For it is these

10. Heb 2.12; Ps 21.23.   11. Gn 18.27.
12. Cf. Rom 8.7.

that our common enemy attacks and enslaves in their weakness, as they willingly succumb to his tyranny.

(8) He says, *He knows that his time is short:* for the time is short, from the fall of the Devil until his judgment and just deserts, when compared to eternity. For the same reason, too, the patriarch Jacob, even though he was a hundred and thirty years old, said when asking something of Pharaoh, "few and evil have been the days of the years of my life."[13]

8. *And when the serpent saw that he had been thrown down to the earth, he pursued the woman who had borne the male child. (2) But the two wings of the great eagle were given to the woman, so that she might fly into the desert, to her own place, where she is to be sheltered for a time, and times, and half a time from the presence of the snake. (3) The snake poured water like a river out of his mouth after the woman to sweep her away with the flood. (4) But the earth came to the help of the woman, and the earth opened its mouth and swallowed the river which the serpent had poured from his mouth. (5) Then the serpent was angry with the woman, and went off to make war on the rest of her offspring, on those who keep the commandments of God and bear testimony to Jesus* (Rv 12.13–17).

9. The present account is a repetition of what has already been said. He does not say that after *the serpent saw that he had been thrown down to the earth,* he immediately *pursued the woman,* but since the serpent saw the troubles in which he was immersed, and that he had fallen out of the angelic rank, he became exceedingly bitter against human beings, and pursued the woman who had borne the savior of humankind, in order to destroy her. *He pursued the woman,* since he knew that the one who was born of her was too powerful to be captured. He was moved with envy against human beings because of their salvation by the Lord. He could not bear such a great reversal, by which he himself had been thrown out of heaven, and human beings by their virtue had gone up from earth to heaven.

(2) He says, *But the two wings of the great eagle were given to the woman, that she might fly into the desert, to her own place, where she is*

13. Gn 47.9.

to be sheltered for a time, and times, and half a time, from the presence of the snake. He says that the woman was not handed over to Satan, but fled *into the desert.* This is Egypt, as was said earlier. (3) So it was that the prophet sought "wings like those of a dove," to "fly away and be at rest in the desert."[14] But more powerful *wings of the great eagle were given* to the all-holy Virgin. He means by *the wings of the eagle* the intervention of the divine angel, who exhorted Joseph to take the child and his mother and escape to Egypt. By this intervention it was as though they reached Egypt on the wings of an eagle. So the serpent, failing in this plot, which he had arranged through Herod, devises another plot against the Virgin, the destruction of her son, and so accordingly he goes on to describe the Lord's cross and death.

(4) He says, *The serpent poured water like a river out of his mouth after the woman, to sweep her away with the flood:* the divine Scripture means allegorically by *the river* temptation or trial, saying somewhere through Jonah, "You cast me into the depths of the heart of the sea, and the rivers surrounded me,"[15] and again in the words of the Lord, "the rain fell, and the rivers rose up, and the winds came, but they did not throw down the house which had been founded upon the rock."[16] Therefore, he calls her trial over the passion of the Lord *a river,* so that through this, he says, he might drown the Virgin. And truly, by what happened to the Lord and the intensity of her sorrow, the serpent had the power to fulfill his purpose. What does Simeon say to her? "And a sword will pierce your own soul, too, so that the thoughts of many hearts may be laid bare."[17] (5) But, he says, *the earth came to the help of the woman, and the earth opened its mouth and swallowed the river which the serpent had poured from his mouth* onto the woman. That the earth swallowed the river indicates that the earth had accepted the trial, that is, the killing of the Lord. But the earth's help did not consist in this, but in restoring the Lord again; for he came to life again after three days, trampling upon death, since it was impossible for him to be held by it,[18] since he was "the author of life," according to blessed Peter.[19] To construe

14. Ps 54.7–8.   15. Jon 2.3.
16. Mt 7.25.   17. Lk 2.35.
18. Cf. Acts 2.24.   19. Acts 3.15.

it in this way, one must read a full stop after *the earth came to the help of the woman*. Then, as though in answer to the question, "in what manner did it help?" *it swallowed up the river,* that is, it received in itself the Lord after the plot against him, and again restored him, and this is how it gave its help. (6) Since, therefore, the serpent also failed to achieve his second plan, what more is there for him to do? He pursued those called sons and brothers of the Lord—that is, the faithful—for these, he says, are *the offspring* of the woman; for the faithful are the sons and brothers of the Lord according to Scripture: "I will proclaim your name to my brothers,"[20] and again, "Here am I, and the children God has given me."[21] So then they also belong to his mother's family; and the Devil made war on them, pursuing them and plotting against them, putting them to death through the tyrants and rulers of the earth, since they were testifying that the Virgin-born was God.

10. (1–2) *I was standing by the seashore. And I saw a beast rising out of the sea, with ten horns and seven heads, with ten diadems upon its horns and blasphemous names upon its head. (3) And the beast which I saw was like a leopard, its feet were like a bear's, and its mouth was like a lion's mouth. And to it the serpent gave his power and his throne and great authority. (4) One of its heads was as though it had been mortally wounded, but its mortal wound had been healed, and the whole earth was astounded behind the beast, and they worshiped the serpent, (5) for he had given his authority to the beast* (Rv 12.18–13.4a).

11. In the vision before this the blessed evangelist had seen a sign in heaven, and behold, *See*, he says, *a red serpent* (Rv 12.3). But now he tells us that he has seen *a beast like a leopard rising out of the sea*. Then in the following vision he again sees *another beast rising out of the earth* with *two horns of a lamb* (Rv 13.11). Therefore, he saw three beasts in all: the first in heaven, the second from the sea, and the third from the land.[22] The first and third are clear to all, for the first is the serpent, the source of all

20. Heb 2.12; Ps 21.23.   21. Heb 2.13; Is 8.18.
22. Oecumenius's interpretation of the three beasts is not consistent. Compare the present passage (7.11.1–3) with 7.3.2–3, and contrast these with 8.3.1–4; 9.5.2; 9.11.3–5; 11.6.3; as noted by de Groote, p. 184.

evil, Satan, who revolted and lifted up his neck[23] against God the sovereign Lord, and the third is the Antichrist. But this beast in the middle, which is now brought before us in the vision, what is he? (2) I think that this one certainly comes after the rebel, and is Satan the serpent, the chief of the rest of the demons; for many were destroyed together with Satan and brought down to earth. And it is clear from this that the divine Scripture means that the ruler of all the demons has been condemned to the sea and nether gloom, as has been explained earlier. Perhaps Scripture in this way figuratively describes the confusion and turmoil in which Satan is embroiled as he recognizes from where he has fallen and where he now is, and that "he is being kept for the judgment of the great day,"[24] as Scripture has it. For if this was not the case, but if he was actually in the sea and in the nether gloom, how was he described in the vision before this as having contrived many things against the Lord and against his mother? Nevertheless, according to the literal narrative—which cannot be impugned—he has been allotted nether gloom and the abyss.[25]

(3) So this second one, the one who is now brought before us, is found in the book of Job, both conversing with God and demanding Job for himself by bringing countless trials on him, and indeed saying that he was there "after roaming about the earth under heaven."[26] And not only the book of Job, but the Lord, too, has mentioned him in the gospel of John when addressing the Jews: "You are of your father the Devil, and you wish to do your father's desires. He was a murderer from the beginning, and has nothing to do with the truth, because there is no truth in him. When he lies, he speaks according to his own nature, for he is a liar and his father,"[27] meaning *the father of the Devil,* that is, [the father] of the one who is now presented to us in the vision, the rebel serpent, as being their leader and the prime mover of the rebellion. In a similar way holy Abraham is called *the father of nations,* as one who established faith for them, according to what was said to him, "I have made you the father of many nations."[28]

23. Cf. Jb 15.25.   24. Jude 6.
25. Cf. 2 Pt 2.4.   26. Jb 1.7.
27. Jn 8.44.   28. Gn 17.5.

Now that these things have been rightly determined, according to my way of thinking, let us return to our subject. (4) He says, *I saw a beast rising out of the sea, with ten horns and seven heads, with ten diadems upon its horns.* He sees the beast rising out of the sea. Its ascent is, as it were, its elevation from the troubled and unstable life of human beings, who have appointed it as despot over themselves. (5) The ten horns witness to its great power, just as the seven heads witness to some of its *wiles* and the origins of its schemes and deceits. For both ten and seven are perfect numbers. (6) The diadems on its horns mark it out as the tyrant over humankind, since we have voluntarily handed ourselves over to it through its deception. (7) He says, *upon its head* are *blasphemous names.* They are rightly *upon its head,* for it rages against itself and against its own head, acting drunkenly against God: it deprives God of the reverence [due to him] and gives it to itself. (8) He says, *And the beast which I saw was like a leopard,* I think because it moves at speed and is quick to devise its plots.

(9) He says, *And its feet were like a bear's,* as they were strong and durable so as to "roam about the earth under heaven"[29] to plot against human beings. He says, *And its mouth was like a lion's mouth.* According to Scripture, "Our adversary the Devil prowls around like a lion, to see whom he can devour."[30] (10) He says, *And the serpent gave it his power.* The power of the rebellious serpent is in his deceptions and wiles, and [the Devil] is the source and teacher of these for him. (11) He says, *And I see that one of its heads was as though it had been mortally wounded, but its mortal wound had been healed.* The inspired evangelist would himself know the meaning of this. As it appears to me, it indicates something of this sort: the mortal blow that the Devil received in one of his heads through the piety of Israel was healed again through the idolatry of the same people. (12) He says, *And the whole earth was astounded behind the beast:* for how is it that even the pious nation of Israel has not stopped worshiping it? Yet this is what is said in Isaiah speaking in the person of God to Israel: "On your account my name is constantly blasphemed among the na-

29. Jb 1.7.
30. 1 Pt 5.8.

tions."[31] Further, they also joined in the worship of the serpent, the fount of all the evil, and the cause of all the great deception and crafty wiles of the beast.

1 2. *And they worshiped the beast,*[32] *and who is able to make war against him?* (2) *And he was given a mouth uttering haughty and blasphemous words, and he was given authority to do this for forty-two months.* (3) *He opened his mouth in blasphemy against God, to blaspheme his name and his dwelling and those who dwell in heaven.* (4) *And he was given authority over every tribe and people and tongue and nation,* (5) *and all who dwell in the world will worship him, every one whose name has not been written in the book of life in heaven, which has been sealed since the foundation of the world* (Rv 13.4–8).

1 3. After he had outwitted Israel, those who had been caught by him contrived a fair address to him, *saying, Who is like the beast and who is able to make war against him?* (2) When all had been defeated and had fallen beneath his feet, he says, *And he was given a mouth uttering haughty and blasphemous words.* By whom was it given? By those people who had been thoroughly deceived and had worshiped him; for boastful talk is a mark of arrogance. For what is more arrogant than saying, "I will ascend to heaven; above the stars of heaven I will place my throne"?[33] And a little later he says, "I shall be like the Most High,"[34] as Isaiah satirizes him. These are plainly blasphemies against God.

(3) He says, *And he was given authority to do this for forty-two months.* Previously we accepted the *forty-two months* as a short time. For all time is short, even if it seems to be very long, when compared to ages of eternity. (4) He says, *And he opened his mouth in blasphemy against God, to blaspheme his name and his dwelling and those who dwell in heaven.* Some of the rebel's blasphemies against God have already been mentioned. By *the dwelling* of God he means the holy angels, because God dwells among them. For if

31. Is 52.5.
32. Oecumenius here omits the words "saying, 'who is like the beast?'" (λέγοντες τις ὅμοιος τῷ θηρίῳ) in Rv 13.4b, though he alludes to them in his comment.
33. Is 14.13.
34. Is 14.14.

it is said of human beings, "I will live in their midst and move among them,"[35] what [less] could be said of the heavenly powers, than that they have God living among them?

(5) *And he was given authority over every tribe and people and tongue and nation, and all who dwell in the world will worship him.* I said earlier that he had received his authority from those human beings who had willingly submitted to his deadly power. Rightly then does he say that *all who dwell in the world will worship him.* Apart from the God-fearing Israel, all the rest of the human race were idolaters, and, though even Israel shared in this, every other race and tribe of people was found to have worshiped the wretch. (6) *Every one,* he says, *whose name has not been written in the book of life in heaven, which has been sealed since the foundation of the world.* The vision has already defined this with great accuracy. For although it said that all who dwell in the world had worshiped the rebellious Devil, there were a few who were untainted by his worship, both from among the gentiles and from Israel, such as Job, his four friends, Melchisedek, and the holy prophets of Israel, and those who were distinguished in the Old Testament for their piety. He says that all had worshiped him, except for those who on account of their worship of God and the exactness and purity of their way of life are written in heaven and are protected by God. (7) This is the meaning of the sealing of the scroll. About this scroll the Lord says to his holy disciples, according to blessed Luke, "Nevertheless do not rejoice in this, that the spirits are subject to you; but rejoice that your names are written in heaven."[36]

14. (1–2) *If anyone has an ear, let him hear: if anyone is to be taken captive,*[37] *he goes; if anyone slays with the sword, with the sword he must be slain. Here is the endurance and faith of the saints* (Rv 13.9–10).

15. He means that *if anyone has* the sense to understand these sayings, *let him hear* what is said and know that he who is preparing to make prisoners of others will be taken prisoner by the

---

35. 2 Cor 6.16; cf. Lv 26.11.
36. Lk 10.20.
37. Oecumenius here omits the second "to captivity" (εἰς αἰχμαλωσίαν), found in the manuscripts of Revelation.

beast and will desert to him of his own accord. For if he finds no support whatever from God, he will be carried away into every kind of evil. (2) If anyone has been prepared for murder, he will undergo spiritual death by his worship of the Devil. (3) He says, *Here is the endurance and faith of the saints:* This is how one escapes being enslaved by the wicked one. (4) May all of us be delivered from this slavery by the grace of God who has called us to know him. To him glory is due for ever. Amen.

CHAPTER EIGHT

FTER MANY digressions and after reverting from these starting points to previous beginnings, he came to the serious business. This was to explain to us the facts about the impious and abominable Antichrist. So it is he who is now brought into the forefront; see what he says about him:

2. *Then I saw another beast rising up from the earth; it had two horns like a lamb, and it spoke like a serpent.* (2) *It exercises all the authority of the first beast in its presence, and compels the earth and its inhabitants to worship the first beast, whose mortal wound had been healed.* (3) *It works great signs, so as to make fire come down from heaven to earth in the sight of human beings* (Rv 13.11–13).

3. He says, *Then I saw another beast rising up from the earth,* from where all human beings have their origin. For the Antichrist is a human being, "whose advent occurs by the action of the Devil," as Paul in his great wisdom believes.[1] (2) *It had two horns like a lamb, and it spoke like a serpent.* He rightly said not that it had the horns of a lamb, but *like those of a lamb,*[2] and he did not say that it was a serpent, but that it spoke like a serpent. Since the wretch pretends to be the Christ (though he is not), he has given him *horns like those of a lamb.* And although he tells of all kinds of profanity like the Devil (but he is not the Devil), he did not say that he was a serpent but that he spoke like a serpent. This being so, the account retained the image in the vision, and attributes to him the form not of a lamb, but like a lamb, nor of a serpent, but like a serpent. For Christ is said to be a lamb, and the Devil is said to be a serpent, but he was neither the one nor the other.

---

1. 2 Thes 2.9.
2. Note the slight difference from the original quotation. The first quotation reads κέρατα δύο ὅμοια ἀρνίῳ, whereas Oecumenius subsequently presents the phrase as κέρατα δύο ὅμοια ἀρνίου, replacing a dative with a genitive.

(3) He says, *It exercises all the authority of the first beast in its presence.* That is, it becomes the successor of the Devil's authority, and it teaches everyone to worship the one *whose mortal wound had been healed.* (4) This has already been mentioned earlier on, and now we need only to notice it. For when he said that *it exercises all the authority of the first beast in its presence* (and he has called the *red serpent* the first of all, which the vision showed depicted in heaven), lest anyone should think that he is now speaking of it as the one which had received the authority of the first beast, he says, I am not speaking of that which is the first of all, but of the later one, which comes before the Antichrist. The vision showed this one *rising out of the sea like a leopard* (Rv 13.1–2). For it was this one's *mortal wound* which was healed, as was said earlier.

(5) And *it works great signs, so as to make fire come down from heaven to earth in the sight of human beings.* The working of signs and wonders by the operation of the Devil is also attested by the apostle, for after saying, "whose advent occurs by the action of Satan," he adds, "with all power and with pretended signs and wonders."[3]

4. He says, *And it deceives the inhabitants of the earth by the signs which it was its task to effect in the presence of the beast, telling the inhabitants of the earth to make an image for the beast, as[4] it had been struck by the sword and had yet come to life, and its task was to give breath to the image of the beast, [so that the image of the beast should even speak, and to cause those who would not worship the beast][5] (2) to be slain. (3) Also it makes all, both small and great, both rich and poor, both free and slave, to be given as a mark (4) the name of the beast or the number of its name. (5) This calls for wisdom: let him who has understanding reckon the number of the beast, for it is a man's number; its number is six hundred and sixty-six* (Rv 13.14–18).

5. He says, *And it deceives the inhabitants of the earth by signs:* for it performs signs, deluding the eyes of the spectators, just as the

3. 2 Thes 2.9.

4. Oecumenius reads ὡς ("as") in place of the text of Revelation, ὅς ("who") or ὅ ("which").

5. The words in square brackets are missing from Oecumenius's text, though supplied by some manuscripts. See de Groote ed., p. 192.

magicians did before Pharaoh. For both they and this one were under the command of one and the same deceptive demon. (2) Rightly did he say that it was working the signs in the presence of the beast. For since it will erect an image as a monument, which it will compel everyone to worship, it will in truth consummate its signs by making the image a god, because it is in virtue of the image that it is able to do these things.

(3) He says, *And its task was to give breath to the image.* For they say that many of the images sweat and appear to speak by the work of the Devil. (4) He says, too, that the Antichrist gives the mark and seal of his own name, without which no one can either buy or sell. (5) He says, *This calls for wisdom: let him reckon the name of the beast,* and by means of the reckoning let him find it. I will not say, he says, that this form of reckoning is strange or unusual, nor that it is named for concealment or double-mindedness, but it is a well-worn method of reckoning known to people, which calculates the number to be six hundred and sixty-six. (6) Although this number applies to many other appropriate names and titles, it applies especially to these: Lampetis, Benediktos, and Titan[6] [all of which fit the number]. Though Titan is spelled with "i," one can also spell it with a diphthong, for if Teitan is derived from *teisis* [τεῖσις, stretching], and the word *teinō* [τείνω] and the future *tenō* [τενῶ], it must properly be written with a diphthong, like *phtheirō* [φθείρω] from *phtherō* [φθερῶ], and *speirō* [σπείρω] from *sperō* [σπερῶ]. (7) "The conqueror"[7] is also a title, for perhaps he gave himself this name, because he will make war and root out the three horns or, in other words, the kings. See what Daniel says about them in his eighth vision. He says, "I considered" his "horns," that is, of the fourth beast, "and see, there came up among them another little horn, before which three of the former horns were uprooted from its presence; and see, in this horn were eyes like the eyes of a man, and a mouth speaking great things."[8] So he is the unstable one, the evil guide, the truly noxious one, the ancient sorcerer, the unjust lamb. Although

6. The numerical value of the letters forming each of these three names adds up to 666, but only if Teitan (Τειτάν) is spelled with a diphthong.
7. The numerical value of the letters of "the conqueror" (ὁ νικητής) is 666.
8. Dn 7.8.

he might have been given these names by his opponents, (8) he will not only not feel disgraced at being called by these names, but will even rejoice in such titles, since he is not ashamed to call himself thus. In hitting at such wicked and abominable choices, the wise apostle says, "whose glory is in their shame."⁹ (9) Since, then, many names have been proposed, anyone can apply to the accursed demon the one that is most appropriate.

6. *Then I looked, and see, the Lamb was standing on Mount Zion, and with him a hundred and forty-four thousand with his Father's name written on their foreheads.* (2) *And I heard a voice from heaven like the sound of many waters and like the sound of loud thunder; the voice I heard was like the sound of harpists playing on their harps,* (3) *and they are singing a new song before the throne and before the four living creatures and the elders. No one could learn the song except a hundred and forty-four thousand who had been redeemed from the earth.* (4) *These are they who have not defiled themselves with women, for they are celibate, these who follow the Lamb wherever he goes; they have been redeemed from among human beings as first-fruits for God and the Lamb,* (5) *and in their mouth no lie was found, for they are spotless* (Rv 14.1–5).

7. The Lord is described in the gospels as addressing the lawless people of the Jews: "Behold, your house is forsaken."¹⁰ For they were no longer worthy of God's presence after their madness with the cross. So how is it that the Lord is now shown by the vision as *standing on Mount Zion,* as though they had repented? The Romans clearly saw to it that their city, the temple, and their race had been completely abandoned when they burned the temple, set fire to cities, ravaged all their land, and enslaved their chief city itself. (2) But now by showing the Lord as having ascended Mount Zion he indicates the return of Israel in the last days through faith, and that the Lord will claim them as his own and take them to himself. For this is the good news they were promised through Isaiah when he says, "The savior will come from Zion and will turn away impiety from Jacob, said the Lord."¹¹ Both the prophet and the apostle are in agreement with

9. Phil 3.19.
11. Is 59.20–21.

10. Mt 23.38; Lk 13.35.

Isaiah: the former sings, "You will make them turn back, you will prepare their presence among your remnant,"[12] and the other writes, "When the full number of the gentiles comes in, then shall all Israel be saved."[13]

(3) *And with him,* he says, there were *a hundred and forty-four thousand with his Father's name written on their foreheads.* Earlier on he called the twelve thousand believers from each of the tribes of Israel a hundred and forty-four thousand. So is he now speaking of these? I do not think so; for he did not name them with the definite article; for he did not say *the hundred and forty-four thousand,* but only *a hundred and forty-four thousand;* and he did not assert that they had remained celibate. For celibacy was not very seriously considered by Israel, as it certainly was later by those from the gentiles. So we must consider those who have now been named to be a mixed company, coming from both Israel and the gentiles, with the majority from the gentiles. (4) To have the name of the Father and of his Son written shows that they are garlanded with a certain divine glory.

(5) He says, *And I heard a sound like harpists singing a new song before the throne and before the living creatures and the elders.* That the sound which was issuing was like that of harpists indicates the sweet God-like harmony of the song. For although "praise is not appropriate in the mouth of a sinner" according to Scripture,[14] it is wholly suitable and in harmony in the mouth of the righteous. (6) He says, *No one could learn the song except a hundred and forty-four thousand who have been redeemed from the earth.* I think that no one was able to hear the mysteries of the new song except those who had been made worthy of singing them, for knowledge is given to each in proportion to their purity. "There are many mansions" (or rewards for the good), says the Lord, "in my Father's house."[15] (7) He calls those who were bought by the blood of Christ *redeemed.* For the precious blood of Christ has been shed on behalf of all people, but unprofitably on behalf of some, that is, those who willingly deprived themselves of the offered salvation. These are they whom the Lord reproaches when

12. Ps 20.13.
14. Sir 15.9.

13. Rom 11.25–26.
15. Jn 14.2.

he says through the prophet, "What profit is there in my blood, if I go down to destruction?"[16] But, for those who were saved and justified, of whom these who are now mentioned are the first-fruits and forerunners, it is so profitable as to be past description. (8) *These are they,* he says, *who have not defiled themselves with women, for they are celibate, these who follow the Lamb wherever he goes. They have been redeemed from among human beings as first-fruits for God and the Lamb, and in their mouth no lie was found, for they are spotless.* The account of the vision bears witness to those in Christ as being excellent and surpassing human nature.

8. *Then I saw another angel flying in mid-heaven, with an eternal gospel to proclaim to those who dwell on earth, to every nation and tribe and tongue and people; and he said with a loud voice,* (2) *"Fear God and give him glory, for the hour of his judgment has come; and worship him who made heaven and earth, the sea and the fountains of water"* (Rv 14.6–7).

9. The mid-heaven symbolizes the high and exalted nature of the blessed angel. (2) He had *an eternal gospel;* for from of old the teaching "Fear the Lord" brought salvation, since "The fear of God is the beginning of wisdom,"[17] but "love is the end."[18] (3) He says one must not fear the formidable and soul-destroying beast, the Antichrist, even if he threatens and does dreadful things. *For,* he says, *the hour of his judgment has come,* and the very one who terrifies those on earth will be punished as never before. (4) He says, *and worship him who made* all creation, and not the wretched and abominable Devil.

10. *Another angel, a second, followed, saying, "Great Babylon has fallen, she who made all nations drink the wine of the wrath caused by her fornication"* (Rv 14.8).

11. By *Babylon* I think he means the confusion of the present life and its vain temptations (for Babylon means "confusion") and the stupidity of the crazy idolaters. What they call "religious frenzy"[19] is reverenced by them. But if you should in fact consider her to be the actual Babylon, you would not be wide of

16. Ps 29.10.
18. 1 Tm 1.5.

17. Prv 1.7.
19. Greek, ἐνθουσιασμὸς.

the mark. (2) He means by *the wine of the wrath caused by her fornication* rebellion against God; according to Scripture, "You destroyed all those who commit fornication against you."[20] This fornication makes any rational argument murky and obscure, for who of sound mind would choose to worship things of wood and stone, and so evoke the wrath of God? Presumably it is about this wine that Scripture says, "Their wine is the wrath of serpents, and the incurable wrath of asps."[21] (3) This Babylon has first herself drunk of the deadly wine, and then she compelled all the nations which she ruled to drink it.

12. *And another angel, a third, followed them, saying with a loud voice, "If anyone worships the beast and its image, and receives a mark on his forehead or on his hand, (2) he also shall drink of the wine of God's wrath, poured unmixed*[22] *into the cup of his anger, and he shall be tormented with fire and brimstone in the presence of the holy angels and in the presence of the Lamb. (3) And the smoke of their torment goes up for ever and ever, and they have no rest, day or night, these worshipers of the beast and its image, and whoever receives the mark of its name." (4) This is the patient endurance of the saints, those who keep the commandments of God and the faith of Jesus* (Rv 14.9–12).

13. The third angel forbids human beings to worship the beast, and to receive his seal. For to worship anyone else as god, other than the real and true God, is most impious. (2) He says, *And he shall drink of the wine of God's wrath, poured unmixed into the cup of his anger.* Blessed David has also mentioned this cup and the wine when he says, "For in the hand of the Lord there is a cup, full of a mixture of unmixed wine, and he tilted it from side to side; but its dregs were not emptied out; all the sinners of the earth will drink them."[23] He calls the wrath of God *wine*, speaking metaphorically not of joy, but of darkness and the changed destiny, by which those who are subject to the wrath of God are inspired. (3) He says, *mixed unmixed:* that is, purely[24] mixed. For

20. Ps 72.27.
21. Dt 32.33.
22. Literally, "mixed unmixed" (κεκερασμένου ἀκράτου).
23. Ps 74.9.
24. Literally, "unmixed" (ἀκράτως), as used previously.

the wrath of God is mixed with loving-kindness and goodness; it is purely mixed. For there is no equivalence between his wrath and his goodness, but his loving-kindness is many times more abundant. For if there were an equality of righteous wrath and goodness, no living person would survive. Because the prophet knew this, he said, "If you, Lord, should take note of iniquities, Lord, who could survive?"[25] (4) That there is much more goodness in God's cup than righteous anger, the same writer again signified when he said, "The Lord is merciful and just, and our God will have mercy on us,"[26] putting his justice in the middle, as if it were constrained by mercy on each side and not being allowed to exercise its own vocation. For the vocation of justice is to award each person what he deserves. (5) After he had once mentioned wine and thus called it wrath, he continued with this image and named the cup as that which is given to sinners from the hand of God. (6) But perhaps someone will say, "How do you speak of God's mercy as abundant in the future judgment when the vision went on to tell us a little later that the penalty for those being punished is eternal? For why does he say, *And the smoke of their torment goes up for ever and ever; and they have no rest, day or night*"? (7) One could reply to this in these words: "It means, my dear fellow, to be tormented eternally, yet not to suffer according to one's deserts. How is this? If anyone deserves fire and darkness but has been condemned to darkness and is punished only by not being given a share in God's bounty, and suffers pain only in this respect, he is certainly not being physically punished. (8) By *the smoke of torment which goes up* he means the breath of sinners which has been exhaled from below in their wailings."

(9) He says, *This is the patient endurance of the saints:* he means that in this time of the Antichrist and in the time of trial their endurance is clearly shown. For when the danger is greatest and the accompanying tribulation, so much greater is the need of endurance. (10) Then the account proceeds as though in answer to a question: who, he says, are these whom you call holy and patiently enduring? *Those*, he says, *who keep the commandments*

25. Ps 129.3.
26. Ps 114.5.

of God and the faith of Jesus. For such people, even in the presence of trials and death, will put everything second to their faith and love of God.

14. *And I heard a voice from heaven saying to me, "Write: Blessed are the dead who die in the Lord henceforth." And the Spirit says, "that they may rest from their labors, for their deeds follow after them"* (Rv 14.13).

15. He blesses those who refused to worship the image of the beast, or to receive the mark on their forehead and their hand, and were therefore put to death; for these have been crowned with the crown of martyrdom and so achieve the same lot as the martyrs.

16. *Then I looked, and there was a white cloud, and on the head*[27] *there was seated one like a son of man, with a golden crown on his head, and a sharp sickle in his hand. (2) And another angel came out of heaven, calling with a loud voice to him who sat on the head, "Put in your sickle and reap, for the hour for reaping has come, for the harvest of the earth is fully ripe." (3) So he who sat on the cloud threw*[28] (Rv 14.14–16).

17. While he sees the Lord dignified to be the son of man, he also sees him riding on a cloud. It is either really a cloud, since this is what the gospel says whose witness I described earlier, or he refers to an angelic power. Scripture says, "He rode on cherubim and flew, he flew upon the wings of the winds."[29] He calls the angels *a cloud,* on account of the height and loftiness of their nature and worth, or perhaps he calls the God-bearer[30] *a cloud* on which he is riding, so giving honor to his human mother. For this is how Isaiah foresees it when he says, "Behold, the Lord is seated on a light cloud and will come to Egypt, and the idols of Egypt will be shaken at his presence."[31] (2) Interpreting this text, Aquila says that the cloud is a "light thickness,"[32] thick, as I imagine, because it is a human being and flesh, and light because it

---

27. Oecumenius's text reads "on the head" (ἐπὶ τῆς κεφαλῆς) instead of "on the cloud" (ἐπὶ τὴν νεφέλην), both here and in the following verse (vv.14–15).

28. The text here omits the rest of the sentence, though it is presumed in the comments that follow.

29. Ps 17.11.

31. Is 19.1.

30. Greek, Θεοτόκος.

32. See Origen, *Hexapla in Is 19:1.*

is pure, blameless, and not weighed down by a single sin, and also because it is a high pathway to heaven for the soul. This is then how you should consider the *cloud*. And it is *white* because of the purity and luminosity of the beings in the vision. (3) And the crown symbolizes the kingship of our Lord Jesus Christ; for Christ is the king both of spiritual and material things, and the crown is golden since it connotes the glory of his kingship in terms of value as we understand it. (4) That he has a sickle in his hand intimates his being seated with authority [to bring in] the end of the age. (5) Why does the angel also say to him, *Put in your sickle and reap, for the hour for reaping has come, for the harvest of the earth is fully ripe; and he threw his sickle,* he says, *and the earth was reaped?* The harvest is described in the gospels as abundant, "but the laborers are few";[33] but there the harvest meant the assembling of the faithful; but here it means the finale of human beings, so that if there were any chaff among them or unfulfilled work or something deserving to be burned, it would be handed over to fire.

18. *And another angel came out of the temple in heaven, and he, too, had a sharp sickle. (2) Then another angel came out from the altar, with power over the fire, and he called with a loud voice to him who had the sharp sickle, saying, "Harvest the clusters of the vine of the earth, for its grapes are ripe." (3) So the angel swung his sickle on the earth and gathered the vintage of the earth and threw it into the great wine-press of the wrath of God; (4) and the wine-press was trodden outside the city, and blood flowed from the wine-press, as high as the horses' bridles, for one thousand six hundred stades* (Rv 14.17–20).

19. The angel with the sickle, who had come out of the heavenly temple, is himself the servant and minister of the coming consummation. And being the heavenly minister of God, he is described as coming out of the heavenly temple. He says, (2) *And another angel came out from the altar, with power over the fire.* And to me it seems that this one has been put in charge of the punishment of the ungodly. (3) Next he says, Send and gather *the clusters of the vine of the earth.* So the harvest mentioned earlier represent-

33. Mt 9.37; Lk 10.2.

ed the righteous and the sinners together at the consummation, whom he will separate, as is said in the gospels—"The winnowing fork of the Lord with which he will clear his threshing-floor and gather the wheat into the granary, but the chaff he will burn with unquenchable fire."[34] The vintage of the grapes symbolizes those who are exceedingly sinful, whom the vision depicts in their drunkenness and madness. (4) From this it is clear that the Lord did not consider it proper that he should gather them as he gathered the first, but that one of the angels should do this. They were immediately thrown outside *into the wine-press of the wrath of God*, without being considered worthy of making any defense, nor of being questioned, or being brought before a law-court, just as in the gospels sinners were introduced who were punished because of their failure to give and share with others.[35] It was of these, I think, that the prophet said, "The wicked will not stand in the judgment."[36] He has called their punishment *a wine-press*, cleverly using the metaphor of the grapes and of the vintage. (5) He says, *And the wine-press was trodden outside the city*, for it was not right for those who were being punished to receive the recompense for their evil deeds in the heavenly Jerusalem, which had been allotted to the saints, and to impair the joy of the saints through sympathy with those who were being justly punished—to say nothing of the great chasm which separates the pious from the impious, according to the words of the patriarch Abraham, which were addressed to the rich man in the gospels.[37]

(6) He says, *And blood flowed from the wine-press*. He rightly spoke of *blood*, to show that in talking of *bunches of grapes* he spoke metaphorically, since they were human beings who were being trampled together and mangled, *as high*, he says, *as the horses' bridles, for one thousand six hundred stades*. (7) Some of God's horses have been handed down to us in Holy Scripture, symbolizing angelic powers with God mounted on them. For the heavenly bridegroom says to his bride in the Song of Songs, "I compare you,

34. Mt 3.12; Lk 3.17.
35. Mt 25.46; Lk 16.19–31.
36. Ps 1.5.
37. Lk 16.26.

my nearest[38] love, to my mare in Pharaoh's chariot,"[39] and the prophet Habakkuk sings to God, "You will come mounted on your horses, and your horsemanship is deliverance."[40] (8) Revelation says that the bridles of these horses are soaked in the blood of the ungodly, who are standing not nearby but at a distance. The whole passage is metaphorical, the symbolism showing the extent of the blood. For those traveling on the broad highway are many times more numerous than those on "the narrow and hard way,"[41] so that they soak even the bridles of the horses, that is, angels, mounted on them ready to inflict punishment.

20. *And I saw another portent in heaven, great and wonderful, seven angels with the final seven plagues, for with them the wrath of God is at an end. (2) And I saw what appeared to be a sea of glass mingled with fire, and the conquerors of the beast and its image and the number of its name, standing beside the sea of glass holding harps of God. (3) And they sing the song of Moses, the servant of God, and the song of the Lamb, saying, "Great and wonderful are your deeds, Lord God, sovereign of all! Just and true are your ways, O king of the nations. (4) Who shall not fear and glorify your name, Lord? For you alone are holy, for all the nations shall come and worship before you, for your judgments have been revealed"* (Rv 15.1–4).

21. He says, *I saw seven angels with seven plagues.* By the number seven he means the many plagues prepared against the sinners, by means of which God's wrath reaches its limit. (2) He says, *And I saw a sea of glass mingled with fire, and the conquerors of the beast and its image and the number of its name, standing beside the sea of glass holding harps of God.* The very wise Paul in one of his writings says, "If anyone builds on this foundation with gold, silver, precious stones, wood, hay, stubble, the quality of each person's work will be tested by fire, because it will be revealed in fire."[42] So then when the sinners with their offerings of inflammable loads of sin are put to the test, will the righteous also be

38. The Greek text here reads "the near one, my near one" (ἡ πλησίον ἡ πλησίον μου), the first phrase being omitted in LXX. It is contrasted with the sinners who are not standing nearby.

39. Song 1.9.   40. Hab 3.8.
41. Mt 7.14.   42. 1 Cor 3.12–13.

tested in fire although they bring along gold and their precious materials? (3) He is now speaking of those who have conquered the beast through thick and thin: they are *standing beside the sea of glass mingled with fire*—glass because of the brightness and purity of the righteous in it, but mixed with fire because of the purging and cleansing of all uncleanness, since even the righteous need to be cleansed. "For we all frequently stumble,"[43] as Scripture says, "and who will be free from uncleanness? no one, not even if their life on earth is but one day."[44] (4) The harps, as has often been said, symbolize the tuneful song of the saints addressed to God.

(5) He says, *And they sing the song of Moses* in its entirety. This was the one he sang when Pharaoh and all his army had been drowned, saying, "Let us sing to the Lord, for he has triumphed gloriously; the horse and his rider he has thrown into the sea; he has become my help and protector for our deliverance."[45] The song is a paean of victory for the punishment of the ungodly and the victory over the Devil and his lawless son, the Antichrist. (6) He says, *And the song of the Lamb,* that is, the appropriate song for the Lord and his righteous judgment against the ungodly; that is why they wonder at the truth and righteousness of the Lord.

(7) He says, *The king of the nations:* Christ is king of all, but since it is said by Isaiah, "And there will be the root of Jesse and one set up to rule over the nations; on him shall the nations hope,"[46] on account of this the divine oracle says both that he is *king of the nations* and that *all the nations will come and worship him,* neatly foretelling the calling of the nations and their faith in the Lord.

22. *After this I saw that the temple of the tent of testimony in heaven was opened,* (2) *and out of the temple came seven angels with seven plagues, clothed with a pure bright stone,*[47] *and girt with golden girdles round their breasts.* (3) *And one of the four living creatures gave the seven angels seven golden bowls full of the wrath of God who lives for ever*

43. Jas 3.2.   44. Jb 14.4–5.
45. Ex 15.1–2.   46. Is 11.10.
47. Oecumenius here reads λίθον ("stone") instead of the usual λίνον ("linen").

and ever; (4) *and the temple was filled with smoke from the glory of God and from his power, and no one could enter the temple until the seven plagues of the seven angels were ended.* (5) *Then I heard a loud voice from the temple telling the seven angels, "Go and pour out on the earth the seven bowls of the wrath of God"* (Rv 15.5–16.1).

23. *The tent of testimony* was the tent constructed in the wilderness by Bezalel, the master-builder of the artifacts made at that time;[48] it was the custom in Holy Scripture to call it thus because it was the tent of the testimonies and commands of God. For in it was the ark of the covenant, the mercy-seat, the table, the altars of incense and of burnt offering, the lampstand,[49] and all that God had commanded blessed Moses to construct, when he said, "And you shall make for me all that I show you on the mountain."[50] For this reason he has used the metaphor of the old tent to describe the nature of the heavenly temple by calling it the *tent of testimony.*

(2) *From there,* he says, *the seven angels came out.* From where else could the heavenly ministers of God be seen coming out except from the heavenly *temple?* (3) He says they had in their hands *seven plagues,* which they were going to let fall on the earth. For many signs will come about on earth at the time of the end, which Christ also mentioned in the gospels when teaching about the end.[51] (4) The clothing of the angels *with a pure bright stone* is a sign of their worth, purity, and radiance, and points to their natural steadfastness for good, since they had indeed put on Christ. For the Lord is named *a stone* in Holy Scripture, as found in Isaiah, "Behold, I am laying in Zion for a foundation a stone, very costly and chosen,"[52] and in the prophet, "The stone which the builders rejected has become the head of the corner."[53] Very wise Paul also advises us to put on this stone: "Put on our" stone "Jesus Christ and make no provision for the flesh, to gratify its desires."[54] For whoever is clothed in this is out of reach of every lust that harms the soul. (5) The girdles symbolize their capability and preparedness, for it is said of them, "Mighty in power are

48. Cf. Ex 35.30.
50. Ex 25.9.
52. Is 28.16.
54. Rom 13.14.

49. Cf. Ex 31.7–8.
51. Mk 13.
53. Ps 117.22.

they who keep his word."⁵⁵ (6) For these seven angels have taken from one of the four living creatures, of whom much was said earlier, the wrath of God in seven golden bowls. "Golden" was well said, for even the wrath of God is precious, bringing with it what is good and more profitable than justice, even if those suffering punishment are in anguish.

(7) He says, *And the temple was filled with smoke from the glory of God and from his power.* The smoke is a sign of the divine wrath, for Scripture says, "Smoke went up in his wrath."⁵⁶ Smoke is indicative of fire; but there is also the smoke that blessed Isaiah saw where he says, "And the lintel shook at the voices of the seraphim as they sang" the Trisagion, "and the house was filled with smoke."⁵⁷ He was describing the wrath of God directed against Jerusalem. (8) The words *from the glory of God and from his power* are a kind of periphrasis for the smoke, as if he said, "it was filled with smoke from the wrath of God," for God himself is the power and the glory, and who could bear his wrath? (9) He says, *And no one could enter the temple until the seven plagues of the seven angels were ended:* for who will mount up on the wrath of God, or who will remain alive when caught in it? "For if no one has stood at the feet of the Lord,"⁵⁸ according to Scripture, scarcely could anyone endure God's wrath. (10) He says, And I heard a command of one who came out that they should *pour out on the earth the seven bowls* of the divine wrath.

24. *The first angel went off and poured out his bowl on the earth, and foul and evil sores came upon those who bore the mark of the beast and worshiped its image. (2) Then the second angel poured out his bowl over the sea, and it became blood like that of a corpse, and every living thing died. (3) The third angel poured out his bowl into the rivers and the fountains of water, and they became blood. (4) And I heard the angel of the waters say, "Just are you, you who are and who were, the Holy One, because of your judgments, (5) for they shed the blood of saints and prophets, and you gave them blood to drink, for they are worthy." (6) And I heard the altar say, "Yes, Lord God, sovereign of all, true and just are your judgments!"* (Rv 16.2–7)

55. Ps 102.20.
57. Is 6.4.

56. Ps 17.9.
58. Jer 23.18.

25. These words could be understood in two ways, either literally of the events that will occur at the time of the end, or allegorically. For when the Lord talked about the signs of the end, he warned his disciples of many of the evils that would then occur. He said, "You will hear of wars and rumors of wars. And nation will rise up against nation, and kingdom against kingdom, and there will be famines and plagues and earthquakes in various places: all this is the beginning of the sufferings,"[59] and after a few verses, "Then there will be great tribulation, such as has not been from the beginning of the world until now, no, and never will be."[60] It is with reference to these that the present sayings might be interpreted as having taken place, when each of the seven bowls was being poured out. (2) The sores that resulted from the first bowl would then symbolize the tribulations and sufferings which were slowly consuming the souls of human beings at that time on account of rumors of wars, while the blood in the sea would stand for those killed in naval battles, and the blood of the rivers and of the waters probably connotes the murders in battles of those encamped beside the waters.

(3) He says, *And I heard the angel of the waters speaking.* God is all-powerful both in showing care for his creation and in supplying what all need for their welfare, so that he does not need anyone to help him in this. For one whose will alone assures the completion of the work, and by whose decree everything has been brought into being—how could such a one stand in need of a fellow-worker and assistant in order to do good? (4) But since he is good, he wishes that the holy angels, too, should be shown kindness by giving aid to those in need. For those who help another in need are not benefiting the recipient so much as themselves. None of the angelic powers was in need and required aid from anybody else. So God ordered that those on earth who were in need of any good thing would be supplied by the holy angels. That is why we earlier recognized the angels as the protectors of the churches. So Daniel in his great wisdom wrote of Michael, the ruler of the angels, as taking care of the tribe of the Jews.[61]

59. Mt 24.6–8.   60. Mt 24.21.
61. Dn 12.1.

(5) The Revelation now explains for us the angel appointed over the waters. For the earthly creation was constructed from the four elements of air, fire, earth, and water. (Some wanted to hold that the heavens were made by a fifth primal body, which they say was ethereal and circular.) Three of the elements, fire, earth, and air, have been generously mixed together for the needs of breathing and other common uses. But even if they say that the ether is wholly the element of fire, yet its abundance and self-sufficiency on earth lurk hidden in its hollows and stones. There are even some who produce fire out of water contained in vessels of glass when they face the rising sun. The earth is the common mother, tomb, and sure home for all. It is only in the case of fresh water, in springs, fountains, wells, and even rivers, that there is not a plentiful supply for everyone, and in the case of the water which comes from above, which is contained in the clouds on high and by divine command gives us rain in due season and nourishes every living thing on the earth. (6) Therefore, since there is not an abundant supply of water for everyone, one of the holy angels is put in charge of it, in order that he may provide those in want with an unfailing sufficiency for their need. When as often it fails or is withheld because of our evil deeds, it results in droughts and famines and the plagues that follow them. (7) It is of this angel appointed by God's providence over the waters, that he says, *I heard him say, "You are just, you who are and who were, the Holy One."* "You who are" signifies that God has no end; "you who were" signifies that God has no beginning; "the Holy One" is he who is altogether just in all things. (8) When he says, *because of your judgments,* he means that those who poured out the blood of the saints should drink blood. For those in war who are encamped by the side of the waters and rivers cannot but drink the water that has been befouled by blood from the bodies of the dying. (9) In harmony with the angel those around the heavenly altar render their thanksgiving to God. The words, *I heard the altar saying this,* denote those ministering at the altar. (10) May it be that we, being set free from all possible afflictions, may render a hymn of thanksgiving to Christ, to whom be glory for ever and ever. Amen.

CHAPTER NINE

HE THREE BOWLS poured out by the three angels accomplished what I have already described. We must now consider what the fourth and fifth have done.

2. *The fourth angel,* he says, *poured out his bowl on the sun, and his task was to scorch human beings with fire,* (2) *and they were scorched by the fierce heat, and they cursed the name of God who had power over these plagues, and they did not repent and give him glory.* (3) *The fifth angel poured out his bowl on the throne of the beast, and its kingdom was put in darkness; people gnawed their tongues in anguish* (4) *and cursed the God of heaven for their pain and sores, and did not repent of their deeds* (Rv 16.8–11).

3. It is not difficult to explain all this by means of the rules of metaphor. The sun scorching human beings would be the drought, the affliction, and the distress of the survivors of wars. (2) When they were weighed down by their hardships, they ought to have asked God for aid and release from their distressing ordeals; for God was able to do this. But, he says, instead they *cursed God and did not repent.* This is why the plagues occurred, so that since they did not acknowledge their master as a result of God's kindnesses to them, at any rate they might acknowledge him as a result of their torments.

(3) He says that the bowl of the fifth angel was poured out *on the throne of the beast, and its kingdom was put in darkness.* The apostle has written about the Antichrist, whom "the Lord will slay by the breath of his mouth,"[1] and Isaiah says, "Let the wicked person be destroyed so as not to see the glory of the Lord,"[2] meaning by "glory" the glorious coming of the Lord. So the statement

1. 2 Thes 2.8.
2. Is 26.10.

that the bowl was poured out *on the throne of the beast* means that the impious tyranny of the Antichrist will come to an end once he has, by God's mercy, been destroyed, and darkness will take hold of all those who are under his command as the result of the unexpected punishment of his accursed tyranny: in distress at what has happened, they will experience darkness in their reasoning.

(4) He says, *They gnawed their tongues* as a result of the fire. This usually happens in any excessive agony, when people have been accustomed to bite their tongues or a part of their body, thinking that in this way they will alleviate much of their agony. (5) They ought to have repented, if not on account of anything else, at any rate because of the downfall of the Antichrist, whom they had elected as king and god for themselves, but instead they cursed the true God because of the destruction of the wretch.

4. *The sixth angel poured out his bowl on the great river Euphrates, and its water was dried up to prepare the way for the kings from the east. (2) And I saw, issuing from the mouth of the serpent and from the mouth of the false prophet, three foul spirits like frogs; (3) for they are demonic spirits, performing signs, which go abroad to the kings of the whole world, to assemble them for war on the great day of God, the sovereign Lord. "See, I am coming like a thief! (4) Blessed is he who is awake, looking after his garments that he might not go naked and his shame be seen!" (5) And he assembled them at the place called in Hebrew Megiddo* (Rv 16.12–16).

5. The sixth angel made the river Euphrates fordable, perhaps by drying up some of its springs, so as to facilitate the passage of the kings through it. But by the work of the Devil and with the consent of God a very large number of kings were brought together for war among themselves. For the Lord said, in the testimony described a little earlier, that wars would take place about the time of the end.[3]

(2) *And I saw,* he says, *issuing from the mouth of the serpent and from the mouth of the false prophet.* He calls the Devil *a serpent,* the Devil, who is the author of all evil. The *false prophet* is either

3. Cf. Mt 24.6.

someone speaking at the instigation of the Devil, or the Antichrist. (3) If he really means the Antichrist, do not be surprised that you meet him again after he had been earlier described as having been destroyed by the Spirit of the Lord, and is now described as still alive, spewing forth demons through his mouth. For all that the evangelist sees are a vision, and he is often shown the first things last and contrariwise the last first.

(4) *And, he says, I saw three spirits like frogs, for they are demonic spirits, performing signs, which go abroad to the kings.* The demons are compared to frogs because they rejoice in the muddy and slimy life of human beings,[4] and because the present murky and flabby life of sinners is preferred by them to the restrained and austere life of the righteous, since the demons are very envious and rejoice in the destruction of the living. (5) The assembling of the kings to make war against each other at the time of the end is a form of trickery on the part of the demons. He calls the day *great,* which means "that moment." For it is truly great and fearful, as Joel also calls it in the words, "before the great and indisputable day of the Lord comes."[5] (6) *See, I am coming like a thief,* says the Lord. *Like a thief* refers to the suddenness and unexpectedness of his second coming.

(7) *Blessed is he who is awake, looking after his garments that he might not go naked.* He has continued with the figure of the thief, so that he says he must guard his garments lest they are lost, meaning by *garments* either the virtuous and honorable life, by which we are made worthy of God's protection, or our bodies, which are to be [kept] chaste and pure. (8) For those who do not keep guard will be ashamed before the angels and the human beings around the divine throne. They will be persecuted in the day of judgment and will be *naked,* bereft of divine aid. (9) He says, And the demons *assembled*[6] *the kings of the earth at the place called in Hebrew Megiddo.* This is to be translated as "a cleft" or "a cleaving."[7] So, then, as a result of the forthcoming slaugh-

---

4. Cf. 2 Pt 2.22.
5. Jl 3.4.
6. In the original quotation the singular was used. Here the plural occurs.
7. This connects the word Megiddo with the Hebrew root *gdd,* meaning "to penetrate" or "cut."

ter and butchery of those assembled in it, he named the place of war Megiddo.

6. *The seventh angel poured out his bowl into the air, and a loud voice issued from the temple, from the throne, saying, "It is done!"* (2) *And there occurred flashes of lightning, voices, peals of thunder, and a great earthquake such as has never occurred since human beings came to be on the earth, so great was that earthquake,* (3) *and the great city was[8] [split into three parts, and the cities of the nations fell down, and great Babylon] was remembered before God to be given the cup of the wine of my God and his wrath. And every island fled away, and no mountains were to be found;* (4–5) *and great hailstones like a hundredweight dropped on human beings from heaven, and they cursed God for the plague of the hail, so very great was that plague* (Rv 16.17–21).

7. *He poured out the bowl* in the air, and *the voice* said, *It is done.* What was done? The command, that is, of God, and his will. (2) When *It is done* had been spoken, there came from the air, *flashes of lightning and voices*—flashes of lightning from on high, and *voices* from those on earth in fear of the lightning. *And peals of thunder and an earthquake.* (3) By the *earthquake* he either means the tumult of the earth, since this also is included in the signs of the end, or he calls the changing of the visible order an *earthquake,* as Haggai said, "Once again I will shake" not only "the heaven" but also "the earth and the sea and the dry land, and I will shake all the nations together."[9] This is why he says that such [an earthquake] has never occurred before.

(4) He says, *The great city was split into three parts, and the cities of the nations fell down* (Rv 16.19). By *the great city* he means Jerusalem, and he clearly contrasts with this the *cities of the nations.* For apart from Israel it is the custom in Holy Scripture to call the rest of humankind *nations.* He calls it *great* because of its renown. All *the cities fell down,* (5) for when the earth was being changed and had become new, how could the cities on it remain standing since they had been defiled by the residence of sinners?

8. There is a lacuna in the text, supplied by the comments that follow; see de Groote ed., p. 216.
9. Hg 2.6–7.

OECUMENIUS

(6) He says, *And great Babylon was remembered before God, to be given the cup of the wine of the fury of his wrath.*[10] It was said earlier, *A second angel followed, saying, "Fallen, fallen is Babylon the great"* (Rv 14.8). In the present passage he is speaking to us about another Babylon, and he gives us to understand that he means not that one, but some other one. And I fancy he is talking about Rome and all the calamities that will later overtake it, as the account will proceed to describe. Therefore he says, *And great Babylon was remembered before God.* That is, the memory of her sins of old, when they persecuted and murdered God's people, came into God's mind. (7) *The cup of the wine of the wrath of God* has already been interpreted. So there is no need to spend any more time on this.

(8) He says, *And every island fled away, and no mountains were to be found.* The churches of the nations are said to be *islands*, as the prophet says, "The Lord has become king; let the earth rejoice; let the many islands be glad."[11] They have been called *islands* as having sprung up and as having overcome the bitterness and brackishness of idolatry. According to another meaning, one might also understand *islands* to be the unclean brigades of demons, as wallowing in this brackish and turbulent life. (9) In referring to the *mountains* as demons he is supported by the blessed poet, singing, "The mountains melted away like wax from before the Lord because he is coming."[12] (10) Therefore, the account tells us that the present brigades of demons will be clean gone and will disappear. But where would the wretched ones flee from the face of God, who holds "in his hand the ends of the earth,"[13] who "has measured heaven in a span and the earth with the palm of his hand"?[14] In vain will those who have been struck by the plagues attempt flight and escape. (11) After these events, and in the face of the violent hail, human beings should have turned to prayers and entreaties. For then all these signs against them would have ceased. But they even went on to curse God, and that is why their troubles were in fact increased.

10. Note the difference between the comment and the original citation.
11. Ps 96.1.   12. Ps 96.5.
13. Ps 94.4.   14. Is 40.12.

8. *Then one of the seven angels who had the seven bowls came and spoke with me saying, "Come, I will show you the judgment of the great harlot who is seated upon many waters, (2) with whom the kings of the earth have committed fornication, and with the wine of whose fornication the dwellers on earth have become drunk." (3) And he carried me away in the Spirit into a wilderness, and I saw a woman sitting on a scarlet beast which was full of blasphemous names, and it had seven heads and ten horns. (4) The woman was arrayed in purple and scarlet, and bedecked with gold and jewels and pearls, holding in her hand a golden cup full of abominations, together with the impurities of the earth's[15] fornication; (5) and on her forehead was written a name, a mystery, "Babylon the great, mother of harlots and of the earth's abominations" (Rv 17.1–5).*

9. After completing the account of the end of the present age and of all that will then happen, the vision turns to something else, as it wishes to show the evangelist what will happen to Rome. (2) It says, *He said to me, "Come, I will show you the judgment of the harlot who is seated upon many waters,"* meaning by "judgment" the way of life and society in which she has decided to live and the way in which she spends her time. He calls her a harlot, because of her fornication and rebellion against God. For this is named fornication by Holy Scripture according to the words of the prophet addressed to the God of the universe, "You have destroyed everyone that commits fornication against you."[16] He calls the nations over whom she rules and presides *many waters,* as he himself goes on to say.

(3) He says, *With whom the kings of the earth have committed fornication.* They are those who had been kings[17] over [the nations], for these are the kings of the earth who have shared in her fornication and mad idolatry. (4) He says, *And the dwellers on earth have become drunk with the wine of her fornication.* For the rest, too, of those she was ruling had joined in the revolt from God, sometimes by her compulsion and sometimes by her example. (5) He

15. Oecumenius here reads τῆς γῆς ("the earth's") instead of αὐτῆς ("her") as in Nestle-Aland, 27th ed., where the critical note shows that τῆς γῆς appears as a variant reading in several NT manuscripts.
16. Ps 72.27.
17. Greek βασιλεύς, a regular title for the emperors of Rome.

says, *And he carried me away in the Spirit into a wilderness.* The wilderness symbolizes her coming desolation. (6) He says, *And I saw a woman sitting on a scarlet beast.* By the *beast* he means the Devil on whom she was relying and by whom she was being controlled. The beast is *scarlet* because it has been made red by the blood of the saints. (7) *The beast was full of blasphemous names.* For the Devil, dedicated only to himself, fails to render the worship due to God. (8) He says, *Having seven heads and ten horns.* He goes on to interpret this, saying that the *heads* and *horns* are the kings who have already reigned over her and who were still going to reign. (9) *And the woman was arrayed in purple and scarlet*—*purple* on account of her reign, *scarlet* because she had shed the blood of many saints. (10) *Bedecked with gold and jewels and pearls:* the text rightly adorns her as a queen with royal adornment. (11) *Holding in her hand a golden cup, full of abominations*—*golden* on account of her honored sovereignty, but nevertheless *full of* idolatry and pollutions by which she was being nurtured and from which she poured her libations to her demons.

(12) He says, *The impurities of the earth's fornication:* for he attributes to her the cause of the idolatry even of the rest of the nations, as the prime worker of evils and of mad idolatry. (13) There was, he says, *written on her forehead,* as if it were an inscription on a monument, saying who she was, that she is *Babylon, the mother of harlots*—*Babylon* because of the turmoil and confusion in her, and the persecutions of the saints (for the name "Babylon" signifies confusion, as has been mentioned), and she is the *mother* of fornication and of rebellion against God. For how can she not be a mother and teacher when she persecutes the gospel and those proclaiming it and persuades the nations to remain attached to their ancestral error?

10. *And I saw the woman, drunk with the blood of the martyrs of Jesus.* (2) *When I saw her, I marveled greatly. But the angel said to me, "Why marvel? I will tell you the mystery of the woman, and of the beast with seven heads and ten horns that carries her.* (3) *The beast which you saw was, and is not, and is going to ascend from the bottomless pit and go to perdition; and the dwellers on earth whose names have not been*

written in the book of life from the foundation of the world will marvel as they behold the beast because it is not and is to come. (4) *This calls for a mind with wisdom"* (Rv 17.6–9).

11. Not only did the harlot have her fill of the blood of the saints, but she also became drunk, since her kings shed so much blood on all sides. (2) *I will tell you,* he says, what *the mystery* is *of the woman and of the beast;* that is, by means of the Revelation he explains to you in mystical fashion these pictorial images. (3) He says, *The beast which you saw was, and is not, and is going to ascend from the bottomless pit:* the Devil *was,* having been brought into existence by God before the beginning of the visible universe to perform good works, just like the rest of the blessed angels. But *he is not,* since the events at the end of the age are shown to the evangelist, when the Devil will go "into the fire prepared for him and his angels."[18] For to be in such a condition is not to have any being at all in the proper sense of the word. (4) Then, since the Antichrist is going to be exhibited by his action at the end-time, he says, *And he is going to ascend from the bottomless pit and go to perdition.* For by means of the Antichrist an ascent, and as it were an increase, will accrue to the Devil, as the Antichrist leads human beings astray and persuades them to worship the Devil, according to what has already been said more than once. (5) Or you can understand *he was and is not* in this way: the apostle, in writing to the Philippians, says, "To all the saints in Christ Jesus who have their being in Philippi,"[19] calling the saints "beings"[20] because they are in Christ and held in God's intimacy and memory.

Therefore if the saints are *beings,* then the wretched Devil is not now *a being,* even if *he was* such before he exalted himself against God, the sovereign Lord of all, and was utterly expelled from his own order. Similarly also the impious, even if they seem to be beings in virtue of their substance and existence, in fact are not beings when it comes to the decree and memory of God. Because this is so, the book of Genesis does not give the genealogy of the descendants of Cain, since through their impiety

18. Mt 25.41.
19. Phil 1.1.
20. Using the present participle of εἰμί in the sense that God is ὁ Ὤν ("he who is"; see Ex 3.14), and those in Christ are οἱ ὄντες ("they who are").

they are not beings. (6) He calls this *perdition* to which the Devil will go, that is, his deserved punishment in Gehenna. For the Lord speaks of those condemned to perish in Gehenna, saying, according to Matthew, "Fear him who can destroy both soul and body in Gehenna."[21]

(7) He says, *And the dwellers on earth will marvel,* not all, but those whose names are not[22] in the book of life. Why *will they marvel? Because he was and is not and is to come,* and *the beast* is being destroyed. Those who had believed in him were panic-struck at his great change. For while wishing to be lord of the world and while proclaiming himself as this, not only will he be deprived of his rule, but he will also receive the deserved result of his wickedness. (8) He says, *This calls for a mind with wisdom.* This is the way, he says, in which the mind is made wise: one needs to understand the riddle of how *he was, and is not, and is going to ascend from the bottomless pit.* For the movement from being to non-being seems to be opposite to ascending again from the bottomless pit, unless one thinks of it in the way which has been explained.

1 2. *The seven heads are seven hills on which the woman is seated; there are also seven kings,* (2) *five of whom have fallen, one is, the other has not yet come, and when he comes, he must remain only a little while.* (3) *As for the beast that was and is not, he is an eighth, but he comes from the other seven, and is going to perdition.* (4) *And the ten horns that you saw are ten kings who have not yet received royal power, but they will have it*[23] *as kings; they are to receive it for one hour, together with the beast.* (5) *These are of one mind and give over their power and authority to the beast;* (6) *these will make war on the Lamb, and the Lamb will conquer them, for he is Lord of lords and King of kings, and those with him are called and chosen and faithful* (Rv 1 7.9–14).

1 3. He says, *The seven heads are seven hills on which the woman is seated:* this is a very clear indication that he is speaking about Rome, for Rome is described as seven-crested, and no other city

21. Mt 10.28.
22. The word "not" is omitted in the manuscripts, but is a necessary emendation by de Groote, in whose ed. see p. 222.
23. Oecumenius here reads ἕξουσιν ("they will have") instead of the accepted text of Revelation, ἐξουσίαν ("authority").

is so called. (2) He says, *There are also seven kings, five of whom have fallen, one is, the other has not yet come, and when he comes, he must remain only a little while.* He reasonably regards the kings as heads; for the kings are the head and summary of the Roman empire. (3) Why did he say, in spite of the very many emperors of Rome, that the beast had only seven heads? He said this since the seven were specially responsible for causing the beast, that is, the Devil, to raise up his head against the Christians, by stirring up persecutions against the church. These were first Nero, second Domitian, then Trajan, Severus, after him Decius, Valerian, and Diocletian. When these were the emperors of Rome, they persecuted the church without restraint, as Eusebius says in the *Chronicles.*[24] (4) He says that of these seven, five have fallen by death: Nero, Domitian, Trajan, Severus, and Decius, but that there was still one, that is, Valerian.

(5) *The other,* he says, *has not yet come, and when he comes, he must remain only a little while.* He means that the other is Diocletian, after whom the seat of empire ceased to be in Rome and was transferred to the city named after the pious Constantine, who himself was responsible for changing the policies of the empire. (6) The evangelist was told everything very accurately, especially with regard to Diocletian, when he said, *And when he comes, he must remain only a little while,* referring to the time spent in his persecution against the Christians. For although he reigned for twenty years, he began the persecution during the last two years before he abdicated.

(7) He says, *As for the beast that was and is not, he is an eighth, but he comes from the seven, and he is going to perdition.* He has placed the Devil both first and also last as a persecutor and of one mind with the seven. For how could the Devil, too, fail to be numbered among them, since it was he who directed the seven to be so very wicked?

(8) He says, *And the ten horns that you saw are ten kings who have not yet received royal power.* Concerning these ten kings, or horns, the prophet Daniel in his great wisdom has marked them out as arising from the rule of the Romans when he said that they will

24. Eusebius, *Chronicle* 2.211–73.

rise up in the last times; in the midst of these the Antichrist will
arise.[25] That is why he says, *They have not yet received royal power, but
they will have it as kings.* He is right to say *as kings,* because of the
early demise and darkness of their reign. (9) Then he goes on to
say, *For one hour they are to receive it with the beast.* He here calls the
Antichrist *a beast.* Earlier on, too, he has called him this, saying,
*Then I saw another beast rising out of the earth; and it had two horns
like those of a lamb* (Rv 13.11). That they reigned over them for
one hour symbolizes either the short span of time of their reign,
or one hour is a figure of speech for a year.

(10) He says, *These are of one mind, and give over their power and
authority to the beast.* For even if the coming ten kings have contrary policies among themselves, in this at least they will be of
one mind, in giving their power and authority to the beast, that
is, the Antichrist. For they will be defeated by him, and he alone
will then rule over them all. But even if contrary to their expecta-
tion they are to be defeated, nevertheless, since the ten will have
the same experience of defeat and destruction, he says they have
one mind. It is as though he was saying that it is by their consent
and agreement that the ten will be defeated by the Antichrist.

(11) He says, *These will make war on the Lamb.* Before their total
destruction by the Antichrist, those whom we are describing will
persecute the church. (12) But Christ will be victor. Evil as they
are, he will hand them over to the more evil Antichrist to death.
Or, according to another interpretation of "Christ will be victor,"
it refers to his slaves' striving until death on behalf of their faith
in him. For he says, they *are called and chosen and faithful*—that is,
the slaves of Christ.

14. *And he said to me, "The waters that you saw, where the harlot is
seated, are peoples and nations and multitudes and tongues. (2) And
the ten horns which you saw and the beast, they will hate the harlot,
and they will make her desolate and naked, and devour her flesh and
burn her up with fire. (3) For God has put it into their hearts to carry
out his purpose and to be of one mind and give over their royal power to
the beast, until the words of God shall be fulfilled. (4) And the woman*

25. Cf. Dn 8.23?

whom you saw is the great city which has dominion over the kings of the earth" (Rv 17.15–18).

15. He said, *The waters where the harlot is seated are peoples and nations,* over which the city clearly has dominion. (2) How will Rome be made desolate by the kings? For we considered that it was Rome which the Revelation meant. Perhaps they will fight against her because she is a queen, secure, populous, and the receiver of tribute. So in the war over her she would have to be a prize of conquest and be ill-treated by all, destroyed by fire and made desolate.

(3) He says, *For God has put it into their hearts to carry out his purpose:* he means that with God's consent she will suffer this at the hands of her adversaries and those who wish to take her. (4) *And,* he says, *to be of one mind and give over their royal power to the beast:* just as with one mind they were handed over as subject to the Antichrist, as has been said previously. He says, *until the words of God shall be fulfilled:* he means that they will be subject to the beast until the punishment of the Antichrist takes place and God's decrees on him through the prophets are fulfilled. (5) In his desire to give a clearer reference to the city whose story he is telling, he adds that *the woman is the great city which has dominion over all.*

16. *After this I saw another angel coming down from heaven, having great authority; and the earth was bright with his splendor.* (2) *And he called out with a mighty voice, "Fallen, fallen is Babylon the great! She has become a dwelling place of demons, a haunt of every foul spirit, and a haunt of every foul and hateful bird, (3) for all the nations have fallen down*[26] *as a result of the wrath due to her fornication: the kings of the earth have committed fornication with her, and the merchants of the earth have grown rich from the extent of her wantonness"* (Rv 18.1–3).

17. He says, *I saw another angel having great authority:* he means that this is the source of the heavenly light that illuminates the earth *with its splendor.* (2) He says, *Fallen is Babylon:* he proclaims God's sentence against her. He says that she was meant to suffer

---

26. The text here reads πέπτωκε ("have fallen down") whereas textual variations in other manuscripts and the later comment read πέπωκε ("have drunk") in line with most manuscripts of Rv 18.3.

this. (3) *And she became a dwelling place of demons:* the destroying demons, as haters of humankind and greedy for blood, wherever they might find men's blood shed, when they were killed in wars or in some other way, spend their time as though exulting in what was happening among them. Therefore, since most people in the city will be destroyed, as he said earlier, it will become for the future *a dwelling place of demons, a haunt of every foul spirit,* a place which keeps careful watch over the behavior of the demons in their enjoyment of it. (4) *And a haunt of every foul bird and of every unclean beast:* such beasts shun the life of human beings and cling to desolate places and so keep themselves secure from those who plot against them and from the pursuit of hunters. These are the sort of things which Isaiah the prophet, too, says about Babylon. He says, "There owls will dwell, and there demons will dance. Satyrs will dwell there, and hedgehogs will build their nests in their houses."[27]

(5) *For all the nations have drunk of the wrath of her fornication:* he means here by *fornication* their insatiable appetite and love of money, for such is the manner of harlots. For those in the aforementioned city were closely joined to all the nations, and when they had subdued them, they ordered them to pay tribute. (6) And their *kings,* he says, have become accomplices and sharers in her love of money, and *the merchants* who traded in her, he says, *have grown rich from her wantonness;* that is, because of her contempt and her loose, gushing, and sloppy lifestyle, they were able to peddle all kinds of wares in her.

18. *Then I heard another voice from heaven saying, "Come out of her, my people, so that you may not participate in her sins and consequently share in her plagues, (2) for her sins are heaped high as heaven, and God has remembered her iniquities. (3) Render to her as she herself has rendered, and repay her double for her deeds in the cup in which she mixed a double draught.*[28] (4) *As she glorified herself and played the*

27. Is 13.21–22.
28. Rv 18.6. The accepted text has ἐκέρασεν κεράσατε, whereas Oecumenius's text omits the imperative verb. Note also that in v.4 NT has ἐξέλθατε, but Oec has ἔξελθε, as in some manuscripts of Revelation. So, too, Oec reads αὐτῶν in place of NT αὐτῆς.

wanton, so give her a like measure of torment and mourning. Since in her heart she says, 'A queen I sit, I am no widow, mourning I shall never see,' (5) *so shall her plagues come in a single day, death and mourning and famine, and she shall be burned with fire, for mighty is the Lord who has judged her"* (Rv 18.4–8).

19. When the divine angels overthrew the city of the Sodomites to execute judgment on those in it and in the neighboring cities—or rather, as Saint Cyril thought,[29] when the Son of God and the Holy Spirit visited there ("for the Father will not judge anyone," as Scripture says, "but has given all judgment to the Son,"[30] of course with the life-giving Spirit being present with him naturally and substantially)—they then said to blessed Lot, "Flee for your life; do not look back or stop anywhere in the region; take refuge in the hills, lest you be consumed."[31] (2) The Revelation now gives us the same teaching. Since it is impossible that in this very great, populous city, Rome, there should fail to be some slaves of Christ, he says to them, *Come out of her, my people, so that you may not participate in her sins and consequently share in her plagues.* To participate in her sins is also to share in her plagues, for the plagues are the result of her sins.

(3) He says, *For her sins are heaped high as heaven:* as one might say, she defiled the air between earth and heaven with her sins. So he says, "God, after being patient for so long, has now woken up to exact repayment." (4) That is why he says, *Render to her double* for her sins, even though God has enjoined us through the all-wise Moses, "You shall not take vengeance twice for the same offense."[32] So why does he himself render double? Double does not here mean twice as much, but because God is benevolent and good, and punishes much less severely than the offense merits, he thinks he has rendered double even when he has rendered a part, and not only double, but also sevenfold. Knowing this, the prophet said, "Render sevenfold into the bosom of our neighbors the taunts with which they have taunted you, Lord."[33] By this petition for sevenfold he is asking God for a due punishment of his enemies. (5) He is now saying, "because she has

---

29. Cyril of Alexandria, *De adoratione et cultu in spiritu et veritate* 1.
30. Jn 5.22.   31. Gn 19.7.
32. Cf. Dt 32.41; Na 1.9.   33. Ps 78.12.

been living in splendor and wantonness in this present life and has taken no thought for God's will, *Render to her.*" For she is saying, "I shall never be deprived of my reign"; for this is the meaning of the *widow,* she who is bereft of her reign; "nor shall I see any evil." Therefore, on account of her boasting all kinds of evil will fall on her at once. (6) For, he says, *God is mighty* and will not be prevented by anyone from bringing judgment and punishment upon her. (7) May we all be free from this by the grace of the one who called us to know him and to hope in Christ, to whom be glory for ever. Amen.

CHAPTER TEN

HE ACCOUNT IN the Revelation is still concerned with Rome. In describing her very great and dramatic change the account continues to dwell on it. So what does it say?

2. *And the kings of the earth, who committed fornication and lived in luxury with her, will weep and wail over her when they see the smoke of her burning, (2) as they stand afar off, in fear of her torment, and say, "Alas! Alas! You great city, Babylon, you mighty city! In one hour has your judgment come."* (3) *And the merchants of the earth are weeping and mourning for her, since no one is buying their merchandise any more, (4) their gold, silver, precious stones and pearls, fine linen, purple, silk, and scarlet, every kind of scented wood, every article of ivory, every article of very costly wood, bronze, iron, and marble, cinnamon, (5) spice, myrrh, frankincense, wine, oil, fine flour and wheat, cattle and sheep, horses and chariots, and slaves, and human souls. (6) The fruit for which your soul has longed has gone from you, and all your dainties and splendor are lost to you, and they will never find her[1] again. (7) The merchants of these things, who gained their wealth from her, will stand afar off, in fear of her torment, weeping and mourning and saying, (8) "Alas, alas, for the great city that was clothed in fine linen and purple and scarlet, adorned with gold and precious stones and pearls! (9) In one hour all this wealth has been laid waste."* And every shipmaster and all who were sailing on the river,[2] sailors and all whose trade is on the sea, (10) *stood far off and cried out as they saw the anguish[3] of her burning, "What city was like the great city?"* (11) *And they threw dust on their heads, as they wept and mourned, crying out, "Alas, alas,*

---

1. Oecumenius reads αὐτὴν (i. e., Babylon) instead of the usual neuter plural αὐτά.
2. Oecumenius here reads ποταμὸν ("river") instead of τόπον ("place").
3. Oecumenius here reads πόνον instead of καπνὸν ("smoke").

for the great city where all who had ships at sea grew rich by her wealth, for in one hour she has been laid waste" (Rv 18.9–19).

3. How variously and neatly has he woven the lament over her and the climax of her grief. Since practically everything is clear, let us simply note what seems to be difficult and go on to the rest. (2) He says, *Horses, chariots, and slaves.* The word for *chariots* is Latin, for since the Romans were ruling, it is not at all unreasonable for the blessed evangelist to use Latin. But the text has turned it into Greek. For *redium*[4] is the Latin for chariot, but he has put the genitive plural case, and one ought to say *rediorum* according to Latin usage, but when turning it into Greek he has written a Greek ending, saying *redōn* [ῥεδῶν], in order that the word may be in a proper form. (3) He says, *Horses, chariots, and slaves,* meaning chariot-horses are suitable for chariots, and slaves, that is, steeds meant for riding.

4. *Rejoice over her, heaven, saints, apostles, and prophets, for God has given judgment for you against her!* (2) *Then an angel*[5] *took up a huge stone like a great millstone and threw it into the sea, saying, "So shall Babylon the great city be thrown down with violence, and shall be found no more;* (3) *and the sound of harpists, minstrels, flute-players, and trumpeters shall be heard in you no more; and no craftsman of any kind shall be found in you from now on; and the sound of the millstone shall be heard in you no more; and the light of a lamp shall shine in you no more;* (4) *and the voice of bridegroom and bride shall be heard in you no more; for your merchants were the great men of the earth, and all the nations were deceived by your sorcery,* (5) *and in her was found the blood of all the prophets and saints who have been slain on earth"* (Rv 18.20–24).

5. The merchants and the kings of the earth and all who had an interest in the city while it was standing and prospering will weep over it, but let the heavens rejoice, that is, the angels in heaven and the souls of the righteous—the latter because God has effected vengeance, and the angels as rejoicing together

4. Oecumenius uses a neuter form, *redium*, whereas the Latin is feminine, *reda* or *raeda*.

5. Oecumenius uses the adjective "mighty" to qualify the stone, not the angel (ἰσχυρὸν rather than ἰσχυρὸς).

with those who were avenged. (2) Again, by dwelling on this in the exposition he emphasizes the suffering of the spiritual Babylon. As all this is clear, there is no need to spend time on what is generally agreed.

6. *After this I heard a loud voice of a great multitude in heaven, crying, "Alleluia! Salvation and glory and power belong to our God, for his judgments are true and just; (2) for he has judged the great harlot who corrupted the earth with her fornication, and he has exacted vengeance from her hand for the blood of his slaves." (3) A second time they cried, "Alleluia! The smoke from her is going up for ever and ever." (4) And the twenty-four elders and the four living creatures fell down and worshiped God, who is seated on the throne, saying, "Amen, Alleluia!" (5) And from the throne came a voice crying, "Praise our God, all you his slaves, you who fear him, small and great"* (Rv 19.1–5).

7. He says, *I heard* what seemed to be *the voice of a great multitude from heaven.* The ranks of the holy angels are innumerable, as one of the fathers spoke of "the ninety-nine sheep,"[6] saying that those who were being preserved and who did not wander away were the angels, and that the one who wandered off was the whole of humanity.[7] (2) They were crying, he says, *Alleluia.* Alleluia is a Hebrew word; it means "Praise, laud God." Accordingly, they sing a song of thanksgiving for the righteous judgment of the spiritual Babylon. (3) *And a second time* they raised the same hymn, and again they uttered it a little further on: by this threefold use of *Alleluia* they were glorifying the holy and venerable Trinity; for this is God.

(4) He says, *The smoke from her is going up for ever and ever.* The hymn *Alleluia* broke midway through the sequence of the argument, since this is indeed the logical order: *And he has exacted vengeance from her hand for the blood of his slaves. And the smoke from her is going up for ever and ever:* he means the *smoke* of the city as being completely burnt up, for smoke indicates fire. (5) When the elders and the living creatures said *Amen,* this shows their approval of the doxology offered by the holy angels, for when

6. Mt 18.12–13; Lk 15.4, 7.
7. Cf. Epiphanius, *In assumptione Christi;* Chrysostom, *De remissione peccatorum;* Origen, *Commentary on Psalms* 18.6.

Amen is translated from Hebrew to Greek it is rendered, "may it be so." (6) He says, *Praise our God, small and great;* for he calls the greater ones *small,* because of their sanctification, and he calls those who are eminent *great.*

8. *And I heard what seemed to be the sound of a great multitude, like the sound of many waters and like the sound of mighty thunderpeals, crying, "Alleluia! For the Lord our God, the sovereign of all, has entered upon his reign.* (2) *We rejoice and exult and will give him the glory,*[8] *for the marriage of the Lamb has come, and his bride has made herself ready; it was granted to her to be clothed with fine linen."* (3) *These are the righteous deeds of the saints.* (4) *And he said to me, "Write: Blessed are those who have been invited to the marriage supper of the Lamb." And he said to me, "These are the true words of God"* (Rv 19.6–9).

9. When the seraphim in words of the divine prophet Isa-iah[9] said "holy" three times, they ascribed the threefold hymn of praise to the one lordship, indicating on the one hand that there were three addressed in the hymns by their peculiar attributes or persons[10] (if it is thought proper to say so), but one in the being[11] of the Godhead. So also here after the blessed angels had previously uttered *Alleluia* thrice, and had ascribed worship to each of the three holy beings,[12] now they go on to sing *Alleluia* to the Holy Trinity, intimating that the holy and glorified Trinity exists in a single being and Godhead.[13]

(2) He says, *For the Lord our God has entered upon his reign:* our Lord Jesus Christ, even before his saving incarnation, reigned with the Father and the all-holy Spirit over those in heaven and on earth, as the only Son and Word of the Father and as the craftsman of the universe. And after the incarnation he is likewise the lord and king of all, since in no way was he limited by his incarnation as far as concerns his supreme rule and reign. (3) But since according to the most wise apostle[14] we do not yet see all things subjected to him, in the age to come all things will

8. Oecumenius here reads indicatives instead of the usual subjunctives.
9. Is 6.3.					10. Greek, πρόσωπα.
11. Greek, οὐσία.				12. Greek, ὑποστάσεις.
13. Greek, μοναδικὴ οὐσία καὶ θεότης.
14. 1 Cor 15.27–28.

be subjected, including those who up to now have been haughtily resisting him, so that even death itself will be made subject to him—for "the last enemy to be destroyed is death"[15]—for this reason the blessed angels rightly say, *The Lord our God has entered upon his reign.* In so doing they refer their hymn of praise to the age to come, as then by the subjection of all things Christ will obtain in its highest perfection his reign over all. Some will make their submission by being punished, others as they come to full knowledge face to face and no longer as they now see "in a mirror or a blurred image."[16]

(4) He says, *For the marriage of the Lamb has come, and his bride has made herself ready:* at the present time the marriage of the Lord to the church is still a courtship and not yet a complete marriage. The blessed apostle symbolizes this when writing the second epistle to the Corinthians, in which he says, "I betrothed you to one man to present you to Christ as a pure virgin."[17] So this is still a matter of courtship; for "I betrothed" is used of courtship. And as a symbol of courtship we receive "the earnest of the Spirit."[18] (5) When, however, the church truly becomes one spirit with Christ, then the marriage is complete, just as the man becomes one body with his wife. For when the wise apostle reflects on physical marriage, he puts it very graphically, saying, "the two shall become one flesh," and then adds, "This is a great mystery, and I take it to refer to Christ and the church."[19] So when the holy angels say, *The marriage of the Lamb has come,* they mean that the marriage consequent on the present courtship will be consummated. (6) The gospel, too, has clearly taught us this on two occasions: firstly it tells the story of the marriage of a king's son, when many had been invited to the banquet, some of whom joined in the feast, but others excused themselves from the supper, and how one who was not wearing "a wedding garment" was chased away.[20] Then also it speaks of the ten virgins, of whom five, whom it calls "prudent," went with the bridegroom into that happy bridal chamber, while the others were shut out,

15. 1 Cor 15.26.
16. 1 Cor 13.12. Oecumenius here reads δι' ἐσόπτου ἢ αἰνίγματι.
17. 2 Cor 11.2.   18. 2 Cor 1.22.
19. Eph 5.31–32.   20. Mt 22.2–14.

since they had not filled their lamps with sufficient oil. Nothing in these events can be understood as referring to the present, but only to the future. So *the marriage of the Lamb has come, and his bride* the church is present, ready to enjoy those ineffable good things resulting from its union with Christ. (7) By *clothed with linen* he means, "having a garment of virtues." It is linen on account of its brightness and plainness, bright because of [the church's] incomprehensible being and way of life, plain in its teachings and thoughts about God. (8) He says, *And he said to me, "Write: Blessed are those who have been invited to the marriage-supper of the Lamb,"* even though some are destined to depart. For we know that although many have been invited in the gospels, some did not attend the spiritual banquet, either by going away, or by being excluded because they did not have "a wedding garment,"[21] as was made clear a short while back. And the divine apostle, too, has said, "Many are called, but few are chosen."[22]

10. *And I fell down at his feet to worship him, but he said to me, "Don't do that! I am a fellow slave with you and your brothers who hold the testimony of Jesus. Worship God. For the testimony of Jesus is the spirit of prophecy"* (Rv 19.10).

11. The accursed and godforsaken Greeks understand that we have a divine doctrine which states that the holy angels, with the approval of God, are the guardians of nations and of churches and of each one of us.[23] Daniel in his great wisdom wrote about the nations: "And I have come because of your words. And the prince of the kingdom of the Persians withstood me";[24] and again, "But I am now returning to make war against the prince of the Persians; and I went forth, and the prince of the Greeks came";[25] and again, "There is none who contends by my side for this [purpose] except Michael, your prince";[26] and again, "At that time Michael will arise, the great prince, who has charge

21. Mt 22.11–12.
22. Mt 20.14.
23. Cyril of Alexandria, *Contra Julianum* 4.
24. Dn 10.12–13.
25. Dn 10.20.   26. Dn 10.21.

over the sons of your people."[27] (2) The present Revelation has spoken previously about the guardians of the churches, with which Saint Gregory agrees when he writes of the holy angels, "I believe that an angel is a guardian of each church, as John teaches me through the Revelation."[28] The prophet has spoken about the angels as guardians of each one, "The angel of the Lord encamps around those who fear him, and will deliver them,"[29] and the apostle also writes about the holy angels, "Are they not all ministering spirits sent forth to serve for the sake of those who are going to obtain salvation?"[30] (3) So when [the Greeks] hear these things being taught as our belief, they say to us, "Why, you fellows, since you have the same belief as we have, do you take offense at our belief which assigns gods as rulers over nations? Those whom you call angels, we call gods: we disagree only about the names, and no longer about the facts; and since you also say ranks of angels are called gods, the difference is not even about names." (4) To them we must reply: "You are damned: both in the worship of the works of your hands, and in having set up as gods only yesterday or the day before those whom you knew to be involved in all kinds of disgraceful conduct, you filched away most of our divine teachings; you took them and mixed them with your deadly doctrines, but, as you took your reason and not God as your guide, you were not able to preserve the overall excellence of our doctrines, but after following them a little way you were shipwrecked somewhere near the start. Wherefore, we and you have nothing in common, just as Scripture says, 'light has nothing in common with darkness or Christ with Beliar.'[31] (5) For when you think of national gods (though really they are unclean demons), you show yourselves as offering reverence to them and wishing to worship them as gods; and when you have deified them, they take no account of God, who has made provision for the care of humankind, but they govern the nations by their own will just as they wish. (6) So you allocated to Ares the fierce and bloodthirsty Scythians and Germans, who had be-

27. Dn 12.1.
28. Gregory of Nazianzus, *Orationes* 42.9.
29. Ps 33.8.
30. Heb 1.14.   31. 2 Cor 6.14–15.

come such under the rule of murderous Ares, the bane of human beings; and you assign the Greeks for their intelligence to Athene, as having obtained their intelligence from her;[32] and you deal similarly with others, assigning the gods to the nations each according to their own natural propensity." (7) But you will understand what we say from the present text. For when the evangelist wished to worship the divine angel, but not to worship him as God (for who knew better than John who is naturally and truly God, and who the angels are, that they are ministers and slaves and creatures of God?), nevertheless [the angel] is shown as refusing to accept even the worship due to an angel, since this is indeed a form of worship, and saying, *Don't do that! I am a fellow slave with you and your brothers who hold the testimony of Jesus.* (8) "Don't do that" is not simply a phrase to prevent an action, but is a positive affirmation. He says that he is himself *a fellow slave* of all who confess themselves slaves of Christ and who testify that God has become incarnate. (9) What, therefore, must we do, most divine angel, when you refuse to be worshiped? He says, *Worship God, for the testimony of Jesus is the spirit of prophecy,* as if he were saying, "Are you trying to worship me, because I told you beforehand the things that are to come? All those who witness to the rule and divinity of Christ are full of prophetic grace, and not I alone. Why, therefore," he says, "do you worship one who has been given the same grace as my fellow slaves? Can the Greeks' beliefs about those who rule over the nations ever be the same as what Christians say about the holy angels?"

1 2. *Then I saw heaven opened, and see, a white horse! He who sat upon it is called Faithful and True, and in righteousness he judges and makes war.* (2) *His eyes are a flame of fire, and on his head are many diadems; and he has a name inscribed which no one but he himself knows.* (3) *He is clad in a robe sprinkled*[33] *with blood,* (4) *and his name is called the Word of God. And the armies of heaven, arrayed in fine white linen, followed him on white horses.* (5) *From his mouth issues a sharp sword with which to smite the nations, and he will shepherd them with*

32. Cf. Homer, *Iliad* 5.31, 455, 844, 846.
33. Oecumenius reads ἐρραμένον ("sprinkled") instead of βεβαμμένον ("dipped").

a rod of iron; he himself is treading the wine-press of the wine of God, of the wrath of God the sovereign Lord. (6) *On his robe and on his thigh he has a name inscribed, King of kings and Lord of lords* (Rv 19.11–16). 13. This is after the hour of the overthrow of Babylon. It is clear what is meant by Babylon; and now this, too, is shown to the evangelist: the fall both of the Antichrist and the serpent, the originator of evil, and the kind of punishment to which they are going at the time of the end and their punishment, together with the overthrow of the kings who will rise at that time against the slaves of Christ. (2) See what he says: *I saw heaven opened, and see, a white horse! He who sat upon it is faithful* and true and just: he sees the Lord as though he was joining in the war in defense of the saints and taking the field against their adversaries. So the vision surrounds him with a general's equipment, giving him a horse and sword and the leadership of the armed hosts.

(3) *And see,* he says, *a white horse* on which the Lord was riding, where the symbolism makes it clear that Christ does not rest upon any except the pure and those unmarked by any stain of sin. So the Lord has called Paul "the chosen vessel, to bear my name before the gentiles and kings of the children of Israel."[34] Therefore, note that Christ rests on and mounts upon those such as Paul describes. (4) He says, *He who sat upon it,* that is, on the horse, *is called Faithful and True, and in righteousness he judges and makes war:* the true one is faithful, as the apostle says of him, "He remains faithful, for he cannot deny himself,"[35] so that he is *Faithful and True,* where two epithets have been used about the same person. (5) That *he judges* righteously and *makes war* on behalf of his slaves against their actual enemies, the prophet bears witness, saying, "Give the king your judgment, O God, and your righteousness to the king's son,"[36] that is, Christ; for Christ is a son of Solomon according to the flesh, to whom the psalm refers, as he goes on to say, "to judge your people with righteousness and your poor with justice."[37] (6) That it is the same one

34. Acts 9.15. Oecumenius omits καὶ ("and") between "kings" and "children of Israel," thus reading βασιλέων υἱῶν 'Ισραήλ (the latter two words being rendered in some English translations as "sons of Israel").

35. 2 Tm 2.13.
36. Ps 71.1.   37. Ps 71.2.

who is also *making war* he shows by arming him in military fashion, with the words, "Gird your sword upon your thigh, O mighty one, in your grace and beauty; exert yourself, and prosper and reign"; and then he adds, "Your arrows are sharp, O mighty one; peoples will fall beneath you."[38] (7) He says, *His eyes are a flame of fire:* the fire of his eyes shows his fury against the enemy. (8) *And on his head*, he says, *are many diadems*, altogether as many as the regiments in heaven and on earth over which he reigns. *He has a name*, he says, *inscribed which no one but he himself knows.* (9) In the seventh section of Exodus God says to blessed Moses, "I, the Lord, appeared to Abraham and Isaac and Jacob, being their God, but I did not make known to them my name, 'the Lord,'"[39] as it is clearly greater than anything which can be comprehended by the hearing of a human being. This is why the Lord told his apostles how those who turn to the knowledge of God must be baptized, saying, "baptizing them into the name"; and when he said *name* he did not use the title "Lord." For he was not able to utter their title, "Lord," but instead of calling them "Lord" he gave relational and descriptive names, saying in relational terms, "into the name of the Father and of the Son," and then adding the descriptive term "and of the Holy Spirit."[40] So with great accuracy in the Revelation, too, he lets the name "Lord" of the only Son be unknown to all and sundry.

(10) He says, *Clad in a robe sprinkled with blood:* for even in the vision the Lord was bearing the marks of his passion, and was showing his all-holy body all but covered with his precious blood. (11) *And his name is called the Word of God:* do you see how after avoiding the name "Lord" above, the vision has now put a descriptive title instead of it, saying, *The Word of God*? (12) *And the armies of heaven, arrayed in fine white linen, followed him on white horses:* for he is the commander-in-chief of the heavenly powers, and thus the Lord has called himself, bearing the title of "Jesus son of Nun,"[41] saying, "As the commander-in-chief of the power of the Lord have I now come."[42] (13) The horses are white for

38. Ps 44.4–6.   39. Ex 6.2–3.
40. Mt 28.19.   41. Jos 5.9.
42. Jos 5.14.

the holy angels, too; for they delight in the pure among human-kind, since they are naturally pure and unstained by any defilement. The clothing of pure white linen shows this.

(14) *And from his mouth,* that is, from the commander-in-chief, *issues a sword:* the divine prophet places the sword "upon the thigh"[43] of the Lord in the passage cited a little earlier, while the vision describes it more accurately and places it in his mouth. In this way it is indicated that by the word of God all things have their being, and he who transgresses this in anything will not go unpunished. *With which to smite the nations:* which *nations?* Those who march with the Antichrist under his command against the slaves of Christ. (16) He says, *And he will shepherd them with a rod of iron:* for the Lord, being goodness itself and mercy, wished to rule these nations, of whom the account speaks, with a shepherd's rod of succor, "to bring them into green pastures and to nourish them beside the waters of comfort."[44] But since they have not wanted this, they will be shepherded *with a rod of iron,* that is, with one that is harsh and deadly. For those who are not changed by the Word can expect only punishment. (17) And because the iron rod indicates harshness and punishment, the prophet, in his desire to hint at the rule of the Romans, of which Daniel said,[45] "Arise, devour much flesh," spoke in regard to God: "You will shepherd them with a rod of iron, and dash them in pieces like a potter's vessel."[46] When the time was favorable, God ruled them with a shepherd's rod, but in the last time he will do so with a rod of iron. (18) *And he himself is treading the wine-press of the wine of the fury of the wrath of God the sovereign Lord of all:* the Lord said in the gospels about his own Father, "The Father judges no one, but has given all judgment to the Son";[47] therefore, the Revelation has been very correct in saying that *he himself is treading the wine-press of the fury of the wrath of God,* for by means of judgment and the requital of the wicked he fulfills his Father's will, and so becomes the fulfiller of the just wrath of the Father.

(19) *On his robe and on his thigh he has [a name] inscribed, King of kings and Lord of lords:* the *robe* is an allegorical description of

43. Ps 44.4. 44. Ps 22.2.
45. Dn 7.5. 46. Ps 2.9.
47. Jn 5.22.

the flesh of the Lord, which has been given life by his mind,[48] according to the holy angels speaking in Isaiah: "Why are your robes red, and your garments like those of one who has come from a fully trodden wine-press?"[49] The thigh clearly indicates his physical birth; for it is written in Genesis, "All the souls who entered Egypt with Jacob, those who came from his thighs. . . ."[50] (20) The symbolism of the writing on his robe and on his thigh shows "Emmanuel" to be king over all.[51] Although the Word was hypostatically united to the flesh and underwent a physical birth from a virgin, he is no less King and Lord of all things in heaven and upon earth, since his dignity was not diminished by his incarnation; for as such he was God, and is God, and will always be so.

14. *Then I saw another angel standing in the sun, and with a loud voice he cried out to all the birds that fly in mid-heaven, (2) "Gather for the great supper of God, that you may eat the flesh of kings, the flesh of captains, the flesh of mighty men, the flesh of horses and their riders, and the flesh of all people, free and slave, small and great." (3) And I saw the beast and the kings of the earth with their armies gathered to make war against him who sits upon the horse and his army. (4) And the beast was captured, and with it the false prophet who in its presence had worked the signs by which he deceived those who had received the mark of the beast and those who worshiped its image. The two were thrown alive into the lake of fire that burns with brimstone. (5) And the rest were slain by the sword of him who sits upon the horse, the sword that issued from his mouth; and all the birds were gorged with their flesh* (Rv 19.17–21).

15. I think that this holy angel who is now spoken of is a herald of the army of the divine battle-order, and that a charge has been sounded to all the holy angels in heaven, whom he figuratively calls *birds* because they are on high and traverse the air, to take part in the killing of the enemies. Of course, even a single angel was not incapable of destroying the whole battle-order of the enemies, as an angel clearly showed when in one night he

48. Greek, νοερῶς.
50. Gn 46.26.

49. Is 63.2–3.
51. Is 7.14.

struck one hundred and eighty-five thousand of the Assyrians.[52] But [all the angels are given the charge] so that all may become sharers in the rejoicing over the enemy. For I think that they, too, are saying with the prophet, "Have I not hated them that hate you, Lord, and do I not pine away over your enemies? I hated them with a perfect hatred; they have become my enemies."[53] (2) When the charge was sounded to the angels flying in mid-heaven, he himself stood in mid-heaven and made proclamation. The sun is firmly fixed in the middle of the seven planets, with three above it and three below it. (3) It either means this, or that the proclamation was being made in the light as though in the Spirit, and that he was speaking of the result of the coming slaughter. The Spirit is a spiritual light, as the prophet teaches, when referring to God and the Father, saying, "In your light we shall see light,"[54] that is, "We shall see the Son in the Spirit."

(4) He says, *that you may eat the flesh of kings:* he calls the joy over the death of the enemies the food of those whom he mentions. In a similar way the Lord, too, talks of joy when he says to his disciples and apostles, "I have food to eat which you do not know,"[55] describing in this way the gladness of those who are going to believe. (5) The Devil and the Antichrist, whom he calls a false prophet of the beastly Devil, together with the kings who marched with them, made war against the Lord and his divine angels, but they were defeated more quickly than a word. What do the divine Scriptures say about them? Isaiah says, "Let the impious one be done away with, that he may not see the glory of the Lord,"[56] meaning his sudden destruction; and the apostle says, "whom the Lord will destroy with the breath of his mouth."[57] What could be quicker than breathing and blowing against the enemies?

(6) He says, *The two were thrown alive into the lake of fire, and the rest were slain by the sword:* what an excellent display of justice! He did not consider the guilty protagonists of the war and their associates to deserve the same punishment. The two, that is, the Devil and the Antichrist, were condemned to the fire, in which

---

52. 2 Kgs 19.35.   53. Ps 138.21–22.
54. Ps 35.10.   55. Jn 4.32.
56. Is 26.10.   57. 2 Thes 2.8.

they will remain alive forever, for this is symbolized by their being thrown into the fire alive. But the rest were put to death by
the sword. To be punished by the sword is certainly far quicker
than by fire. (7) Once he has started to mention the kind of
punishment that the Devil will suffer, to maintain the continuity
of the account he goes on to describe what [the Devil] has suffered from the incarnation of the Lord. Keeping a grasp on this
sequence, he has more to say about the Lord's incarnate presence, and he says:

16. *I saw an angel coming down from heaven, holding the key of the
bottomless pit and a great chain in his hand.* (2) *And he seized the serpent, the ancient snake, who is the Devil and Satan, and bound him for
a thousand years,* (3) *and threw him into the pit, and shut it and sealed
it over him, that he should no longer deceive the nations, till the thousand years were ended. After that he must be loosed for a little while, to
deceive the nations again* (Rv 20.1–3).

17. For this is what he goes on to say. Surely the Revelation is
not telling us about the thousand years of the ungodly Greeks
and the transmigration of souls and the water of Lethe and I do
not know what nonsense and silly talk, when it says that the Devil
will be bound for *a thousand years* and released again and deceive the nations? Forget about such worthless doctrines which
are fitting for Greek crookedness! (2) What then does he say?
The prophet tells us, "For a thousand years in your sight, Lord,
are like yesterday which is past, and a watch in the night."[58]

So, then, the thousand years are reckoned as one day in the
eyes of God. The second epistle of blessed Peter says the same
thing, when he writes, "But do not ignore this one fact, beloved,
that with the Lord one day is as a thousand years, and a thousand
years as one day."[59] (3) So this is how it is: blessed Isaiah calls the
whole incarnation of the Lord "a day," saying, "In a time of favor I listened to you, and in a day of salvation I helped you."[60]
Nor is this all: the psalmist, too, calls it a day and an early morning, saying somewhere, "This is the day that the Lord has made;

58. Ps 89.4.   59. 2 Pt 3.8.
60. Is 49.8.

let us rejoice and be glad in it"[61] with the joy of our salvation; elsewhere he sings, "in the morning you will hear my voice; in the morning I will stand by you, and you will see me."[62] For our prayers have been deemed acceptable and worthy of the vision of God and the Father. They have become so by the intercession and atonement of the Lord. And again he says about Jerusalem, "God will help her in the early morning."[63] (4) The incarnation of the Lord has become the day and early morning, when "the sun of righteousness" (as Malachi calls him) shone upon us,[64] and brought us "the light of knowledge."[65] Zechariah prophesied about this divine light, saying, "When the rising of the sun dawned upon us from on high, to shine upon those who sit in darkness and in the shadow of death."[66] In accord with this the prophet also said, "The Lord is God, and he has shone upon us; bind the festal procession together with branches, up to the horns of the altar."[67]

Since all this has already been explained, we must proceed to the matter in hand. (5) Since I have already said that a day is reckoned "as a thousand years" by God, and again that the earthly residence of the Lord has been called "a day," he says this day is *a thousand years,* as though there is no distinction with God between one day and a thousand years. (6) It was in this period of the Lord's incarnation that the Devil was bound, so that he was unable to oppose the savior's divine miracles. This was why the destructive demons recognized these spiritual bonds and cried out, "What have you to do with us, Son of the living God? Have you come to torment us before the time?"[68] The Lord, too, when talking of stripping off the bonds, said, "Or how can anyone enter a strong man's house and plunder his goods, unless he first binds the strong man? Then indeed he may plunder his house."[69] (7) Since, as was said, we have considered the incarnation of the Lord and his earthly residence to be both *one day* and

61. Ps 117.24.
62. Ps 5.4. The LXX reads σοι . . . ἐπόψομαι ("I shall look to you"); Oecumenius reads ἐπόψει με ("you will see me").
63. Ps 45.6.
64. Mal 4.2.
65. Hos 10.12.
66. Lk 1.78–79; cf. Zec 14.6–7.
67. Ps 117.27.
68. Mt 8.29.
69. Mt 12.29.

a thousand years, such a number being used indifferently in Holy Scripture in mystical fashion, see what the Revelation says:

I saw another angel coming down from heaven, holding the key of the bottomless pit and a chain, and he says, he seized the Devil and *bound him and threw him into the pit.* (8) As if in a sketch on a canvas, the evangelist perceives the spiritual actions of the Lord against the Devil. Since it was not possible for a human being such as John to see spiritual events, they are depicted for him in physical terms—an angel with a chain binding the Devil and throwing him into the bottomless pit. For this is how the book of Job, too, expressed in physical terms the Devil's venture and God's consent: it depicted the Devil begging God to give him [Job], and it depicted God as making a suitable response to his request and giving him Job, and then went on to write the story. So you will be right in thinking that I am now doing the same.

(9) He says, *That he should no longer deceive the nations, till the thousand years were ended:* for the Lord's sojourn on earth had to provide rather more succor and care so that the unclean demons might be prevented from exercising the same influence on human beings as they had in the time preceding the incarnation. He says, (10) *After that he must be loosed for a little while.* What sort of *little while* does he mean? That between the incarnation of the Lord and the end of the present age; for this is short, even if it may seem to be very long, when reckoned and compared with the past and the future. For if in the "last" hour, even in "the eleventh" hour,[70] our Lord appeared in bodily form to us, according to the belief of Holy Scripture, the time until the end has rightly been called short, after which [the Devil] will be bound again with an eternal and endless bond. (11) But even now that he has been released, bind again, Lord, his wiles against us. For you are our king, and to you is due glory for ever. Amen.

70. Mt 20.6, 9.

CHAPTER ELEVEN

 HE REVELATION continues in the same pattern. For he says,

2. *Then I saw thrones, and they sat upon them, and judgment was committed to them; and I saw the souls of those who had been beheaded for their testimony to Jesus and for the word of God, and who had not worshiped the beast or its image and had not received its mark on their foreheads or their hands. They came to life and reigned with Christ for a thousand years. This is the first resurrection.* (2–3) *Blessed and holy is the one who has a share in the first resurrection. Over these souls the second death has no power, but they shall be priests of God and of Christ, and they shall reign with him for a thousand years.* (4) *And when the thousand years are ended, Satan will be freed from his prison and* (5) *will come out to deceive the nations in the four corners of the earth* (Rv 20.4–8).

3. The previous chapter had said that after the vision had once made mention of the Devil, in order to retain some continuity in the account, it went on to describe not only what the Devil will suffer at the end of the present age, but also his spiritual sufferings in the time of the Lord's incarnation. The vision continues with this theme and describes in greater detail the Lord's incarnate visit to us; this is now our present concern. (2) For he says, *Then I saw thrones, and they sat upon them, and judgment was committed to them:* he sees in his vision the holy apostles "seated on twelve thrones" and "judging the twelve tribes of Israel,"[1] according to the promise made to them. Although this will be more fully effected in the age to come, it has already happened in some way in the time of the incarnation. For those who put their trust in the Lord and so received a share in countless benefits con-

---

1. Mt 19.28.

demned those who refused to hasten to the faith and so, though taught by the grace given to the apostles, did not attain the true worship of God, but rather devised a cross and death for him.

(3) He says, *And the souls of those who had been beheaded for their testimony to Jesus and for the word of God:* the verb *I saw* in the phrase "those seated upon thrones and judging the rest of mankind" is to be understood here, too. By *those who had been beheaded* he means those who had been killed with an axe.[2] He is speaking figuratively about those who had put to death their own bodies because of their faith in Christ, and who endured very much because of it. For they expelled them from the synagogues, assaulted them with countless abuses, and plundered their personal possessions, when they put their faith entirely in Christ, as the wise apostle testifies.[3] The Lord also spoke of them, "Blessed are you when they revile you and persecute you and utter all kinds of evil against you falsely on my account."[4] (4) If you follow the sequence of the argument and subject every thought in obedience to Holy Scripture, you will understand that those who did not worship *the beast* and did not receive *its mark or its image,* are those who did not agree with the rest of the Jews in their plots against the Lord, and who refused to obey the propositions of the abominable and blasphemous Devil. For this is to worship him and *his image.* For by the word *image* he means the imprint of [the Devil's] will in the hearts of the Jews. He also means that this *mark* includes both control and action. For the head, of which the forehead is a part, stands for control, and the hand stands for action.

(5) *They came to life and reigned with Christ for a thousand years:* as was said earlier, he again calls the Lord's domicile on earth *a thousand years,* during which they were living their spiritual life, and reigning together with Christ, as they gave orders to demons, cured diseases, and worked countless miracles. For it is not simply by being present with Christ, the king of glory, that a person reigns together with him.[5] So the prophet said of them, "When the

2. "Those who had been beheaded" renders οἱ πεπελεκίσμενοι, literally, those who had been "cut off with an axe" (πέλεκυς).

3. Cf. Heb 10.34.

4. Mt 5.11.   5. Cf. 2 Tm 2.10–12.

Heavenly One gives the orders, kings will be covered with snow in Salmon."[6]

(6) *The rest of the dead did not come to life,* he says, *until the thousand years were ended:* he calls *dead* those who have persisted in unbelief, about whom the Lord also said, "Leave the dead to bury their own dead."[7] So the unbelievers did not *come to* the spiritual *life* until the time of the incarnation had ended, which is the *thousand years;* for they came to life only after this. How? By the coming and presence of the Holy Spirit. For by then most of the Jews had come to faith in Christ, who did not believe in him when he was physically dwelling and moving among them. (7) The event was most divinely ordered, beyond the hope of any human mind. For when the Son[8] had been proclaimed and made known in the old covenant as well as by his incarnation and his countless divine signs and miracles, the Holy Spirit had not yet been clearly revealed to human beings. There was only a report about the Spirit in the old covenant, but there was no manifest and perceptible work of the kind which specially leads people to faith, as there was of the Son, even though the Spirit was being made known to those who had attained the depth of vision, because everything which has been done and effected has been accomplished by the Holy Trinity. (8) The Lord clearly proves this, saying somewhere, "The Father has told me what I am to say and what I am to speak,"[9] and again, "I can do nothing on my own,"[10] referring the events to the Trinity; and again in John, "The Son of man can do nothing of his own accord, but only what he sees his Father doing";[11] and elsewhere he asserts, "If I cast out demons by the Spirit of God."[12] (9) But since, as I have said, there was no perceptible work of the Holy Spirit available to human beings, it was arranged that almost all people should receive faith in Christ by the coming and the power of the Paraclete and of God the Father, in order that it might be clear to everyone that the Spirit was of the same substance[13] as

6. Ps 67.15.
7. Mt 8.22.
8. Some manuscripts read "the Father" (ὁ Πατήρ).
9. Jn 12.49.   10. Jn 8.28.
11. Jn 5.19.   12. Mt 12.28.
13. Greek, ὁμοούσιος.

the Father and the Son, and possessed of the same power. (10) Of course, in the whole period of the incarnation not more than "a hundred and twenty" are recorded as having been believers.[14] This was the number reckoned by Acts of those assembled in the upper room. Even if the power of the teaching of Christ had reached many others, their faith was maintained by the coming of the Spirit. (11) So one might find that, just as when seed has been scattered the rain comes down and the sun shines upon all the seeds that up to this time have been hidden unnoticed in the earth, and then they spring up and become visible, because they were wholly stored up in the earth, so, too, the same thing happens at the coming of the Holy Spirit. All those in whom the teaching of the Lord had been sown sprang up into faith. So the Revelation accurately says that *the rest of the dead did not come to life until the thousand years had ended.*

(12) He says, *This is the first resurrection,* that is to say, which results from faith: the second will be the universal bodily resurrection. Therefore, (13) *Blessed is the one who has a share in the first resurrection:* for we shall all have a share in the second, whether we like it or not. (14) But he says that *the second death will not have any power* over those who share in the first resurrection, that is, the faithful. What sort of death is this? It is that quite clearly which results from sin and is followed by punishment. For just as he has spoken of the first and the second resurrection, so he speaks of the first and second death. The first one is the physical death, which separates the soul and the body, but the second death is the spiritual death, resulting from sin. The Lord said of this, "Do not fear those who kill the body; but rather fear him who can destroy both body and soul in hell."[15] (15) The faithful, he says, *shall be priests of God and of Christ:* all the faithful were appointed priests of the evangelical word, about whom the prophet, striking the prophetic lyre, said, "You will make them rulers over the whole world."[16] *And they shall reign with him for a thousand years,* which are the years of the incarnation, as I have said more than once.

(16) *And when,* he says, *the thousand years are ended,* that is,

14. Acts 1.15.   15. Mt 10.28.
16. Ps 44.17.

when the Lord has completed his course in the flesh and has gone back into heaven, the Devil will be set free from his spiritual bonds and will again *deceive the nations.* For it has already been said that the dwelling of the Lord with human beings nullified the activity of the Devil. But once the Lord has gone up into heaven, both the Devil himself will carry on his own customary activity, and human beings on earth in their usual way will follow their free will. In the face of the Devil's attempts to deceive everybody, some obey him, while others who refuse to do so struggle against the evil one. (17) But perhaps someone will say, "Why in the world was the Devil, whose assault was restrained and held in check by the bodily presence of the Lord, again set free to deceive us upon earth? For would it not have been better for him to have been bound, and for human beings to continue undeceived?" (18) To such a one we should reply, "Why do you not rather say, 'Why did the Devil come into being at all, or when he had been created and then transgressed, why was he not utterly destroyed, to prevent him getting access against human beings?' And how, my good fellow, would the contestants have been trained without any opponent? And how would the might of athletes have been shown if there were no competitors? (19) For slothful human beings, giving way to their desires, go all awry when left to themselves without the presence and provocation of the Devil, whereas the people of God and noble contestants would be unfairly treated if they were not able publicly to display their courage in the face of their sufferings. So it turns out that whereas the slothful would have no benefit if Satan did not exist, the noble would suffer great unfairness. For Satan is a kind of trainer of human beings, providing an opportunity for the contestants to receive a crown of victory. For those who love sin, who in the absence of the Devil use their own laziness as a substitute for the Devil, have not been at all unfairly treated, as I have said. So in spite of himself he does good to some, and does no harm, or very little, to others. (20) But on account of you and me, 'the slaves of sin,'[17] irresponsible and irresolute, in order that we might suffer little or no further harm from the

17. Rom 6.16.

activity of the Devil, you wanted patriarchs and prophets, apostles and evangelists, those who had persevered in their witness to Christ unto death and had kept loyalty with him, as well as confessors and pastors who had faithfully guided the churches, and the most steadfast ascetics, and every righteous person perfected in the faith of Christ, 'of whom this world was not worthy'[18]—you wanted them all to be deprived of glory. The noble contenders for virtue alleviate the penalty of those sinners who for quite a short time suffer harm. A single person who acts rightly is more honored by God than countless others who break faith."

(21) Both events have been effected in the best and most inspired way—the impious assaults of the Devil were checked during the bodily presence of the Lord, and after the Lord's ascension into heaven the Devil was freed to test human beings. For if Satan had been allowed to display all his activity when the Lord was dwelling on earth, he would not have permitted people either to hear his divine teachings or to learn who it is who is naturally and truly God, or the nature of the holy worship due to him, or the difference between evil and goodness. He would also have prepared the cross for him before the time, even before he began his teaching. If this had happened, the incarnation of the Lord and such a wonderfully glorious mystery would have been incomplete, or rather useless. (22) But after those on earth had been taught these things while the Devil was in bondage, they were then able to use their own free will, and to continue the fight against the adversary on the basis of acknowledged and recognized ways both of evil and of good. For one who knows the good and that which is not so good is entirely free to choose either this or that. But one who does not know what he could do, is like a man wounded in a night battle who does not realize that he has been hit, and therefore does not recognize his own destruction. For the one who knows his adversaries has the opportunity to choose what he wishes, but there is no such opportunity for one who is ignorant.

For God created human beings in the beginning with free will and controlled by their own reasoning powers. (23) But be-

18. Heb 11.38.

cause they first needed to know good and evil, so that in this way there may be room for free will, see what Moses the divine lawgiver says in Deuteronomy to the disobedient people of the Israelites, "See, I have set before your eyes this day life and death, good and evil,"[19] so that the choice may be freely made between both. Again he says in Exodus, "If you hearken attentively to my voice and do all that I say to you."[20] And what about Isaiah, who sets forth the same teaching near the beginning of his prophecy, saying in the person of God, "If you are willing and listen to me, you shall eat the good of the land, but if you refuse and do not listen to me, you shall be devoured by the sword; for the mouth of the Lord has spoken this"?[21]

4. So much then for this. After saying earlier that *the Devil will come out to deceive the nations,* he now identifies the nations and their leaders. He says, *Gog and Magog gather them for war* (Rv 20.8); the war is that against the saints. (2) For after completing the account of the saving incarnation, he has returned to the place from where he set out to explain those things to us. He started with the Devil and the Antichrist, and the defeat and punishment of the nations which collaborated with them. (3) So he is now going to supply what was earlier left unsaid. He links Gog to the rest of the nations who fought with the Antichrist, saying,

5. *And he came out*[22] *to deceive all the nations which are at the four corners of the earth,* with whom he now includes *Gog and Magog, to gather them for war; their number is like the sand of the sea.* (2) *And they marched up over the broad earth and surrounded the camp of the saints and the beloved city. But fire came down from God out of heaven and consumed them,* (3) *and the Devil, their deceiver, was thrown into the lake of fiery brimstone, where the beast and the false prophet were, and they will be tormented day and night for ever and ever* (Rv 20.8–10).

6. The blessed prophet Ezekiel also told us about Gog and Magog, describing the evil end of evil men. These will be some

---

19. Dt 30.15.   20. Ex 23.22.
21. Is 1.19–20.
22. Oecumenius reads aorist ἐξῆλθε where NT has future ἐξελεύσεται.

of the nations and their leaders at the end of the age,[23] but they do not now exist, or they are some of the present nations called by other names in holy Scripture. So these will be allies of detested Satan in his fight against the slaves of Christ. (2) *And they will surround the beloved city,* that is, the church. But *fire from heaven* will destroy them all, and after the end has been reached, Satan, the origin of all the evil, together with the Devil and the Antichrist, will be thrown *into the lake of fire,* that is, Gehenna. (3) For the reader should recognize that the present Revelation has already told us of three [adversaries]: one was the dragon, the originator of the evil, shown in heaven; the second was the beast coming up out of the sea, which we considered to be second to Satan, but superior to the rest of the demons; and the third was the Antichrist, whom he also calls the *false prophet.* But it was said shortly before about the second one, the Devil, and the Antichrist, that *the two of them were thrown into the lake of fire burning with brimstone.* But now he is talking about Satan, or the Devil, whom earlier he called a *serpent.* (4) He says, *And they will be tormented day and night for ever and ever.* So you who read this essay will know that we were quite right to consider *the thousand years* during which the Devil was bound and thrown into the bottomless pit and was then set free again, to refer to the incarnation of the Lord and his dwelling upon earth, in which the Devil's activity was for a short time restricted. For now he has shown that the punishment of the Devil and of those deceived by him is not for *a thousand years,* but for ever and ever, and that there will be no release of the evil one.

7. *Then I saw a great white throne and the one who sat upon it, from whose presence earth and sky fled away, and no place was found for them.* (2) *And I saw the dead, great and small, standing before the throne, and some little scrolls*[24] *were opened. Also another little scroll was opened, which is the little scroll of life. And the dead were judged by what*

23. Cf. Ezek 38–39.
24. See n. 4 in chapter 6 (on Revelation 10.1–4) for the difference between the three types of scrolls. In the present text on all three occasions the form βιβλίον ("little scroll") is used, but in the comment the text is quoted with βίβλοι ("scrolls") rather than βιβλία.

was written in the little scrolls according to their works (Rv 20.11–12).
8. He says *a white throne*, bright and flashing as with lightning.
By the flight of heaven and earth the account symbolizes their
change and transformation. For "the heavens will pass away with
a loud noise,"[25] according to blessed Peter and according to the
prophet who says, "In the beginning, Lord, you laid the foundation of your earth, and the heavens are the work of your hands.
They will perish, but you endure; they will all wear out like a
garment. You will wrap them up like a cloth, and they will be
changed,"[26] presumably referring to their passing and destruction. What these sayings describe as their "change," the Revelation called "flight," so that no place was found for them. For
where could they be found when they had been cast down in destruction? Although he has here spoken of their change, a little
further on he says that they will be new.[27]

(2) He says, *And I saw the dead, great and small, standing before
the throne:* by *great* he means the righteous, calling them *great*
not in virtue of their physical size, but because of the glory and
brightness of their goodness, and by *small* he means the sinners
as being worthless on account of their baseness and meanness.
(3) *And scrolls were opened. Also another little scroll was opened, which
is the little scroll of life.* The Lord says in the gospels that the way
leading to destruction is broad and spacious, and many travel on
it, while the way that leads to life is narrow and constricted, and
there are few[28] not only who walk along it but who even find it.
This is why he saw many scrolls and a single scroll: the many are
those in which all human beings are written, because of the multitude of those involved, but there is one scroll of life, in which
are those chosen from the rest who are blameless in virtue and
travel along the entire length of the steep and rugged path of
virtue.

(4) And all of those written in the scrolls, he says, were judged
in accordance with their own individual works. In the beginning of the sixth chapter he mentioned another little scroll, too,
which he called *a miniature scroll*. But now he talks of *a scroll* and
a little scroll of life, so that there are three different scrolls. By *a*

25. 2 Pt 3.10.   26. Ps 101.26–27.
27. Cf. Rv 21.1, 5.   28. Cf. Mt 7.13–14.

miniature scroll he means that in which are the exceedingly impious, as we considered there: the little scroll of life is that in which are the exceedingly righteous and just, and *the scrolls* are those which contain all human beings who are somehow midway between evil and goodness. (5) He is talking about the resurrection. For to say, *And I saw the dead before the throne* receiving their rewards and being judged *according to their works,* is to speak of the resurrection. For he saw the dead rise up and receive their just recompense, and he goes on to describe how the resurrection took place.

9. He says, *The sea gave up the dead in it, Death and Hades gave up the dead in them, and all were judged by what they had done.* (2) *Then Death and Hades were thrown into the lake of fire,*[29] (3) *and if anyone's name was not found written in the scroll of life, he was thrown into the lake of fire.* (4) *Then I saw a new heaven and a new earth; for the first heaven and the first earth had passed away, and the sea was no more.* (5) *And I saw the holy city, the new Jerusalem, coming down out of heaven from God, prepared as a bride adorned for her husband* (Rv 20.13–21.2).

10. Those who do not believe in the resurrection of the body mock us and our teaching that these bodies of ours rise again from the dead, considering it to be not only implausible but absolutely impossible. They say that each of our earthly bodies consists of the four elements: fire, water, earth, air. When dispersed by death, our bodies go back to those things of which they originally consisted. For example, the fiery component in us proceeds to its corresponding element and becomes entirely fire, the watery component to water, and the other pair to their own particular elements. (2) "So when these have once been mixed up and combined with their own substances, how is it possible that what has been mixed together to form a compound be restored as bodies, as you profess, unless you were to say that things of one kind are raised to become things of another kind?" (3) In answer to these people one could quote the text of Holy

---

29. A sentence is here omitted from the quotation, but is duly commented on. The sentence, occurring in Rv 20.14 in the NT, is as follows: οὖτος ὁ θάνατος ὁ δεύτερός ἐστιν, ἡ λίμνη τοῦ πυρός.

Scripture, O people, "you are wrong, and you do not know the power of God,"[30] by whose will the universe was brought into being, and whose decree is the only completed work, as was said earlier. For in what way is it easier to bring beings into existence from non-being than to separate them again once they have been brought into being and mixed either in themselves or with other beings, and to apportion to each its own characteristics? (4) For in fact we, too, effect this, when we often skillfully separate wine which has been mixed with water. The sun, too, draws off drinkable and sweet water from the sea by means of steams and vapors, but leaves alone that which is heavy, earthy, briny, and bitter. But above all it is God alone who is able to do whatever he wills. (5) Therefore, if God brought into being things which are not, why is it not easy for him to separate again what was completely mixed together with the elements simply by his own will, and to assign its own identity to each body, even if this proves impossible for human beings? For just as it is impossible for you and me to separate the illumination of fire from its burning, it is possible for God—for Scripture says, "The voice of the Lord, who cuts into two a flame of fire"[31]—so it is impossible for you and me to separate what has been mixed together, but it is easily possible for God.

(6) The present text of the Revelation now sets before us this amazing doctrine, saying, *The sea gave up the dead in it* from the sea. This is the element of water, signifying all that is made of water.[32] So he means that what is made of water gave up all that was mixed in it from the watery nature of human bodies. (7) He says, *Death and Hades gave up the dead in them.* He calls the earth *death* since our bodies are dissolved in it, so that the blessed prophet by a periphrasis calls death "the dust of death," saying, "He brought me down to the dust of death."[33] Accordingly, the earth also has given up all of our earthy substance in it. (8) In addition, *Hades also gave up the dead* in it, calling the air and fire

30. Mt 22.29.
31. Ps 28.7.
32. The punctuation of de Groote has here been slightly altered; see his edition, p. 264, where he places a period after "water" and links the participial phrase ("signifying . . .") to the following sentence.
33. Ps 21.16.

Hades from their incorporeal and invisible [nature]. For air is invisible in its lightness, except when it becomes dense, and fire lurks invisibly in wood until it is kindled externally. But also the element of fire is ether, which is invisible to us when obscured by the covering of much air. Or perhaps he calls fire *Hades* because it destroys and disfigures those it attacks, so that many learned writers call it obscure.[34] (9) So the resurrection takes place when each of the elements has rendered back all of the human composition they contained. After this, he says, *They were all judged by what they had done.*

(10) He says, *Then Death and Hades were thrown into the lake of fire,* that is, Death was destroyed, together with the formless and incorporeal existence of the souls in death, once the resurrection had taken place and each soul had received its own particular body. He has explained this in a somewhat figurative way and has symbolized their destruction by saying that Death and Hades had been thrown into the lake of fire. The prophet Hosea also writes this, saying, "O Death, where is your justice?[35] O Hades, where is your sting?"[36] (11) He says, *The lake of fire is the second death;* for it has been said earlier that the first death is physical death, the separation of the soul and body, but the second is spiritual death, the punishment and retribution due to those for whom sin is their mother. (12) But he also says that all who were born in their sins and who were not considered worthy to be written in the book of life have suffered the same. Do not be surprised that he said earlier that those who are "medium sinners" have been thrown into the lake of fire with the Devil and the Antichrist. For a different punishment is meant there, just as there is a different kind of fiery heat: one is a sort of continuous burning heat, the other is less so and mild, even though both are called fiery heat. You must understand me there, too, as meaning this.

(13) He says, *Then I saw a new heaven and a new earth; for the first heaven and the first earth had passed away, and the sea was no*

---

34. The text reads ἄδηλον, but some manuscripts read ἀείδηλον, which could be taken to mean "destructive."
35. The LXX has ἡ δίκη ("justice"), whereas Paul (1 Cor 15:55) reads τὸ νῖκος ("victory").
36. Hos 13.14.

more: Peter says something like this in the second of his epistles, saying, "According to his promises we wait for new heavens and earth."[37] He does not mean that the heaven and the earth and the sea have been destroyed and have disappeared and that others have been created in their place, but that the present ones have thrown off their decay and have become new, as though they have taken off an old and squalid garment and the accompanying dirt. For everything is called new which was not formerly of such a kind, but has now become so. Then creation will be purified from all decay, which was imprinted on it by human transgression. (14) The divine apostle is a most trustworthy witness of these things when writing to the Romans about creation, "For the creation waits with eager longing for the revealing of the sons of God; for the creation was subject to futility, not of its own will, but on account of him who subjected it, in hope that creation itself will be set free from its bondage to decay and obtain the glorious liberty of the children of God."[38] But not only he, but the blessed prophet, too, sings about heaven and earth according to the testimony recently cited, "They will all wear out like a garment; you will wrap them up like a cloth, and they will be changed."[39]

(15) He says, *And I saw the holy city, new Jerusalem, coming down out of heaven from God, prepared as a bride adorned for her husband:* by Jerusalem he symbolizes the blessed lot and dwelling of the saints. He called this figuratively *Jerusalem* both here and later, and he has fittingly adorned it with magnificence, so that from what is said about the perceptible Jerusalem we may turn our thoughts to the spiritual blessedness of the saints and their way of life.

11. *And I heard a loud voice from heaven*[40] *saying, "See, the dwelling of God is with human beings. He will dwell with them, and they shall be his people, and God himself will be with them as their God. (2) He will wipe away every tear from their eyes, and death shall be no more, neither*

---

37. 2 Pt 3.13.   38. Rom 8.19–21.
39. Ps 101.27.
40. Rv 21.3. Oecumenius here reads οὐρανός ("heaven") instead of the usual "the throne" (ὁ θρόνος).

shall there be any more mourning or crying or pain, for the former things have passed away. " (3) *And he who sat on the throne said, "See, I am making all things new." And he said, "Write it down, for these words are trustworthy and true"* (Rv 21.3–5).

12. Was I not right in saying earlier on that the vision figuratively calls the lot of the saints and their residence there the spiritual *Jerusalem?* See, it has now disclosed the symbolism, saying, *See, the dwelling of God is with human beings. He will dwell with them, and they shall be his people, and God himself will be with them as their God.* The apostle made this clearer when he said, "Then we who are alive, who are left, shall be caught up in the clouds to meet the Lord in the air; and we shall always be with the Lord."[41]

(2) He says, *He will wipe away every tear from their eyes.* Isaiah the prophet said something like this, saying, "In his might he has swallowed up death for ever, and God has again removed every tear from every face."[42] For if, according to the divine apostle, "pain and grief and sighing have gone away"[43] in that blessed life of the saints, what will be left to cry over, once these have gone?

(3) He says, *The former things have passed away:* he means that the suffering of the saints has come to an end. Now they are receiving the reward of their labors. (4) He says, *See, I am making all things new:* for if the heaven and earth and sea are new, human beings also are new, and their joy and glory are new, now no longer afflicted by tears or grief or disgrace, since everything will be new. (5) "Do not think, John," he says, "that what has been said and shown to you is imaginary or false because of its exceedingly wide scope. Everything is trustworthy and true. So write them down."

13. *And he said to me, "It has been done! I am Alpha and Omega, the beginning and the end.* (2) *I myself will freely give to the thirsty from the fountain of the water of life. He who conquers shall have this heritage, and I will be his God and he shall be my son.* (3) *But as for the rest,[44] the faithless, the polluted, murderers, fornicators, sorcerers, idolaters, and all*

41. 1 Thes 4.17.
42. Is 25.8.
43. Is 51.11 (not from a Pauline epistle).
44. Oecumenius here reads λοιποῖς ("the rest") instead of δειλοῖς ("cowardly"), which he has in his later comment in 11.14.6.

lies, their lot will be in the lake that burns with fire and brimstone, which is the second death" (Rv 21.6–8). 14. He said, *It has been done! What has been done?* The things that have been spoken about, in which there is nothing false. He has written, *It has been done,* instead of "it will be done." (2) He says, *I am Alpha and Omega, the beginning and the end:* since he again resumes what he said earlier, let us also follow in his footsteps and pick up again what we said earlier: *Alpha and Omega, the beginning and the end,* indicate the unoriginate and infinite nature of God. For since there is nothing in this life which does not have an origin, he has used for our benefit *the beginning and the end* instead of "unoriginate and infinite."

(3) He says, *I myself will freely give to the thirsty from the fountain of the water of life:* the Lord says in the gospels, "Blessed are those who hunger and thirst for righteousness, for they shall be satisfied."[45] Accordingly, "to him *who has such a thirst I will give* life *freely.*" (4) Why did he say *freely,* when the saints attain to the future life by means of countless acts of sweat and toil? Why, then, does he say that he gives it *freely?* He says it to indicate that no one can ever contribute anything worthy of future prosperity, even by completing innumerable tasks. This is also what the apostle explained, saying, "I consider that the sufferings of this present time are not worth comparing with the glory that is to be revealed to us."[46]

(5) He says, *He who conquers* the sufferings and the wicked beast, the Devil, *shall have this heritage.* (6) This then is the victor's lot. *But as for the cowardly and the faithless,* and so on, *their lot shall be in the lake* of fire. He calls *cowardly* those who are weak in every good work on account of their voluntary baseness. (7) He says, *and all lies:* he did not say "liars," but "lies," that is, those who act contrary to nature and falsify the natural beauty of virtue and turn it to spurious transformed forms of evil. (8) That the fire is *the second death* has been mentioned earlier.

15. *Then one of the seven angels who had the seven bowls full of the seven last plagues came and spoke to me, saying, "Come, I will show*

45. Mt 5.6.
46. Rom 8.18.

you the wife of the Lamb." (2) And in the Spirit he carried me away to a great, high mountain, and showed me the holy city Jerusalem coming down from heaven from God, (3) having the glory of God. Its radiance was like a most precious jewel, like jasper, clear as crystal. (4) It had a great, high wall, with fifteen[47] gates, and at the gates twelve angels, and names were written on them which are the names of the twelve tribes of the sons of Israel; (5) on the east three gates, on the north three gates, and on the south three gates. (6) And the wall of the city had twelve foundations, and on them were the twelve names of the twelve apostles of the Lamb (Rv 21.9–14).[48]

16. He says, *Then one of the seven angels came:* what *seven* are these? They are those of whom I have had much to say earlier on. (2) *Come,* he says, *I will show you the wife of the Lamb:* he means to signify "the church of the first-born who are enrolled in heaven,"[49] which he also calls the heavenly *Jerusalem.* Paul spoke about this when writing to the Hebrews, "For you have not come to a mountain that may be touched, with blazing fire, and darkness, and gloom, and a tempest, and the sound of a trumpet, and the words of a voice; those who heard it implored that nothing further should be spoken to them. For they could not endure the order that was given, 'If even a beast touches the mountain, it shall be stoned.' Indeed, so terrifying was the sight" that [Moses] said, "'I am filled with fear and trembling.' But you have come to Mount Zion and to the city of the living God, the heavenly Jerusalem, and to innumerable angels in festal gathering, and to the church of the first-born who are enrolled in heaven, and to a judge who is God of all."[50] (3) By speaking of the assembly of all the holy people as a unity, namely, the church, and of the heavenly *Jerusalem,* the text depicts the blessedness of the saints, and their life which will be in God and with God, as is meant by describing it in material and grandiose terms, so leading our mind to consider its spiritual glory and brightness in this present setting.

47. The later comment has "twelve."
48. Oecumenius has omitted mention of the gates on the west, which appear in the New Testament.
49. Heb 12.23.
50. Heb 12.18–23.

(4) He says, *And in the Spirit he carried me away to a high moun-tain, and showed me the holy city Jerusalem coming down out of heav-en from God, having the glory of God:* for it is not without spiritual grace that the human mind can ever be so exalted as to com-prehend the glory of the saints. This is naturally the church, as though the life of the righteous and their situation, both here and in the future, is *a great, high mountain.* For there is nothing on ground-level or abject with them, but everything is high and lifted up. For Scripture says of them, "The rulers of the earth who belong to God were highly exalted."[51]

(5) He says, *Its radiance,* that is, Christ, the "sun of righteous-ness,"[52] *is like jasper:* jasper, as was also said earlier, is green, and so exhibits the life-giving and quickening gift of Christ, who "opens his hand and fills every living thing with satisfaction."[53] For green is the origin of all earthly nourishment. But the jasper was also as *clear as crystal,* exhibiting the purity and holiness of Christ, "for he had committed no sin, and no deceit was found in his mouth,"[54] according to the prophecy of Isaiah. (6) Again, Christ is himself a wall of the saints, that is, of the church, since he is our defense and shelter and succor.

(7) He says it has *twelve gates,* symbolizing the divine apostles who proclaimed to us the entrance into faith in Christ. (8) *And at the gates twelve angels:* I am convinced that the divine angels worked with the holy apostles to bring the world to faith; for if the law of Moses was spoken by means of angels—as the apostle says, "For if the message declared by means of angels was valid"[55] —surely the preaching of the gospel even more so had the coop-eration of angels?

(9) He says, *And names were written on them which are the names of the twelve tribes of Israel:* historically Israel is those who were born from Jacob the patriarch, but spiritually it means those who walk by the faith of our father Abraham. The apostle witnesses to this when he says, "And he is the father of the circumcised, not only of those who are circumcised but also of those who follow in the footsteps of the faith of our father Abraham."[56] Israel is

51. Ps 46.10.   52. Mal 4.2.
53. Ps 144.16.   54. Is 53.9.
55. Heb 2.2.   56. Rom 4.12.

interpreted as "the mind seeing God," or being clear-sighted.[57] Who rather than the believers have had a vision of God in their mind or have become clear-sighted by the abundant operation of the Spirit? So the names of these have been engraved on the gates of the city. (10) The twelve tribes indicate the full complement of the faithful. For after calling the believers *Israel,* he has mentioned, too, the number of their full complement, by saying *twelve tribes,* and he says that they came from the four corners of the world through *three gates* [on each side]. For the blessed apostles have mentioned the whole Trinity, proclaiming to the nations [the persons of the Godhead] as being of the same substance,[58] and "baptizing them into the name of the Father and of the Son and of the Holy Spirit."[59]

(11) *And the wall of the city,* he says, *had twelve foundations:* for Christ, whom we have considered to be a *wall,* relies on the preaching of the apostles, and stands upon them like "a precious cornerstone,"[60] according to Scripture. (12) And on them, that is, on the foundations, are *the twelve names of the twelve apostles of the Lamb:* he has at last revealed the symbolism by clearly saying that he means the apostles are *the gates* and *foundations* of the holy city, the church. (13) May all of us stand firm in their teaching and "avoid the unhallowed chatter of the falsely called knowledge"[61] of the heretics, by the grace of "Christ our master"[62] and "chief shepherd,"[63] to whom be the glory for ever. Amen.

57. See n. 15 at 2.5.5.
59. Mt 28.19.
61. 1 Tm 6.20.
63. 1 Pt 5.4.

58. Greek, ὁμοούσιος.
60. 1 Pt 2.6; Is 28.16; Eph 2.20.
62. Mt 23.10.

CHAPTER TWELVE

HE BLESSED evangelist's account continues with the holy, heavenly Jerusalem, describing its size, measurement, decoration, and the rest of its situation. He says,

2. *And he who talked to me had a measuring rod of gold to measure the city and its gates and wall.* (2) *The city lies foursquare, its length the same as its breadth, and its height is the same; and he measured the city with his rod as twelve thousand stadia; its length and breadth and height are equal.* (3) *He also measured its wall, a hundred and forty-four cubits by a man's measure, that is, an angel's.* (4) *The wall was built of jasper, while the city was pure gold, like clear glass.* (5) *The foundations of the wall of the city itself were adorned with every kind of precious stone; the first foundation was of jasper, the second sapphire,* (6) *the third chalcedony,*[1] *the fourth emerald, the fifth onyx, the sixth carnelian, the seventh chrysolite, the eighth beryl, the ninth topaz, the tenth chrysoprase, the eleventh jacinth, the twelfth amethyst.* (7) *And the twelve gates were twelve pearls, one for each, each of the gates being made from a single pearl, and the street of the city was pure gold, clear as transparent glass.* (8) *And I saw no temple in the city, for its temple is the Lord God, the sovereign of all, and the Lamb* (Rv 21.15–22).

3. The rod, with which he measured the holy city, was for measuring the earth; it was gold because of the worth both of the angel who was doing the measuring and of the city which was being measured. (2) He says, *And the city lies foursquare, its length the same as its breadth, and its height is the same:* the foursquare structure, as those who know about these things hold, is a cube and is so named. It is also foursquare at ground level, but since it is also foursquare and equilateral in all its dimensions, they say that the cube signifies stability. Stable and immutable are the awards for

---

1. The text here has καρχηδών, instead of the usual χαλκηδών.

the saints, whose blessedness cannot be effaced by any kind of change. (3) He describes the size of the city on a par with the great honor due to the saints, and shows that even if they were far fewer than the multitude of the sinners, they were not so few in number as not to fill so great a city.

(4) He says, *He also measured its wall, a hundred and forty-four cubits by a man's measure, that is, an angel's:* in many passages according to the custom of Holy Scripture, the angels are called men.[2] This is clear from the interpretation of the archangel Gabriel as "man of God." And the prophet said, "Lord, you will save men and beasts,"[3] calling the angels "men," and men "beasts." For compared with the intelligence of the angels, we men are irrational beasts. For by "men" and "beasts" he did not mean, as one might think, real men and actual beasts. The apostle said about the beasts, "Is it for the oxen that God is concerned?"[4] So according to the prophet, men are to be considered as "beasts," and angels as "men." According to Luke, the Lord also called the angels "men" when he said, "Let your loins be girded and your lamps burning, and you yourselves be like men who are waiting for their master's return from the marriage feast."[5] (5) Therefore, in many passages angels have been called "men" according to the above evidence, and they have their gaze directed to God. This is why he says, *a man's measure, that is, an angel's.* The saying symbolizes that although the divine is in every way incomprehensible (for we have concluded earlier that Christ is the *wall* of the city), yet in the judgment of the majesty of God human beings become angels. On account of this the wall of the city has been measured by an angel's cubit and not a human one. The hundred and forty-four cubits are a sort of mystical number determined by the wisdom of the angels, by which the exact measurement was made.

(7) He says, *The wall was built of jasper:* we have already taken jasper to be the quickening and vivifying [power] of Christ. (8) *And the city,* he says, *was pure gold, like clear glass:* gold, be-

2. Greek, ἄνθρωποι, "human beings."
3. Ps 35.7.
4. 1 Cor 9.9.
5. Lk 12.35–36.

ing put alongside brilliance and transparency, is compared with the worth and purity of the saints in their works and words. (9) *And the foundations,* he says, *of the wall of the city itself were adorned with every kind of precious stone:* as for the foundation of the wall, the Lord is the wall, as has often been said. We spoke earlier of the holy apostles, as though Christ relied on their teaching and depended on them according to the promise he gave, in which he says, "And see, I am with you always, to the close of the age."[6] These *foundations,* that is, the apostles, have therefore *been adorned* with every virtue—for the precious stones express virtue —since they have in fact become pure by the preaching of the gospel, by their struggles on behalf of Christ, and by their love for him even to death. (10) But if anyone would wish to quibble about the stones—for one may argue about such a vision—let us be content to say a little more: according to the law of Moses the high-priests were clothed in embroidered garments, invested with a full-length robe, an ephod, a turban, a sash, a girdle, and other things.[7] By their dress they communicated in mystical symbolism awe and dread. They also had the "breast-piece of judgment,"[8] which was attached to the ephod by embroidered cords. (11) The design of the breast-piece was "a doubled piece of cloth, a span long and square,"[9] in which were set twelve stones with the names of the sons of Israel, in four rows. Some of these stones were placed here in the foundations of the wall; others were given another name[10] and not included with these. Eight stones in the breast-piece of judgment were like those in the foundations here: jasper, sapphire, emerald, carnelian, chrysolite, beryl, topaz, and amethyst. Four of the stones in the foundations were not included in the breast-piece of judgment. They were chalcedony, sardonyx, chrysoprase, and jacinth.

(12) And there were also *the gates* of the city, which we took to be the apostles, *each formed from a single pearl.* The pearl, too, has now been shown to be new since it was not included with the stones of the breast-piece, so that one may see those who were

6. Mt 28.20.   7. Ex 29.5–6.
8. Ex 28.15.   9. Ex 28.16.
    10. Greek γωνιαῖοι (literally, "in an angle") here appears to mean that four stones had different names in Exodus and Revelation.

recently named to be more precious than those set in the breast-piece in the old covenant, by which the holy apostles are shown to have had a knowledge of the old covenant and were well acquainted with the injunctions prescribed in it—so the wise apostle could say, "As to righteousness under the law, I am blameless"[11]—and they are well acquainted with the commandments of the new covenant, too, and have come to a rich understanding of it, which is far clearer and more precious than the knowledge of the old covenant. The requirements of the law were a kind of shadow, but truth is found in the requirements of the new covenant. This is symbolized by the mixture of stones of the old covenant and the new precious stones in the foundations of the city, which, as was said, represent the apostles. (13) And this is what the Lord said in the gospels: "Therefore, every teacher of the Law who has become a disciple in the kingdom of heaven is like a householder who brings out of his treasure things new and old."[12] (14) There were, too, he says, *the gates* of the city, which again we took earlier to be the apostles, *each formed from a single pearl*, signifying their worth, purity, and brilliance.

(15) He says, *And the street of the city was pure gold, like clear glass:* it has already been said that gold and the purity and transparency of glass suggest the worth and purity of the life of the saints. (16) He says, *And I saw no temple in it, for its temple is the Lord God, the sovereign of all, and the Lamb:* what is the need of a temple when God is present with the saints and in a way sharing his life with them, and is seen by them face to face, insofar as he may be approached? For the divine apostle has called the knowledge of God in the present life as being "in a mirror" and "dimly," but that in the future it will be "face to face."[13] (17) One might reasonably ask, "Why did he mention God the sovereign Lord, and the Father, the Lord, and the Lamb, the Son of God, without making mention of the Holy Spirit?" (18) To such a questioner one must reply, "My good man, by saying *the Lord* and *God* he has named the Father and the Son and the Holy Spirit—for this

11. Phil 3.6.
12. Mt 13.52.
13. 1 Cor 13.12.

is *God*[14]—and by saying further, *the Lord God, the sovereign of all*, he indicated the Holy Trinity by the three titles." (19) But one might go on to ask: "Why, therefore, after mentioning the venerable Trinity in the words *The Lord God, the sovereign of all, is its temple*, does he separately specify for us *the Lamb*, who is Christ, so that we no longer think of the Trinity?" (20) "This is nonsense," I would tell him. This is not what we are being taught. By mentioning both the Holy Trinity and the Lamb, the account indicates both that the incarnate Son is one person of the Holy Trinity, and that the Son completes the Holy Trinity in his humanity and is not now apart from his humanity in heaven. He indicated, somewhat obscurely, the incarnate Son by the word *God*, who is the Son, and by *the Lamb* he again meant the same Christ, incarnate and of the same essence as we are, animated by a rational soul, in the flesh with which the Word is hypostatically united.[15]

4. *And the city has no need of the sun or the moon to shine upon it, for the glory of God illuminated it, and its lamp is the Lamb.* (2) *And by its light shall the nations walk; and the kings of the earth bring their glory and honor into it,* (3) *and its gates shall never be shut by day—and there shall be no night there* (Rv 21.23–25).

5. He says, *And the city has no need of the sun:* for those who enjoy the divine and spiritual light have no need of perceptible light: in their new abode the saints are aware of their spiritual blessings. (2) *And by its light*, he says, *shall the nations walk*—not only the nations, but also the saints from Israel who have believed. But since those from the nations are much more numerous, his reference to the majority indicated both Jews and gentiles. (3) *And the kings of the earth bring their glory and honor into it:* he calls all the saints *kings of the earth,* of whom Scripture says, "When the Heavenly One gives the orders, kings will be covered with snow in Salmon,"[16] as has been mentioned earlier.

---

14. Greek ταῦτα here refers to the three descriptions (ὀνομασίαι) of God the sovereign Lord.
15. Greek, ἡμῖν ὁμοούσιος ("of the same substance with us"). The Word (Λόγος) is united hypostatically or personally (Greek, καθ ᾽ ὑπόστασιν) with his human nature.
16. Ps 67.15.

Whatever, therefore, these have of glory and honor—by which he means their virtuous exploits—they will dedicate to that holy city, as though he said that their virtuous good deeds continue with the life of the saints.

(4) He says, *And its gates shall never be shut by day:* there is a double thought here: either this means that there will be peace and freedom from fear, so that there will be no need of a guard over the city and the gates need never be closed or secured by bars, or that the apostolic teachings (for we have called the apostles "gates") will not be silent there, and that the apostles will be there, too, as teachers of new and more divine doctrines to the saints. For since they are "sons of the day and of light,"[17] the righteous will revel in the divine and illuminating praises and mysteries since they are constantly wrapped in daylight and the light of divine brilliance. (5) He says, *There shall be no night there:* if the divine brilliance was ever interrupted, it would then also be night. But if it is impious to suggest this, since the divine light operates without interruption, how can it ever be night for the saints?

6. (1–2) *They shall bring into it the glory and the honor of the nations. But nothing common shall enter into it, nor anything which causes*[18] *abomination or falsehood, but only those who are written in the Lamb's book of life.* (3) *Then he showed me a river of the water of life, bright as crystal, flowing from the throne of God and of the Lamb.* (4) *Between the city's street and the river on either side was a tree of life bearing twelve kinds of fruit, yielding its fruit each month, and the leaves of the tree were for the healing of the nations.* (5) *There shall be nothing accursed any more, but the throne of God and of the Lamb shall be in it, and his slaves shall worship him; they shall see his face,* (6) *and his name shall be on their foreheads.* (7) *And night shall be no more; they will have no need of light from a lamp or the sun, for the Lord God will give them light, and they shall reign for ever and ever. Amen* (Rv 21.26–22.5).

7. By *the glory and honor of the nations,* which are brought into

17. 1 Thes 5.5.
18. The text here reads the neuter (πᾶν . . . ποιοῦν βδέλυγμα) instead of the usual masculine, "he who practices abomination" ([ὁ] ποιῶν βδέλυγμα).

the holy city, he meant metaphorically those from the nations who had been held in esteem and had accomplished deeds worthy of life; for these will be brought into the heavenly Jerusalem and will share life in it with the saints. (2) He says, *But nothing common shall enter into it, nor anything which causes abomination, but only those who are written in the book of life:* for "what fellowship has light with darkness,"[19] or a sinner with the righteous people of God? They are separated by a great chasm, the Lord told us in the gospels.[20] He says, (3) *Then he showed me a river of the water of life, bright as crystal, flowing from the throne of God and of the Lamb* through the middle of the street of the city. A *river of life* would be the rich and abundant graces of Christ, which have unceasingly been shed on the saints and are borne along like a river and flowing over them.

(4) He says, *On either side of the river was a* fruitful *tree of life bearing fruit each month:* the Lord is the tree of life according to what the writer of Proverbs says about wisdom; he says, "She is a tree of life to those who lay hold on her,"[21] and wise Paul told us, "Christ is the power of God and the wisdom of God."[22] He means that not only are the saints enriched by Christ's gracious gifts, but they also have him dwelling in them and with them, which is the crown of highest bliss. Christ, the *tree of life,* produces for the saints continuous and uninterrupted fruit and gifts, so that honor follows on honor and they are never without the divine flow of gifts. (5) He says, *And the leaves of the tree were for the healing of the nations: the leaves* of life are those who are dependent on Christ and hold close to him—patriarchs, prophets, apostles, evangelists, martyrs and confessors, those who at the right time perform the priestly service of the gospel,[23] pastors of the church, and every righteous soul; all these have now found healing for their souls, and all good things will be added to the saints.

(6) He says, *There shall be nothing accursed any more:* for at present even though the accursed things are very much in flight, nevertheless we are constantly embroiled in them, as thousands of occasions [for sin] arise in us, both knowingly and in ignorance;

19. 2 Cor 6.14.
21. Prv 3.18.
23. Cf. Rom 15.16.

20. Cf. Lk 16.26.
22. 1 Cor 1.24.

but then the saints will be pure and free from every defilement of both soul and body. (7) He says, *And* the kingdom *of God will be in the city*: for this is *the throne*. (8) He says, *And* the saints *shall worship him* with a worship that is not burdensome, but a worship of pleasure and spiritual joy. This will result from their beholding his face, (9) for, he says, *they shall see his face: they shall see* him insofar as he is accessible to human nature. (10) He says, *And his name shall be on their foreheads:* the present saying symbolizes God's unceasing remembrance of them and communion with them. For since God is imposed and inscribed on them, he will always be present with the saints. This is clear, too, from what Paul said, "And we shall always be with the Lord."[24]

(11) He says, *And there is no more night,* as the saints have no need of the light of the sun or of a lamp, when the divine light gives unceasing illumination. (12) And *they,* that is, the saints, *shall reign for ever:* wisest Daniel bears witness to this, saying, "The saints of the Most High shall receive the kingdom and possess it for ever and ever."[25]

8. *And he said to me, "These words are trustworthy and true. And the Lord of the spirits of the prophets has sent his angel to show his slaves what must soon take place. And see, we*[26] *are coming soon." (2) Blessed are those who keep the words of the prophecy of this book. (3) It is John*[27] *who is hearing and seeing these things. And when I heard and saw them, I fell down to worship at the feet of the angel who showed them to me. (4) And he said, "Don't do that: I am a fellow servant with you and your brethren and the prophets, and with those who keep the words of this book. Worship God"* (Rv 22.6–9).

9. He said, *These words are trustworthy:* that is, they are true. *And the Lord of the spirits of the prophets:* by the *spirits of the prophets* he means the prophetic graces, as wisest Paul says, "And the spirits of prophets are subject to the prophets,"[28] and as the blessed prophet Isaiah says, "Because of fear of you, Lord, we have con-

---

24. 1 Thes 4.17.
25. Dn 7.18.
26. The text here, and in the comment, reads the plural, instead of the usual "I am coming."
27. "I" (ἐγώ) is omitted in the text.
28. 1 Cor 14.32.

ceived and suffered birth-pangs; we have brought forth the spirit of your salvation, which you have brought about on earth."[29]

(2) He says, *To show his slaves what must soon take place:* for by means of John and his writings everyone has learned what he saw. He was right to say *soon,* for all time is short (as I said earlier) when compared with the infinite future ages, even though one might think it excessively long. (3) This is why he added, *See, we are coming soon: blessed are those who keep the [words] of this prophecy:* for those who are keeping them through their God-fearing life are eager to avoid falling into the punishments described.

(4) He says, *And when I heard and saw them, I fell down to worship at the feet of the angel:* this has been interpreted earlier, when we also showed that the doctrines of the atheistic Greeks concerning the national gods among them had nothing in common with the purest doctrines of the church.

10. *And he said to me, Do not seal up the words of the prophecy of this book, for the time is near.* (2) *Let the evildoer still do evil, and the filthy still be filthy, and the righteous still do right, and the holy still be holy.* (3) *See, I am coming very soon, bringing my recompense with me, to repay everyone for what he has done.* (4) *I am Alpha and Omega, the first and the last, the beginning and the end.* (5) *Blessed are those who wash their robes, so that they may have their right to the tree of life and enter the city by the gates* (Rv 22.10–14).

11. He says, *Do not seal up these words,* that is, do not keep them to yourself, nor shut them up and guard them in the treasury of your mind, but reveal them to everyone. (2) He says, *For the time is near:* he means something like this: the time when these words will have to be heard is not very far off, as it once was, but it is not yet here now; nor is the time suitable for earnest prayer to be made as a result of them, for what is the use of making prayers for those who go on striving to act wickedly or virtuously? It is inopportune to teach by words those who are learning by deeds. But why does he say *it is near?* It is not delaying for long, nor is it already here. (3) He says, *Let the evildoer still do evil, and the filthy still be filthy.* He is not commanding or prescribing the doing of

29. Is 26.18.

evil or being filthy, but he means this: a short time is still available to people; so let all go on doing what they have been accustomed to do, and let them use their own free will as they wish,
either for evil or for good. So he goes on to say, *Let the righteous
still do right, and the holy still be holy.* (4) *See, I am coming soon, bringing my recompense with me, to repay everyone for what he has done: I am
coming,* says the Lord, in his second coming, bringing with him
what he must render to each, whether it is good or evil.

(5) He says, *I am Alpha and Omega, the first and last, the beginning and the end:* there has been sufficient comment on this earlier on: so let us pass over it now. (6) He says, *Blessed are those who
wash their robes, so that they may have their right to the tree of life:* he
calls their bodies *robes.* Therefore, *blessed* are those who live well
and keep themselves pure from all filth of sin. For they who have
lived in this way will have the right to attain to the tree of life
and to rest upon it: the Lord is the *tree of life,* as was said earlier.
(7) And *that they may enter the city by the gates:* and by means of the
gates, that is, by the apostolic teachings and lessons, they will become partakers of the life and bliss of the saints.

1 2. *Outside are the dogs and sorcerers and fornicators and murderers and idolaters, and everyone who loves and practices falsehood.* (2) *I,
Jesus, have sent my angel to you to witness to these things in the presence
of the churches. I am the root and the offspring of David; I am the bright
morning star.* (3) *The bride says, "Come,"*[30] *and let him who hears say,
"Come." And let him who is thirsty come; let him who wishes it receive the
water of life as a gift.* (4) *I witness to everyone who hears the words of
the prophecy of this book: if anyone adds to it, God will add on him the
plagues described in this book,* (5) *and if anyone takes anything away
from the words of the prophecy of this book which have been written in
this book, God will take away his share of the tree of life and of the holy
city* (Rv 22.15–19).

1 3. He says, *Outside are the dogs:* it is the custom in Holy Scripture to call those who have prostituted themselves *dogs* on account of their shamelessness and impurity. For the law of the
priest Moses in Deuteronomy says, "You shall not bring the hire

_____

30. Oecumenius has omitted "the Spirit and" (τὸ πνεῦμα καί) from the NT
text, but he comments on these words in 12.13.8.

of a harlot or the price of a dog into the house of the Lord your God for any vow of yours,"[31] for such people are like dogs in their shamelessness, as a heathen wise man also testifies, saying, "Keep far from murder of every kind and a woman's adulterous couch, and swearing by the gods, and youths' shameless beds."[32] Therefore, *the dogs*, whoever they may be, are *outside* the holy city and the life of the righteous. For what do they have in common with the righteous folk of God?

(2) He says, *Everyone who loves and practices falsehood* will be *outside: falsehood* means everything which is contrary to nature. Virtue is natural, since from the beginning the Creator has sown in us the seed of virtue when he formed us, but wickedness is contrary to nature. For just as in our bodies good health is natural, and disease is unnatural, and sight and hearing are natural, but blindness and deafness are unnatural, so in the soul virtue is natural and evil is unnatural; health is analogous to virtue, and disease to evil. (3) Consequently, evil is a lie, because it often falsely claims to be virtue: brashness is taken to be fortitude, evil-doing to be prudence, idleness temperance, and meanness justice. All these are evils, wearing a mask of virtue, and so he casts those who practice the falsehood of evil *outside* the holy precincts.

(4) He says, *I, Jesus, have sent my angel to you to witness to these things in the presence of the churches:* he means by *witness,* to attest solemnly, not in secret, nor in a corner, but in the hearing of the churches everywhere, so that no one could make an excuse of ignorance for being willfully wicked.

(5) He says, *I am the root and the offspring of David,* but it would seem to have been more appropriate to say, "I am the branch which has sprung up from the root of David." But, on the contrary, he has now called himself *the root of David,* and not only the *root* but also *the offspring,* as was said earlier. A *root* is also the origin of everything, including *David,* so that he is, and is considered to be, God; but he is also the *offspring* of David, sprung from him according to the flesh, insofar as he is, and is considered to be, a human being. This is who he is. "To say the same things more than once is not irksome to me, but is safe" for those who

---

31. Dt 23.18.
32. A literal rendering of two anonymous hexameter verses.

read, as the divine apostle says somewhere of his words.[33] (6) So therefore he is "Emmanuel"[34] in his divinity and in his humanity, each of the two natures being complete according to their respective qualities, without confusion, without change, immutable, unimaginable.[35] We believe that after the inexpressible union there is one person, one hypostasis, and one activity,[36] "even if the difference of the natures, from which we say that the ineffable union has been effected, may not be overlooked," as well as the peculiar quality of each nature, according to the words of our blessed father Cyril.[37]

(7) He says, *I am the morning star:* he may mean the sun, since Malachi has called him "the sun of righteousness,"[38] and the prophet in his psalm says, "Fire fell upon them"—that is, on the high priests of the Jews—"and they did not see the sun"[39]— that is, Christ, "the sun of righteousness." Or he may mean "the morning star": he is called this by Peter in his second epistle, saying, "Until the day dawns and the morning star rises in your hearts."[40]

(8) He says, *The Spirit,* that is, the prophetic spirit, *and the bride*—the whole church in every place—*say, "Come!"* We are enjoined to seek the second coming of the Lord, but also to put it into prayer. For the one who says, "Your kingdom come,"[41] to God is asking for the kingdom of Christ, which is also the kingdom of the Father and of the Spirit. (9) He says, *And let him who hears say, "Come":* he means, "let everyone who hears the present words, including you, John, utter a prayer for the kingdom of the coming of Christ." In saying this he is urging everyone to follow the works and practice of righteousness. For no one who is not himself conversant with righteousness could pray for the coming of Christ, since he will then be required to give an account of what he has done in his life.

33. Phil 3.1.
34. Is 7.14.
35. The four adverbs reflect the four adverbs of the Chalcedonian Definition of Faith, but the last two are different from those in the Definition.
36. Greek: πρόσωπον, ὑπόστασις, ἐνέργεια.
37. Cyril of Alexandria, *Ep. ad Iohannem Antioch.* 8.
38. Mal 4.2.   39. Ps 57.9.
40. 2 Pt 1.19.   41. Mt 6.10.

(10) He says, *And let him who is thirsty come; let him who wishes it receive the water of life as a gift:* "when the time of my coming arrives," says the Lord, "put your mouth to the spring of life by the practice of virtue." "And all of you who have no money, come, buy, and drink without money and without price,"[42] Isaiah enjoins us, addressing us with the same words as the Lord. It was said earlier that the acquisition of virtue involves sweat and toil; but he now says, *receive* it as *a gift,* since "the sufferings of this present time are not worth comparing with the glory that is to be revealed to us,"[43] according to the words of very wise Paul. (11) *I bear witness,* he says, *to everyone who hears* these present *words:* that is, I promise solemnly not to add anything to them, so that he may not bring upon himself the plagues spoken of herein, nor take anything away from them, so that he may not be deprived of his share of the *tree of life* and *of the holy city,* both of which are described in this book. (12) See what the evangelist has then added to make his account trustworthy and revered:

14. *He who testifies to these things says, "Surely I am coming soon"* (Rv 22.20).

15. The very thing which Paul said—"I am already on the point of being sacrificed, the time of my departure is at hand"[44] —he himself is now saying: "I who am teaching these things," he says, "and who solemnly testify to them, am henceforth at the end of this present life, so that no one should be left with any suspicion of the truth of the account." (2) For who would ever choose, and certainly not the great John, to fabricate words as coming from God, as though he was not to undergo the death common to us all and to depart into God's hands more evidently than those who are still among the living? Therefore, he says, "I am writing these things," all but saying to Christ, who calls me to be transformed, *Yes, I am coming soon.*

16. *Amen. Come, Lord Jesus* (Rv 22.20).

17. Since, earlier on, the prophetic *Spirit* said to him, *Let him who hears say* to the Lord, *"Come,"*[45] in obedience to his command

42. Is 55.1.   43. Rom 8.18.
44. 2 Tm 4.6.   45. Rv 22.17.

he says, *Amen. Come, Lord Jesus,* as if he said, "Yes, master, Christ, hasten for us the salvation of your second coming."

18. *The grace of the Lord Jesus be with all the saints. Amen* (Rv 22.21).

19. The impure had already been removed from the life of the saints and admission into the spiritual Jerusalem. How could *the grace* of Christ our God come upon the excommunicate? (2) Christ, grant us to share [in this grace] by your goodness alone. For it is right for you to be glorified now and for ever. Amen.

20. As for this divine Revelation, some say, wagging their tongues brashly and ignorantly, that it was not composed by the divine John the evangelist and theologian. They listen to this tradition as though they have secretly received it. (2) But I think they say this not from ignorance nor from any secret revelation, but only from simplicity and, if one may dare to say it, from cowardice and a passionate love for earthly things, showing by their denials their fear of what is absolutely incontrovertible. For in the face of the explicit testimony of the blessed and holy fathers, who is able to contradict their testimony or somehow to reach the conclusion that this is certainly not the case? (3) For the great Basil in his writings against Eunomius refutes his godless blasphemies and nonsense.[46] The divine theologian referred to these in his fourth book, "in which he mentions on the authority of the divinely inspired Scriptures both the problems and solutions to the controversies about the Son" by means of the Old and New Testaments. He starts by saying, "If the Son is God by nature, and the Father is also God by nature, the Son is not one God and the Father another, but they are the same."[47] And later on,[48] "Moses said about the Son, 'I am has sent me,'[49] and John the evangelist said, 'In the beginning was the Word,'[50] and he said 'was' not once only, but four times, and again elsewhere he said, 'he who is from God'[51] and 'he who is in the bosom of the

46. Ps-Basil, *Adversus Eunomium* 4.   47. Ibid., 4.1.
48. Ibid., 4.2.   49. Ex 3.14.
50. Jn 1.1.   51. Jn 8.47

Father,'⁵² and elsewhere, 'he who is in heaven,'⁵³ and in the Revelation, 'he who is and who was and is to come.'"⁵⁴ He made no distinction between authors, but he followed the testimony of Paul and repeated it. (4) If then this Revelation was composed by some other John, as the nonsense of the majority has it, the great Basil also would have written his books on the Revelation with the name of its author. But after first listing the books of Moses, and then those of the apostle and theologian, as those, too, of the apostle Paul, he had no need to refer to anyone else in addition to these. These then are the incontrovertible words of the great and holy Basil. (5) The great Gregory, surnamed "the Theologian," whom they call "the Organizer," when he was making his defense in the presence of the hundred and fifty bishops,⁵⁵ clearly and truly wrote, "When will you inherit my holy mountain?" and he went on to say, "I am convinced that others preside over other churches, as John teaches me in Revelation."⁵⁶ (6) And Eusebius Pamphyli, in the third book of his *Ecclesiastical History*, says somewhere,⁵⁷ "This, then, was the situation of the Jews at that time," and goes on to say, "It is recorded that at that time John the apostle and evangelist was still alive, and was sentenced by Domitian the son of Vespasian to live on the island of Patmos on account of his witness to the divine word. Indeed, Irenaeus, when writing about the number of the name of the Antichrist as given in the book of John called Revelation, uses these very words in the fifth book of his *Against the Heresies*, saying about John: 'If it seems right at the present time for this name to be openly announced, it would have been mentioned by the one who actually saw the Revelation.'"

52. Jn 1.18.　　53. Jn 3.13.
54. Rv 1.8.
55. At the Council of Constantinople, A.D. 381.
56. Gregory of Nazianzus, *Orationes* 42.8–9.
57. Eusebius, *Ecclesiastical History* 3.1.1 and 3.18.1–3.

INDICES

INDEX OF PROPER NAMES

INDEX OF HOLY SCRIPTURE

Old Testament